# The
## School
### Librarian's
# BOOK OF LISTS

# *The*
# *School*
# *Librarian's*
# *BOOK OF LISTS*

## Jane E. Streiff

**THE CENTER FOR APPLIED
RESEARCH IN EDUCATION**
West Nyack, New York 10995

**Library of Congress Cataloging-in-Publication Data**

Streiff, Jane E.
    The school librarian's book of lists / Jane E. Streiff.
      p.  cm.
    Includes bibliographical references.
    ISBN 0-87628-811-5
    1. School libraries—Administration—Miscellanea.  2. School
libraries—Book lists.  I. Title.
Z675.S3S824  1992
027.8—dc20                                    92-12720
                                                   CIP

ISBN 0-87628-811-5

**THE CENTER FOR APPLIED
RESEARCH IN EDUCATION**
West Nyack, New York 10995

Printed in the United States of America

# ACKNOWLEDGMENTS

I am grateful to the following persons, members of the Albany area writers' group, for their encouragement, advice, and support: Pauline Bartel, Jackie Craven, David Drotar, Joyce Hunt, Kate Kunz, Peg Lewis, Marie Musgrove, Jim Nehring, and Donna Tomb.

The members of my high school faculty writers' group also served as a sounding board and a source of moral support: Asta Roberts, founder and leader of the group, Ann Connolly, Teri Goldrich, Richard Hughes, Lyn Jerry, Jim Nehring, Mary Ann Mitchell, Robin Rapaport, and James Yeara.

Several Albany area librarians were especially helpful with suggestions of "the best" to be included in this book: Joan Barron, Melissa Borys, Pat Grimwood, Ginger Hewett, Shirley Schenmeyer, and Nancy Smith.

Finally, I wish to express my appreciation to JoAnn Davies for her helpful suggestions and to the dedicated staff at the Bethlehem Public Library who offered invaluable assistance in tracking down information.

My gratitude to all.

# ABOUT THE AUTHOR

Jane Streiff is the media center director at Bethlehem Central High School in Delmar, New York. She started her career in education as a classroom teacher of English and social studies in Colorado. Those early years in the classroom contributed greatly to an appreciation for the centrality of the school library to the educational program of a school. A family move from Colorado to New York state prompted a change in her career, and she decided to prepare for school librarianship, a decision she has found to be both professionally and personally rewarding.

After receiving a B.A. degree from Cornell College in Mt. Vernon, Iowa with majors in English and sociology, Ms. Streiff attended the graduate school of political science at Columbia University on a Lydia Roberts Fellowship. Upon moving to New York she earned her M.L.S. at the State University of New York in Albany.

Her professional association memberships include the American Library Association, the American Association of School Librarians, the New York Library Association, and the Eastern New York School Library Media Association, as well as both local and state teacher's associations. Presently she is serving on a district-wide technology committee and on the Media Advisory Council of the Albany-Schoharie-Schenectady Board of Cooperative Educational Services.

Ms. Streiff is the author of *The Secondary School Librarian's Almanac: Month-by-Month Activities, Displays, and Procedures for the Entire School Year* (The Center for Applied Research in Education, 1989).

# ABOUT THIS BOOK

We librarians are fond of telling our students that the librarian is the most important source of information in their library. We urge them to seek assistance if they encounter any difficulty in locating materials. We know that the human factor is still the most viable link between resources and people, no matter how carefully we have organized materials or how accurately we have shelved them.

We carry a formidable burden of information around in our heads. That data is related to our collection and to our professional work as well as to those questions we have learned through experience that are most frequently asked. To many students it is close to magic when we can walk directly to a shelf and find the exact resource desired or when we can respond with the very clue they need to complete their puzzling research assignment.

However, with the proliferation of information and the diversity and sophistication of our students' information needs, many of us are now approaching maximum mental storage capacity. What we need is not more information in our heads, but easier access to that information through proper sources.

*The School Librarian's Book of Lists* is a compendium of information that we must recall each day in our work. It contains lists of recommended books and periodicals, tips to assist us in daily routines, a glossary of library terms, access to professional agencies and networks, and sources for successful library skills lessons. Those lists which are appropriate for sharing with teachers and students are also presented in reproducible form.

I have not ranked the recommended titles in these many lists, and readers are sure to wonder why their favorites may not be included. I have made an effort to include only in-print materials while recognizing that many useful titles are already in place in most school libraries. Librarians using this resource are encouraged to add to or delete from these lists, thus customizing the book for maximum usefulness in their libraries.

Here is a ready reference tool specifically for the librarian working in a school setting. It is designed to put the answers to our most frequently encountered questions right at our fingertips.

*Jane E. Streiff*

# CONTENTS

# The
## School
### Librarian's
# BOOK OF LISTS

# section 1

# THE HIT PARADE

You remember The Hit Parade . . . those were the favorite tunes, the ones you could hum, the ones everyone talked about and recommended to friends. Here, too, we have selected titles that should meet popular demand. You will recognize some "golden oldies," but our intent is to add to those familiar titles lists of fresh, new, useful materials.

There are seventeen categories in this section of the *School Librarian's Book of Lists,* ranging from the ready-reference collection, so necessary in our daily tasks, to groups of titles representing diverse special interests.

The lists in these various categories are made up of materials in different formats. Bibliographic information will appear with each citation, along with a brief annotation. Since prices vary with time and among vendors, they have not been indicated. If a title appears in this "parade," we are recommending it for your school library collection. In some cases we have quoted reviews, and you may wish to read those reviews in their entirety. Many of the lists are appropriate for duplicating and sharing with students and faculty. You are encouraged to do so.

# READY REFERENCE

The following titles offer you a selection from which to choose those resources you would find most useful at a reference desk. Some reference tools need to be readily accessible as you try to answer quickly the questions your students so often ask. Many times this involves directing them to further sources. If you keep a handy log of reference questions, with notations about the sources used with the student and the success of the quests, you can soon tailor your reference desk collection to your needs. A small collection may serve you well, if thoughtfully selected. Since answering a reference question often involves putting the question in a framework of who, why, where, what, or when, the titles listed in section 2, Funny You Should Ask! Where the Answers Are, are also appropriate candidates for your "ready reference" collection.

## List 1–1.  Ready Reference Materials: Annotated List

*Benet's Reader's Encyclopedia.* **Third Edition. HarperCollins, 1987. ISBN: 0-06-181088-6.** First copyrighted in 1948, this one-volume encyclopedia still serves as one of the most valued sources of useful information ever published. A complete and practical reference for all those wonderful bits of information that delight the inquiring mind. Students completing English assignments are sure to get the start they need with this source. One of my personal favorites.

Berkman, Bob I. *Find It Fast: How to Uncover Expert Information on Virtually Any Subject.* **HarperCollins Publishers, 1989. ISBN: 0-06-0455194-1.** Highly recommended by *Library Journal,* this title covers electronic data sources as well as traditional listings. *Library Journal:* "This book goes way beyond the walls of libraries and out into the offices of experts of all types." With all the tips included for accessing information from government agencies, this source will delight secondary social studies teachers.

*Cambridge Biographical Dictionary.* **Cambridge University Press, 1990. ISBN: 0-521-39528-3.** Nineteen thousand entries help you answer reference questions about people. This source covers famous and infamous persons from ancient to modern times.

*Compton's Multimedia Encyclopedia.* **Encyclopaedia Britannica, 1990.** This is the CD-ROM format of the twenty-volume print encyclopedia: not just a digital version of print, but complete with color graphics, sound, and movement. *The Computing Librarian* review (2/91) calls this electronic encyclopedia "truly the state of the art." Fast and easy access to reference material. *Booklist* says of it, "stimulating and innovative." With the equipment to access this encyclopedia at your reference desk, you would need no other.

*The Cover Story Index, 1960–1989.* **Edited by Robert Skapura. Highsmith, 1990. ISBN: 0-917846-02-8.** The popular news stories covered by this index are taken from *Time, U.S. News and World Report,* and *Newsweek.* Access to the stories is by subject index, and the usefulness of this source is in its access to in-depth coverage of a student's topic. There may be some frustration involved in acquiring the hard copy of the article, but a bonus lies in the development of the subjects over the span of years indexed.

*Dictionary of Historic Documents.* **Facts On File, 1991. ISBN: 0-8160-1978-9.** This valuable "dictionary" describes and explains the major state and social pronouncements that have proved to be important in history from 1700 B.C. to modern times. There are over twenty-two hundred influential documents included. Reviewed in *Library Journal* (5/1/91).

*Editorial Research Reports.* **Congressional Quarterly, Inc.** With quarterly indexes. Published four times a month. Fourteen-page overviews of topical issues; also included are graphics and bibliographies. Keep them in binders at the reference desk. Bound volumes are available.

*The Electronic Atlas.* **Apple II Geography Software, 1991.** With the political geography of the world changing so rapidly, consider an electronic atlas that can be revised easily. This selection features options from the atlas on disk to a class management tool. Six programs in the series.

*Facts On File.* **Serial. Weekly News Index. Cumulated annually. Facts On File, Inc.** This source includes a current atlas and the $8\frac{1}{2}'' \times 11''$ size makes the maps easily reproducible and useful to elementary and secondary pupils. If you familiarize yourself with the sidebar table of contents on each edition, you will be knowledgeable about world events. The obituary information is particularly useful. Three-ring binders keep the editions in place.

*Fiction Catalog.* **12th edition. H. W. Wilson, 1991. ISBN: 0-8242-0804-8.** With purchase of the new edition one receives four annual supplements. This annotated list of English language fiction titles will be useful for selection and collection development, but it is also important as a resource at the reference desk. Indexes offer access to titles by author, title, and subject.

*The Guinness Book of Answers: The Complete Reference Handbook.* **7th edition. Facts On File, Inc., 1990. ISBN: 0-8160-2559-2.** Dictionary-style entries answer thousands of questions. *School Library Journal* recommended it in May 1990 as a source "offering unique and valuable information."

*Historic Documents [of 1991].* **Annual. Congressional Quarterly Inc., 1991. ISBN: 0-87187-665-5-2SG.** The important documents, reports, and resolutions that chronicle international events of the past year. A free "Historic Quotes" [1991] poster will help you direct students to the full texts of the speeches that are quoted. Consider purchasing the new index to all editions in the series (ISBN: 0-871-566-7).

**Lesko, Matthew.** *Information U.S.A.* **Viking, 1990.** This will help high school students to identify government sources of information. The names, addresses, and phone numbers will help them access information for reports on government, public policy, and consumer affairs, to name just a few topics. The "Sampler" section of the book will give you an idea of the scope and depth of the directories offered.

*The Lincoln Writing Dictionary for Children.* **Harcourt Brace Jovanovich, Inc. 1988. ISBN: 0-15-152394-0.** For grades 3–8. This attractive dictionary has several important features that make it useful for younger students. Quotations show correct word usage; direction is offered regarding the best use. There is a wonderful guide for the user. The 750 well-placed illustrations include beautiful drawings, photos, and fine art.

**Mattson, Catherine M.** *Contemporary Atlas of the United States.* **Macmillan, 1990. ISBN: 0-02-897281-3.** This handsome atlas was favorably reviewed by *School Library Journal* in its reference book roundup 1991. Sixty-two maps present "a unique view of America." Charts, graphs, and tables accompany the map and text, offering a wealth of information about the United States, its history and peoples.

*New York Public Library Desk Reference.* **Prentice Hall, 1989. ISBN: 0-13-620444-9.** This single volume reference purports to answer the questions most frequently asked of the librarians at the New York Public Library. The information is organized into twenty-eight categories which include such topics as weights and measures, first aid, and legal information. The preface cites an interesting paradox. Vartan Gregorian writes: "New technologies are whetting our appetite for more and better books." But, he says, as information grows, use diminishes because we have to sift through more of it. He believes the book is unique and valuable, preferable to an electronic database because of cost, portability, and readability.

*The 1992 Guinness Book of Records.* **Facts On File, Inc., 1991. ISBN: 0-8160-2643-2.** Revised regularly, this edition is the first American edition. With three hundred color photographs it is one of the world's best selling books. It offers the superlatives in many diverse categories.

*Rand McNally Children's Atlas of the Universe.* **Edited by Elizabeth G. Fagan. Rand McNally, 1990. ISBN: 0-628-83408-8.** Easy to read and well indexed, this resource will be useful for students researching planets, stars, and galaxies. It includes satellite photographs, drawings, and charts.

*The Random House Encyclopedia.* **Random House, 1990. ISBN: 0-394-58450-3.** Two sections: quick-reference and a "Color-pedia" section with over eighteen hundred pages of longer articles and illustrations. *The Washington Post* reviewer called it "the most beautiful book of information I have ever seen."

*Sears List of Subject Headings.* **14th edition. H. W. Wilson, 1991. ISBN: 0-8242-0803-X.** Your new edition of *Sears* is as valuable at the reference desk as at your cataloging station. Purchase two copies, if you can, so that one can be made available to your students as they search the catalog.

*Subject Guide to Books In Print.* **Annual edition. R. R. Bowker.** Useful at your reference desk for the student who wants to find additional titles on a topic, for preparing a bibliography, and for using your interlibrary loan service. Available on compact disc for use on CD-ROM equipment.

***The Universal Almanac.*** **Edited by John W. Wright. Universal Press, 1991. ISBN: 0-8362-7985-9.** You have a favorite almanac, selected for its coverage, or format, or good indexes. Here is one to consider, since no reference desk is complete without an almanac. I like the "Essential documents in U.S. history" section and the chronology of American history and of the year's important events. The geographical information is good, with a glossary of common geographical words and terms. Recently I searched for the elevation of selected cities for one of our science teachers. It was difficult to sort out in the atlases, but the desired information was here. Social studies teachers often need national and world rankings according to diverse indexes. Again, the information was here, for TV show, crime, costs of hospital care, and a myriad of other topics.

***Your Reading: A Booklist for Junior High and Middle School Students.*** **Seventh edition. Edited by James E. Davis and Hazel K. Davis. National Council of the Teachers of English, 1988. ISBN: 0-8141-5939-7.** A good choice for your reference post for use in reading guidance. This resource is intended for student use. The titles are presented in sixty-one different subject categories, organized within the categories alphabetically by author's name. Title and author indexes are included. There are brief descriptions of the books listed. This resource covers books from 1983 through 1987.

# List 1–1. Ready Reference: Reproducible List

*Benet's Reader's Encyclopedia.* Third edition. Harper/Collins, 1987.

Berkman, Bob I. *Find It Fast.* Harper/Collins, 1989.

*Cambridge Biographical Dictionary.* Cambridge University Press, 1990.

*Compton's Multimedia Encyclopaedia.* Encyclopaedia Britannica, 1990.

*The Cover Story Index, 1960–1989.* Highsmith, 1990.

*Dictionary of Historic Documents.* Facts On File, Inc., 1991.

*Editorial Research Reports.* Congressional Quarterly, Inc., Serial.

*The Electronic Atlas.* Apple II. Geo-Soft, 1991.

*Facts On File.* Facts On File, Inc., Serial.

*Fiction Catalog.* Twelfth edition. H. W. Wilson, 1991.

*The Guinness Book of Answers.* Seventh edition. Facts On File, 1990.

*Historic Documents of 1991.* Congressional Quarterly, Inc., 1991.

Lesko, Matthew. *Information U.S.A.* Viking, 1990.

*The Lincoln Writing Dictionary for Children.* Harcourt Brace Jovanovich, Inc., 1988.

Mattson, Catherine M. *Contemporary Atlas of the United States.* Macmillan, 1990.

*New York Public Library Desk Reference.* Prentice Hall, 1989.

*The 1992 Guinness Book of Records.* Facts On File, Inc., 1991.

*Rand McNally Children's Atlas of the Universe.* Rand McNally, 1990.

*The Random House Encyclopedia.* Random House, 1990.

*Sears List of Subject Headings.* Fourth edition. H. W. Wilson, 1991.

*Subject Guide to Books In Print.* R. R. Bowker, Annual.

*The Universal Almanac.* Universal Press, 1991.

*Your Reading: A Booklist for Junior High and Middle School Students.* Seventh edition. NCTE, 1988.

# FOR THE TEACHER

> "And gladly wolde he lerne, and gladly teche."
> CHAUCER
> *The Canterbury Tales*

As the cost of materials increases, the teachers on your staff will count on you more often for professional selections.

Although building your collection with students in mind may be your primary responsibility, it is necessary to include in your library solid resources that focus on the profession of teaching and educational administration as well as those titles that will serve to keep your colleagues abreast of practical developments in their fields. Daily we are reminded of that aspect of our job which casts us in the role of educational consultant. Here, then, is a list of materials to help us to help our staffs. Many of the titles in this list are related directly to promoting the integration of library skills and library use into the curriculum.

## List 1–2.  For the Teacher: Annotated List

Aker, Sharon Zardetto, et al. *The Macintosh Bible.* Goldstein & Blair, 1991. ISBN: 0-940235-11-0. A reference manual that "covers it all," according to the review in *Apple Library Users Group Newsletter* (1/91). Nineteen chapters take the user from hardware through the system software. One may obtain a companion package for this book which provides access to public-domain software (*The Macintosh Bible Software Disks*).

Boyer, Ernest L. *High School: A Report on Secondary Education in America.* Harper and Row, 1983. ISBN: 0-06-015193-5. The report of the Carnegie Foundation for the Advancement of Teaching.

Butzow, Carol M. and John W. Butzow. *Science Through Children's Literature: An Integrated Approach.* Libraries Unlimited, 1989. ISBN: 0-87287-667-5. Preschool through grade 3. A sourcebook of titles which integrate scientific concepts with interesting storylines. Includes discussion of whole language approach to teaching.

*Career Discovery Encyclopedia.* 6 vols. Ferguson, 1990. ISBN: 0-89434-106-5. Middle school: 500 careers, 500 illustrations. Reviewed in *Booklist* (5/90). Includes black-and-white photos of people at work with addresses of contacts. Cross-referenced to related jobs and articles.

*Career World. Real World.* Serial. Nine monthly issues. Teachers' edition. General Learning Corp. Connecting with the vo-tech teachers on your staff. Aimed at middle school and older. Interviews with people about their jobs; articles on job-related issues.

*Educational Rankings Annual 1991.* Edited by Lynn C. Hattendorf. Gale, 1991. ISBN: 0-8103-7808-6. Covers fifteen hundred national, regional, local, and international lists and rankings of schools; indexed topically and alphabetically.

Franklin, Carl and Susan Kinnell. *Hypertext/Hypermedia In Schools: A Resource Book.* ABC-CLIO, 1990. ISBN: 0-87436-563-5. A practical handbook that explains the hardware and software and how to apply this new technology in the school. The authors salute the "revolution," thereby suggesting that using hypertext/hypermedia in education can drastically change our methods. The instructional design available through this new technology does encourage and assist students in managing their own learning. A very informative, challenging resource with many ideas for successful projects. The glossary will put you in touch and prove useful to both beginning and advanced users.

Fry, Edward B., et al. *The New Reading Teacher's Book of Lists.* Prentice Hall, 1985. ISBN: 0-13-615543-X. Contains extensive word lists which make this book a practical tool for reading teachers across grade levels.

Goldberg, Natalie. *Writing Down the Bones: Freeing the Writer Within.* Shambhala Publications, Inc., 1986. ISBN: 0-87773-375-9. An important book for teachers who write or who teach writing. A book about how to create.

Haglund, Elaine and Marcia L. Harris. *On the Day.* Libraries Unlimited, 1983. ISBN: 0-87287-345-5. Chronological listing of personalities, places, and events. Reproducible activity sheets and task cards. Very useful for planning enrichment activities in the elementary grades.

Heller, Dawn Hansen and Ann Montgomery. *Winning Ideas from Winning Schools.* ABC-CLIO, 1989. ISBN: 0-87436-527-9. Innovative high school programs that have received awards. Recommended by *School Library Journal* (2/90).

Hunter, Beverly and Erica K. Lodish. *Online Searching in the Curriculum. A Teaching Guide for Library/Media Specialists and Teachers.* ABC-CLIO, 1988. ISBN: 0-87436-516-3. Mastering online searching, for teachers and their students. *Online Searcher* (Winter/89) says "topics chosen are challenging and relevant to teenagers."

Laughlin, Mildred Knight and Patricia Payne Kardaleff. *Literature-Based Social Studies: Children's Books and Activities to Enrich the K–5 Curriculum.* Oryx, 1991. ISBN: 0-89774-605-8. Whole language is now on everyone's tongue. This book is "just the resource needed," according to *School Library Journal* (4/91).

*Literature and Life: Making Connections in the Classroom.* Edited by Patricia Phelan. NCTE, 1990. ISBN: 0-81-12962-5. The articles in this book deal with specific grade level activities to foster the integration and appreciation of literature in the classroom. Helpful for language arts teachers who are intent upon enriching their curriculum and promoting creative listening, writing, and reading skills.

**Means, Beth and Lindy Lindner.** *Clear and Lively Writing, Creative Ideas and Activities, Grades 6–10.* **Libraries Unlimited, 1988. ISBN: 0-87287-645-4.** A source for good ideas as well as getting across the practical aspects of writing.

**Nehring, James.** *"Why Do We Gotta Do This Stuff, Mr. Nehring?" Notes from a Teacher's Day in School.* **M. Evans and Company, 1989. ISBN: 0-449-90536-5.** Entertaining and thought-provoking for educators interested in the problems of school reform. You are sure to recognize someone in Amesley Junior-Senior High!

**Price, Janet R., Alan H. Levine, and Eve Cary.** *The Rights of Students.* **Third edition. (An American Civil Liberties Handbook). Southern Illinois University Press, 1988. ISBN: 0-8093-1423-1.** Good to be informed on this issue.

*Public Education: It's a Bull Market.* **Produced by Hobart Swan. Filmakers Library, 1990.** A film that disturbingly presents the influence of business on education.

*Scholarships, Fellowships, and Loans. 1992–93.* **Edited by Debra Kirby. Gale, 1991. ISBN: 0-8103-8347-0.** The source for high school students as well as those professionals who are advising them regarding higher education.

**Streiff, Jane E.** *Secondary School Librarian's Almanac: Month-by-Month Activities, Displays, and Procedures for the Entire School Year.* **The Center for Applied Research in Education, 1989. ISBN: 0-87628-783-6.** The suggested lesson plans and activities make this a useful resource for teachers as well as librarians.

*Thesaurus of ERIC Descriptors.* **Oryx, 1990. ISBN: 0-89774-561-2.** Designing strategies for searching the ERIC database.

*Thinking Your Way to Better SAT Scores.* A professional Development Video Seminar for Educators. Half-inch or three-quarter-inch format. PBS Video. 1989. Grades 3–12. Prepared and produced by Dr. Gary R. Gruber as a teacher training program or for actual test preparation with students.

**Toffler, Alvin.** *Powershift: Knowledge, Wealth, and Violence at the Edge of the 21st Century.* **Bantam Books, 1990. ISBN: 0-553-05776-6.** The third in Toffler's trilogy of important books that examine powerful changes in our society. First *Future Shock* dealt with the process of change; then *The Third Wave* explored the directions of change. Now *Powershift* helps us understand the global power struggles that will determine who will control, and how changes will be controlled.

**Wells, Shirley E.** *At-Risk Youth: Identification, Programs, and Recommendations.* **Libraries Unlimited, 1990. ISBN: 0-87287-812-0.** VOYA (12/90) lists this as an excellent volume for any educator looking for information on this topic. The author presents characteristics of at-risk youth, identification checklists, descriptions of programs that tackle the problem, and practical recommendations to school districts, teachers, and parents. The basis of the book is research in more than one hundred districts and state departments of education.

**Wigginton, Eliot.** *Sometimes a Shining Moment: The Foxfire Experience.* **Double-day, 1985. ISBN: 0-385-13358-8.** An inspirational book for teachers and other educators, written by the teacher-author-publisher of *Foxfire* magazine.

*Young Children.* **Serial. Journal of the National Association of Young Children.** A magazine that focuses on children from birth to age eight. Offers free lists of books, brochures, videos, and posters.

**Zinsser, William Knowlton.** *Writing to Learn.* **Harper and Row, 1988. ISBN: 0-06-091576-5.** In the preface to this book, the author tells us "knowledge is not as compartmented" as he once thought it was, that "it's not a hundred different rooms inhabited by strangers; it's all one house." This book, which complements *On Writing Well,* is all about writing across the curriculum, about interdisciplinary instruction.

# List 1–2.  For the Teacher: Reproducible List

Aker, Sharon. *The Macintosh Bible.* Goldstein & Blair, 1991.

Boyer, Ernest. *High School: A Report on Secondary Education in America.* Harper and Row, 1983.

Butzow, Carol. *Science Through Children's Literature.* Libraries Unlimited, 1989.

*Career Discovery Encyclopedia.* Ferguson, 1990.

*Career World.* Serial. Field Publications.

*Educational Rankings Annual 1991.* Gale, 1991.

Franklin, Carl. *Hypertext/Hypermedia in Schools: A Resource Book.* ABC-CLIO, 1990.

Fry, Edward, et al. *The New Reading Teacher's Book of Lists.* Prentice Hall, 1985.

Goldberg, Natalie. *Writing Down the Bones: Freeing the Writer Within.* Shambhala, 1986.

Haglund, Elaine. *On the Day.* Libraries Unlimited, 1983.

Heller, Dawn. *Winning Ideas from Winning Schools.* ABC-CLIO, 1989.

Hunter, Beverly. *Online Searching in the Curriculum.* ABC-CLIO, 1988.

Laughlin, Mildred. *Literature-Based Social Studies: Children's Books and Activities to Enrich the K–5 Curriculum.* Oryx, 1991.

*Literature and Life: Making Connections in the Classroom.* NCTE, 1990.

Means, Beth. *Clear and Lively Writing, Creative Ideas and Activities, Grades 6–10.* Libraries Unlimited, 1988.

Nehring, James. *"Why Do We Gotta Do This Stuff, Mr. Nehring?"* M. Evans, 1989.

Price, Janet. *The Rights of Students.* Third edition. Southern Illinois University Press, 1988.

*Public Education: It's a Bull Market.* Filmakers Library, 1990. (Film)

*Scholarships, Fellowships, and Loans, 1992–1993.* Edited by Debra Kirby. Gale, 1991.

Streiff, Jane E. *Secondary School Librarian's Almanac.* The Center for Applied Research in Education, 1989.

*Thesaurus of ERIC Descriptors.* Oryx, 1990.

*Thinking Your Way to Better SAT Scores.* PBS Video, Produced by Dr. Gary Gruber, 1989. (Video)

Toffler, Alvin. *Powershift.* Bantam Books, 1990.

Wells, Shirley. *At-Risk Youth: Identification, Programs, and Recommendations.* Libraries Unlimited, 1990.

Wigginton, Eliot. *Sometimes a Shining Moment.* Doubleday, 1985.

*Young Children.* Serial. National Association of Young Children.

Zinsser, William. *Writing To Learn.* Harper and Row, 1988.

# ABOUT BOOKS AND AUTHORS

> "Books will speak plain when counsellors blanch."
>
> FRANCES BACON
> *Essays: Of Counsel*

The following list focuses on resources that are more than simple bibliographies. These titles will guide the user to stories, plots, or themes that meet particular needs.

The authors enrich their recommendations with ideas for introducing books to children, stimulating reading, and relating themes to the curriculum.

## List 1–3. About Books and Authors: Annotated List

*Beacham's Guide to Literature for Young Adults.* **Volumes 1–5. Beacham Publishing Company.** Contents: Vol. 1–3, 1989. ISBN: 0-933-833-11-3, classic novels, biographies, and nonfiction. Vol. 4, 1989. ISBN: 0-933-833-16-4, science fiction, mystery, mythology, and adventure. Vol. 5, 1991. ISBN: 0-933-833-25-3, fantasy and Gothic titles. Features of this resource include illustrations from the book, an analysis of the literary devices, an overview of the work, an analysis of the characters and themes, and a biographical sketch of the author.

**Bernstein, Joanne E. and Masha Kabakow Rudman.** *Books to Help Children Cope with Separation and Loss: An Annotated Bibliography.* **Volume 3. R. R. Bowker, 1989. ISBN: 0-8352-2510-0.** Using books to help students accept loss that may arise from many causes. Selected readings for adults and a section on bibliotherapy. A directory of organizations and support groups may be helpful for your students.

*Bookwhiz Jr.* **Grades 3–6. Educational Testing Service, 1990.** Disks for the Apple computer. Program and game which include a database of one thousand books (fiction and nonfiction). *School Library Journal* (6/90) reviews this resource favorably and suggests it will encourage reading.

*DiscLit: American Authors.* **Twayne's United States Authors Series and OCLC American Authors Catalog. G. K. Hall & Company and OCLC.** CD format; full text of 143 Twayne volumes as well as the bibliography of literary criticism from OCLC. A compact disc tool which will be excellent for introducing information retrieval by CD-ROM.

**Freeman, Judy.** *Books Kids Will Sit Still For. The Complete Read-Aloud Guide.* **Second edition. R. R. Bowker, 1990. ISBN: 0-8352-3010-4.** Ages 3–12. The list of books is "right on target," according to *School Library Journal.* Entries include plot summaries. There are essays here on reading aloud, booktalking, creative dramatics and children's literature, storytelling, and celebrating books.

**Gallo, Donald R.** *Speaking for Ourselves: Autobiographical Sketches by Notable Authors of Books for Young Adults.* **NCTE, 1990. ISBN: 0-8141-4625-2.** Eighty-seven writers. These vignettes offer substance for students who like to read books by particular authors and want to learn more about them and for adults who like to understand the personalities of writers and to know more about the craft of writing.

**Gillespie, John T. and Corinne J. Naden.** *Juniorplots 3: A Book Talk Guide for Use with Readers Ages 12–16.* **R. R. Bowker, 1987. ISBN: 0-8352-2367-1.** Plot summaries of all the important incidents and characters in the suggested titles. Includes passages for discussion.

**Gillespie, John T. and Corinne J. Naden.** *Seniorplots: A Book Talk Guide for Use with Readers Ages 15–18.* **R. R. Bowker, 1989. ISBN: 0-8352-2513-5.** You, if you are in a high school, and your teachers may find this source useful for preparing book talks and assisting students to find the reading materials they want. At this level we are not generally called upon to give book talks, but this may be an activity you enjoy and would like to promote. Done well such talks will promote library use. About eighty books are included, divided into twelve subject and genre areas. Additional titles are suggested and bibliographies of reviews are included.

***Good Books, Good Times.*** **Selections by Lee Bennett Hopkins, pictures by Harvey Stevenson. Harper and Row, 1990. ISBN: 0-06-022527-0.** For grades K–3. A book about the joys of reading books, in poetry form. A fun and slightly crazy book. Watercolor paintings.

**Howard, Elizabeth.** *America As Story: Historical Fiction for Secondary Schools.* **ALA, 1988. ISBN: 0-8389-0492-0.** Books in these bibliographies were selected by the author and a review panel from standard selection sources and the suggestions of educators. The format is: bibliographic information, plot, comment, and suggestions for reports and activities. The titles are arranged by chronology in American history. One hundred fifty-four books are included here; they are indexed by author and title. The grade range is 6–12. Annotations arouse one's interest. The author comments on the historical relevance of the book. Keep this at the reference desk and encourage students to use it.

**Kennedy, DayAnn M. and Stella S. Spangler and Mary Ann Vanderwerf.** *Science and Technology in Fact and Fiction. A Guide to Children's Books.* **R. R. Bowker. 1990. ISBN: 0-8352-2708-1.** From a large databank of possible titles to meet your collection needs, indexed by reading level, author, title, and subject. Can be used by students to research their topics. Sixty-one categories are included with brief descriptions of the titles listed. Covers books in print 1983–1987.

**Kimmel, Margaret and Elizabeth Segel.** *For Reading Out Loud: A Guide to Sharing Books With Children.* **Delacorte, 1988. ISBN: 0-385-29660-6.** Three hundred books are described by plot and interest appeal. The authors include "suggested listening levels." The recommended materials can be used through grade eight.

**Landsberg, Michele.** *Reading for the Love of It.* **Prentice Hall. 1987. ISBN: 0-13-579822-1.** A discussion of the importance of reading, how to deal with the books the author identifies as "bad" books, censorship, stereotypes, etc. She selects four hundred "best" books, from beginning readers through books for teenagers.

**McCaffery, Larry.** *Across the Wounded Galaxies: Interviews With Contemporary American Science Fiction Writers.* **University of Illinois Press, 1990. ISBN: 0-252-01692-0.** Lively conversation with ten of our foremost writers. Some discussion of writing techniques and theory.

**Reed, Arthea J. S.** *Comics to Classics. A Parent's Guide to Books for Teens and Preteens.* **International Reading Association. 1989. ISBN: 0-87207-798-5.** Ages 10–20. This selection is organized in broad themes, and into categories of ages 10–13, 13–15, 15–18. Also discussed are the computer as a literacy aid and making TV work for the youngster. A buying guide to magazines is helpful, too. You will find the author's chapter on school libraries and borrowing books interesting. Checklists are provided for parents to determine the adequacy of their child's school library.

**Rochman, Hazel.** *Tales of Love and Terror: Booktalking the Classics, Old and New.* **ALA, 1987. ISBN: 0-8389-0463-7.** Brief descriptions of books with diverse settings and reading levels. Relates books by theme to reader interest.

**Sierra, Judy and Robert Kaminski.** *Twice Upon a Time: Stories to Tell, Retell, Act Out, and Write About.* **H. W. Wilson, 1989. ISBN: 0-8242-0775-0.** This is a book about the art of storytelling, creative dramatics, and writing, for those teachers and media specialists working with children ages 8–12. The introductory chapters deal with techniques. Twenty stories are included for the reader's use. Fifty more stories and poems are suggested in a bibliography. (For teachers and media specialists working with children ages 3–8, Sierra's book *The Flannel Board Storytelling Books* is recommended. Also from H. W. Wilson, 1987.)

**Smith, Charles A.** *From Wonder to Wisdom: Using Stories to Help Children Grow.* **New American Library. 1989. ISBN: 0-453-00697-3.** How make-believe can be used to teach children about life, to help them face difficulties, and to learn about themselves. The author draws upon both classics and modern stories to illustrate his ideas. This source should help elementary teachers and media specialists improve their storytelling skills, respond to children's questions, and help them deal with controversial problems through storytelling. The author is a specialist in human development. Two hundred and fifty children's books are reviewed and related to universal themes. "Storybreaks" appear throughout the book.

*Something About the Author.* **(SATA). Annual. Gale. ISSN: 0276-816-X.** Facts and pictures about authors and illustrators of books for young people. Includes early writers through contemporary writers. The "something" includes personal data, career information, the author's writings, works in progress, and "sidelights," which are interesting comments often provided by the author or illustrator. Bibliographies lend access to more information. Especially useful in the middle school. For the high school buy selected volumes of *Dictionary of Literary Biography,* also published by Gale Research.

**Spirt, Diana L.** *Introducing Bookplots 3: A Book Talk Guide for Use with Readers Ages 8–12.* **R. R. Bowker, 1989. ISBN: 0-8352-2345-0.** This source not only lists books and summarizes their themes, but also provides information about audiovisual aids.

*The VOYA Reader.* **Edited by Dorothey M. Broderick. Scarecrow Press, 1990. ISBN: 0-8108-2331-4.** Called "an excellent conceptual guide to library services for young adults" in *Booklist* (1/1/91).

*What Do I Read Next?* **By Neil Barron, Wayne Barton, Kristen Ramsdell and Steven A. Stilwell. Gale Research, 1991. ISBN: 0-8103-7555-9.** Descriptions of fifteen hundred new titles. Thoroughly indexed.

*World Authors, 1980–1985.* **Edited by Vineta Colby. H. W. Wilson. 1990. ISBN: 0-8242-0797-1.** Look for information on the entire *World Author* series. This latest includes 320 contemporary authors.

*The Writer's Chapbook: A Compendium of Fact, Opinion, Wit and Advice From the 20th Century's Preeminent Writers.* **Edited from** *The Paris Review* **interviews and introduced by George Plimpton. Viking, 1989. ISBN: 0-670-81565-9.** For your teachers and older students. Wide-ranging topics, with a gold mine of information about the authors, their work habits, and personalities. Included are gems like E. B. White's comment about writing for children: "Anyone who shifts gears when he writes for children is likely to wind up stripping his gears."

# List 1–3. About Books and Authors: Reproducible List

*Beacham's Guide to Literature for Young Adults.* Volumes 1–5. Beacham Publishing Company, 1989 and 1991.

Bernstein, Joanne E. *Books to Help Children Cope with Separation and Loss.* R. R. Bowker, 1989.

*Bookwhiz Jr.* Educational Testing Service, 1990. (Computer software)

*DiscLit: American Authors.* G. K. Hall & Co. and OCLC. (Compact disc)

Freeman, Judy. *Books Kids Will Sit Still For.* Second edition. R. R. Bowker, 1990.

Gallo, Donald R. *Speaking for Ourselves.* NCTE, 1990.

Gillespie, John T. and Corinne J. Naden. *Juniorplots 3: A Book Talk Guide for Use with Readers Ages 12–16.* R. R. Bowker, 1987.

Gillespie, John T. *Seniorplots.* R. R. Bowker, 1989.

*Good Books, Good Times.* Harper and Row, 1990.

Howard, Elizabeth. *America As Story: Historical Fiction for Secondary Schools.* ALA, 1988.

Kennedy, DayAnn M. *Science and Technology in Fact and Fiction.* R. R. Bowker, 1990.

Kimmel, Margaret. *For Reading Out Loud.* Delacorte, 1988.

Landsberg, Michele. *Reading for the Love of It.* Prentice Hall, 1987.

McCaffery, Larry. *Across the Wounded Galaxies.* University of Illinois Press, 1990.

Reed, Arthea J. S. *Comics to Classics.* International Reading Association, 1989.

Rochman, Hazel. *Tales of Love and Terror: Booktalking the Classics, Old and New.* ALA, 1987.

Sierra, Judy. *Twice Upon a Time.* H. W. Wilson, 1989.

Smith, Charles A. *From Wonder to Wisdom.* New American Library, 1989.

*Something About the Author.* Gale Research Co., Annual.

Spirt, Diana L. *Introducing Bookplots 3: A Book Talk Guide For Use with Readers Ages 8–12.* R. R. Bowker, 1989.

*The VOYA Reader.* Scarecrow Press, 1990.

*What Do I Read Next?* Gale Research, 1991.

*World Authors, 1980–1985.* H. W. Wilson, 1990.

*The Writer's Chapbook.* Edited from *The Paris Review.* Viking, 1989.

# FOR THE RELUCTANT READER

Synonyms for *reluctant* are *disinclined, hesitant,* and *shy.* How do you transform such a student into one who is bold and confident, one who is willing and inclined towards reading? Of course you do not perform miracles, and you often cannot learn about all the barriers, imaginary or real, that individuals may find between themselves and the act of reading. However, as the school media specialist, you want to include in your collection materials that will appeal to those children who are wary of reading. We know that nonprint materials may prove to be the lure as we attempt to captivate interest. The computer, especially, seems to be an outstanding tool for encouraging children to read. Computer programs entice many learners as no other medium can. Their appeal may be the association many make with games and adventure. Well-chosen software offers the student the opportunity to interact and to work at his own speed. Almost everyone will experience a degree of success. LiBretto reports in the third edition of *High/Low Handbook: Encouraging Literacy in the 1990s* (cited in the list below) that studies indicate early introduction of computers as tools for solving problems decreases the number of retentions and remediations.

There are many periodicals cited throughout this book that review the latest computer software and nonprint materials as well as books: *School Library Journal, Booklist, Media and Methods, The Computing Teacher,* and *The Reading Teacher.*

Here are several lists. The first is a guide to your selection of titles. The lists that follow are specific titles suggested for your collection organized by grade level.

## List 1–4. For the Reluctant Reader: Annotated List

**Carlin, Margaret F., Jeannine L. Laughlin, and Richard D. Saniga.** *Hear No Evil, See No Evil, Speak No Evil: An Annotated Bibliography for the Handicapped.* **Libraries Unlimited, 1990. ISBN: 0-87287-717-5.** Available on disks for Apple, Mac, and IBM computers. Lengthy annotations advise whether the titles discuss the handicaps appropriately. Readability is discussed.

Cummins, Julie and Blair Cummins. *Choices: A Core Collection for Young Reluctant Readers,* Volume 2. John Gordon Burke, Inc., 1990. ISBN: 0-934272-22-0. Reviewed in *Journal of Youth Services in Libraries* (Winter 1991). For grades 2–6. Two hundred seventy-five titles published between 1983 and 1988. These are books that could be used for whole language. Two-paragraph annotations. Interest and reading levels are indicated.

Gallant, Jennifer Jung. *Best Videos for Children and Young Adults. A Core Collection for Libraries.* ABC-CLIO, 1990. ISBN: 0-87436-561-9. Here are the video versions of those stories most likely to entice young readers.

*High/Low Handbook: Encouraging Literacy in the 1990's.* Third edition. Edited by Ellen V. LiBretto. R. R. Bowker, 1990. ISBN: 0-8352-2804-5. Recommended highly by *VOYA, School Library Media Quarterly,* and *School Library Journal.* The material about criteria for selection of computer software for the reluctant reader is very helpful. Over seventy of the "best" computer programs are cited.

Pilla, Marianne Laino. *Resources for Middle-Grade Reluctant Readers. A Guide for Librarians.* Libraries Unlimited, 1987. ISBN: 0-87287-547-4. For grades 4–6. Selection includes suggestions for the disinclined reader as well as the reading disabled.

Pilla, Marianne Laino. *The Best: High/Low Books for the Reluctant Readers.* Libraries Unlimited, 1990. ISBN: 0-87287-532-6. Available on disk for Apple, Mac, and IBM computers. Books in print for grades 3–12, plus some old favorites. Entries include bibliographic information, annotations, and reading and interest levels.

*High-interest Books for Teens.* Edited by Joyce Nakamura. Gale, 1988. ISBN: 0-8103-1830-X. Thirty-five hundred books of interest to teens, accessible by over five hundred subjects. Cites reviews.

*High Interest—Easy Reading.* Edited by William McBride. NCTE, 1990. ISBN: 0-8141-2097-0. For use by students, grades 7–12. Four hundred fiction and nonfiction titles, published in the last three years.

Moss, Joyce and George Wilson. *Films for Young Readers: Children's and Young Adults Books on Film and Video.* Gale, 1991. ISBN: 0-8103-7893-0. This resource takes its reviews from our standard selection tools and offers in-depth descriptions of popular films and videos (about twelve hundred titles).

*Quick Picks for Great Reading.* Published annually by ALA Graphics.

### Grades K–5

Anderson, Joan. *Harry's Helicopter.* Photographs by George Ancona. Morrow, 1990. ISBN: 0-688-09186-5. Photos illustrate a fantasy! Harry has daydreams, and they become real.

Barber, Antonia. *The Mousehole Cat.* Illustrated by Nicola Bayley. Macmillan, 1990. ISBN: 0-02-708331-4. This book received a starred review from *Booklist* (10/1/90). A beautiful book to encourage the most reluctant reader.

**Bunting, Eve.** *Is Anybody There?* **Lippincott, 1988. ISBN: 0-397-32303-4.** Story about a latchkey kid who comes home to find that things are missing.

**Conford, Ellen.** *Jenny Archer to the Rescue.* **Illustrated by Diane Phalmisciano. Little Brown, 1990. ISBN: 0-316-15351-6.** Jenny wants to practice her first aid skills. The "emergencies" she creates become humorous escapades.

**Fox, Mem.** *Guess What?* **Illustrated by Vivienne Goodman. Harcourt Brace Jovanovich, 1990. ISBN: 0-15-200452-1.** A guessing game book that will be fun for individual readers or for use at storytime.

**Peterson, P. J. and Betsy James.** *The Fireplug Is First Base.* **Dutton, 1990. ISBN: 0-525-44587-0.** Comics and text. It is amazing when little brother Flea finally gets to bat. Everyone is surprised.

**Shannon, George.** *Stories to Solve: Folktales from Around the World.* **Illustrated by Peter Sis. Beech Tree Books, 1991. ISBN: 0-688-10496-7.** Successfully used by elementary librarians and teachers to entice and intrigue the young reader. The brief problems and mysteries need solutions. Sure to promote lively discussion and encourage reading.

**Yolen, Jane.** *Sky Dogs.* **Illustrated by Barry Moser. Harcourt Brace Jovanovich, 1990. ISBN: 0-15-275480-6.** The Indian legend about the discovery of the horse is told here beautifully. The watercolor illustrations provide a sense of grandeur.

## Grades 6–8

**Barron, T. A.** *Heartlight.* **Philomel Books, 1990. ISBN: 0-399-22180-8.** An offbeat science-fiction story. Grandfather, eighty years old, is an astronomer working on a highly secret project. He says, "A person's life should be like a prism: inhaling light . . . exhaling rainbows." Mystery and adventure for grandfather and Kate, who loves him.

**Davis, Jenny.** *Sex Education.* **Orchard, 1988. ISBN: 0-531-08356-X.** Caring for a pregnant, troubled teenager.

**George, Jean Craighead.** *On the Far Side of the Mountain.* **Dutton, 1990. ISBN: 0-525-44563-3.** *Kirkus* calls this sequel to *My Side of the Mountain* "excellent" and "satisfying." More of Sam Gribley's survival skills in the Catskill Mountains.

**Grosser, Morton.** *The Fabulous Fifty.* **Atheneum, 1990. ISBN: 0-689-31656-9.** The boys in a club win a trip to New York City. The year is 1921, and the scenes of immigrant neighborhoods are realistic. America, the melting pot!

**Jackson, Alison.** *My Brother, the Star.* **Illustrated by Diane Dawson Hearn. Dutton, 1990. ISBN: 0-525-44512-9.** *School Library Journal* says, "Leslie is likeable and believable as he deals with his peers and family."

**Mazer, Norma Fox.** *C, My Name Is Cal.* **Scholastic, 1990. ISBN: 0-590-41833-5.** An easy read for middle schoolers, with good dialogue and an appeal to boys. Friendship survives.

**McDonald, Collin.** *Nightwaves: Scary Tales for After Dark.* **Dutton, 1990. ISBN: 0-525-65043-1.** Natural and supernatural, eerie and thrilling, stories that feature youngsters.

**Shriver, Jean Adair.** *Mayflower Man.* **Delacorte, 1991. ISBN: 0-385-30295-9.** Resourceful Caleb, a thirteen-year-old living in New Hampshire, comes up with a plan to save the family farm.

### Grades 9–12

**Crichton, Michael.** *Jurassic Park.* **Knopf, 1990. ISBN: 0-394-58816-9.** A "sort-of" science fiction adventure; fast-paced, dealing with real life dinosaurs in an amusement park. Received a starred review in *Booklist*.

**Hall, Lynn.** *Halsey's Pride.* **Charles Scribner's Sons. 1990. ISBN: 0-684-19155-5.** For ages 12 and up. ALA recommended.

**Klein, Norma.** *No More Saturday Nights.* **Knopf, 1988. ISBN: 0-394-91944-0.** *School Library Journal* calls it "a lively pick for popular reading." Tim takes on raising his baby, even though he is trying to go to college.

**Lyons, Mary E.** *Sorrow's Kitchen, The Life and Folklore of Zora Neale Hurston.* **Charles Scribner's Sons, 1990. ISBN: 0-684-19198-9.** Ages 12 and up. ALA recommended.

**McClung, Robert M.** *Hugh Glass, Mountain Man.* **Morrow Junior Books, 1990. ISBN: 0-688-08092-8.** A great survival novel based upon the story of a legendary hero of the West. Glass was abandoned by his companions on a hunting expedition; the story covers his perilous struggle for survival and "a final reckoning."

**Paulsen, Gary.** *Canyons.* **Delacorte, 1990. ISBN: 0-385-30153-7.** There is a mystic element here, as two boys from different centuries, and different cultures, meet. Set in Texas and featuring Apache culture.

**Pullman, Philip.** *The Tiger in the Well.* **Knopf, 1990. ISBN: 0-679-80214-2.** This is a sequel to *Ruby in the Smoke* and *The Shadow in the North*. Sally, a businesswoman and mother, is enmeshed in a web of evil in nineteenth century London. Historically accurate and detailed.

**Thompson, Julian F.** *Herb Seasoning.* **Scholastic, 1990. ISBN: 0-590-43023-8.** Humor and fantasy. *Booklist* recommends this selection.

# List 1–4. For the Reluctant Reader: Reproducible List

Carlin, Margaret. *Hear No Evil, Speak No Evil: An Annotated Bibliography for the Handicapped.* Libraries Unlimited, 1990.

Cummins, Julie. *Choices: A Core Collection for Young Reluctant Readers.* Volume 2. John Gordon Burke, 1990.

Gallant, Jennifer Jung. *Best Videos for Children and Young Adults.* ABC-CLIO, 1990.

*High/Low Handbook: Encouraging Literacy in the 1990's.* Edited by Ellen V. LiBretto. R. R. Bowker, 1990.

Pilla, Marianne Laino. *Resources for Middle-Grade Reluctant Readers.* Libraries Unlimited, 1987.

Pilla, Marianne Laino. *The Best: High/Low Books for the Reluctant Readers.* Libraries Unlimited, 1990.

*High-Interest Books for Teens.* Edited by Joyce Nakamura. Gale, 1988.

*High-Interest—Easy Reading.* Edited by William McBride. NCTE, 1990.

Moss, Joyce. *Films for Young Readers: Children's and Young Adults Books on Film and Video.* Gale, 1991.

*Quick Picks for Great Reading.* ALA Graphics.

## Grades K–5

Anderson, Joan. *Harry's Helicopter.* Morrow, 1990.

Barber, Antonia. *The Mousehole Cat.* Macmillan, 1990.

Bunting, Eve. *Is Anybody There?* Lippincott, 1988.

Conford, Ellen. *Jenny Archer to the Rescue.* Little Brown, 1990.

Fox, Mem. *Guess What?* Harcourt Brace Jovanovich, 1990.

Peterson, P. J. *The Fireplug Is First Base.* Dutton, 1990.

Shannon, George. *Stories to Solve: Folktales From Around the World.* Beech Tree Books, 1991.

Yolen, Jane. *Sky Dogs.* Harcourt Brace Jovanovich, 1990.

## Grades 6–8

Barron, T. A. *Heartlight.* Philomel, 1990.

Davis, Jenny. *Sex Education.* Orchard, 1988.

George, Jean Craighead. *On the Far Side of the Mountain.* Dutton, 1990.

Grosser, Morton. *The Fabulous Fifty.* Atheneum, 1990.

Jackson, Alison. *My Brother, the Star.* Dutton, 1990.

Mazer, Norma Fox. *C, My Name Is Cal.* Scholastic, 1990.

McDonald, Collin. *Nightwaves: Scary Tales for After Dark.* Dutton, 1990.

Shriver, Jean A. *Mayflower Man.* Delacorte, 1991.

### Grades 9–12

Crichton, Michael. *Jurassic Park.* Knopf, 1990.

Hall, Lynn. *Halsey's Pride.* Charles Scribner's, 1990.

Klein, Norma. *No More Saturday Nights.* Knopf, 1988.

Lyons, Mary E. *Sorrow's Kitchen, the Life and Folklore of Zora Neale Hurston.* Charles Scribner's, 1990.

McClung, Robert M. *Hugh Glass, Mountain Man.* Morrow, 1990.

Paulsen, Gary. *Canyons.* Delacorte, 1990.

Pullman, Philip. *The Tiger in the Well.* Knopf, 1990.

Thompson, Julian F. *Herb Seasoning.* Scholastic, 1990.

# Intellectually Challenging Resources

Especially demanding of media specialists are those students whose imaginations are keen and lively and whose cognitive skills outdistance their peers'. They are often searching on their own for materials to stretch their minds and enrich their experiences. Often they focus on special interests and request new materials to take them further in their quests. They are not always those students who excel in every area of school life, but they have a drive to meet the challenge of their inquiring minds. Generally they can cope with the complexities of language and respond with imagination to different points of view. We strive to help them understand the world around them. Often we simply make good writing available to them; other times we may suggest a selection in a nonprint medium.

This list of resources will assist you in acquiring titles to meet the demands of these students. Following that are lists of specific titles to consider for your collections.

## List 1–5. Intellectually Challenging Resources: Annotated List

**ALA Youth Division. Lists and Awards: Printed annually in *Booklist: Best Books for Young Adults, Children's Notable Books, Newbery and Caldecott Showcase, Fiction for the Gifted,* and *Editor's Choice*.** Look for "outstanding" lists from ALA for the college bound, and "outstanding" lists of fiction, biography, nonfiction, theater, etc.

**Gallant, Jennifer Jung. *Best Videos for Children and Young Adults: A Core Collection for Libraries*. ABC-CLIO, 1990. ISBN: 0-87436-561-9.** Journals are now including videos in their reviews, but the use of television as a teaching aid in schools has grown to such an extent that our teachers are constantly searching for the newest and best. This source presents an annotated list of 350 videos that have received awards or consistently high reviews. The targeted audience, use, and full bibliographic information are offered.

***Good Reading*. 22nd edition. Edited by Arthur Waldhorn, Olga S. Welber, Arthur Zeiger. R. R. Bowker, 1985. ISBN: 0-8352-2100-8.** The "one hundred significant books" listed at the beginning of this reference will be useful for selection of "classics." Additionally, the books in the lists are arranged by broad categories (historical periods, literary types, etc.) and are cross-referenced. A brief essay introduces each section.

Hauser, Paul and Gail A. Nelson. *Books for the Gifted Child*. Volume 2. R. R. Bowker, 1990. ISBN: 0-8352-2467-8. Selection for grades Primary–6. Covers books published from 1980 through 1987. This source offers long reviews of the titles, which makes it particularly useful.

Jarnow, Jill. *All Ears: How to Choose and Use Recorded Music for Children*. Penguin, 1991. ISBN: 0-1401-1254-5. A guide to good listening. Offers "listening age appeal" ratings. Targeted for parents but the access to catalogs and the tips for locating recordings are helpful for librarians and teachers. The "all ears sampler" contains well-annotated suggestions. While mostly for elementary age levels, they contain some suggestions "for all ages." Source, format, target ages, materials, artists, and style of recording are helpful features of the annotations.

## Grades K–5

Allen, Marjorie N. and Shelley Rotner. *Changes*. Illustrated with photographs by Shelley Rotner. Macmillan, 1991. ISBN: 0-02-700252-7. Called a "multi-leveled concept book" by *The Bulletin of the Center for Children's Books*. A fine selection for your young naturalists, it explores growth sequences in nature.

dePaola, Tomie. *Bonjour, Mr. Satie*. Illustrated by the author. Putnam, 1991. ISBN: 0-399-21782-7. Higher-level thinking skills will be necessary to recognize the many subtleties in this story within a story. Different artists are here in this story told by Mr. Satie (a very sophisticated cat.)

*Dinosaurs!* Video. Golden Book Video, 1987. This video presentation will stimulate interest in the subject through clever animation and live-action. At thirty minutes it may be too long for the little ones.

Kaye, M. M. *The Ordinary Princess*. Pocket Books, 1989. ISBN: 0-671-69013-2. A princess receives a gift from a fairy, decreeing her to be ordinary. Readers will see that it is who you are, not how you look, that truly counts in life.

Macaulay, David. *Black and White*. Houghton Mifflin. 1990. ISBN: 0-395-52151-3. A 1991 Caldecott medal winner, and a 1990 ALA Notable Children's Book. Various sources indicated "all ages" as the target audience. This bold, unusual book will stretch children's imaginations.

Provensen, Alice. *The Buck Stops Here: The Presidents of the United States*. Harper, 1990. ISBN: 0-06-024786-X. Lots of information here presented in short verses.

*The Velveteen Rabbit*. Video. Random House, 1985. Meryl Streep narrates this charming tale. This 26-minute video features pastel drawings. Producer: Clay Sites.

**Whitmore, Arvella.** *The Bread Winner.* **Houghton Mifflin, 1990. ISBN: 0-395-53705-3.** The story of a gritty girl who keeps her family together through hard work and perseverance. Reviewed in *The Reading Teacher* (5/91).

### Grades 6–8

**Avi.** *The True Confessions of Charlotte Doyle.* **Orchard, 1990. ISBN: 0-531-05893-X.** Charlotte is a thirteen-year-old passenger on a transatlantic voyage in 1832, traveling without her parents. She keeps a journal of her intriguing, mysterious adventure.

**Cormier, Robert.** *Beyond the Chocolate War.* **Knopf, 1985. ISBN: 0-394-97343-7.** This sequel to *The Chocolate War* is replete with plots and subplots, subtle and intense. Sure to engage with its look at the darker side of human nature.

**Dalton, Annie.** *Out of the Ordinary.* **HarperCollins, 1990. ISBN: 0-06-021425-2.** A novel about a fifteen-year-old who takes care of a unique child from a parallel world. *Kirkus Reviews* calls this first novel "thought-provoking."

**Greenberg, Jan and Sandra Jordan.** *The Painter's Eye: Learning to Look at Contemporary American Art.* **Delacorte, 1991. ISBN: 0-385-30319-X.** *Kirkus Reviews* says of this beautiful book that it is a "mind-expanding book—not easy, but rewarding." Terms and concepts are explained, quotes by the artists are included, as are black-and-white and color plates. (*Kirkus*, 6/15/91)

**Park, Ruth.** *Things in Corners.* **Viking, 1991. ISBN: 0-670-822265-6.** There are five stories in this collection of fantastic fiction set in Australia. For readers who like the supernatural this is an excellent recommendation.

***Pegasus.*** **Video. Hi-Tops Video, 1990.** Intriguing, dramatic telling of the popular Greek myth. Mia Farrow narrates this 25-minute video; Ernest Troost wrote the music.

**Stine, R. L.** *Phone Calls.* **Archway, 1990. ISBN: 0-671-69497-9.** A comedy of errors, with a plot based on the phone calls of a group of teenagers. *School Library Journal* recommends it (10/90): the "character development is excellent."

**Tchudi, Susan J.** *The Young Writer's Handbook.* **Charles Scribner's Sons, 1984. ISBN: 0-684-18090-1.** Procedures for the beginning writer in the areas of journal-writing, themes, letters, reports, etc. The intriguing first chapter asks: "Why Write?" This is for your students who cannot resist writing, generally going beyond anything required in school.

### Grades 9–12

**Adams, Douglas.** *Last Chance to See.* **Harmony Books, 1991. ISBN: 0-517-58215-5.** Readers are familiar with Adams' excursions through time and space in the Hitchhikers' trilogy. Here he travels with zoologist Mark Carwardine around the world in search of rare and endangered animals.

***Center Stage: One-Act Plays for Teenage Readers and Actors*.** HarperCollins, 1990. ISBN: 0-06-022171-2. Ten plays that feature teenagers, written by award-winning authors. These are thought-provoking plays for sheer reading enjoyment or for performance. The final play allows the reader to write his or her own ending.

**Gilbar, Steven. *The Open Door: When Writers First Learned to Read*.** David R. Godine, Publisher, Inc., 1989. ISBN: 0-87923-809-7. A delightful book with a preface by Barbara Bush in which she writes: "Few things in life are as important as being able to read." The author has selected twenty-nine writers for this collection. He has prefaced each writer's own words with a succinct biographical sketch. Photographs of the writers are included. Each selection reinforces the concept that books and reading do influence lives.

**Harrington, Philip. *Touring the Universe Through Binoculars*.** John Wiley and Sons, Inc., 1990. ISBN: 0-471-51337-7. One hundred years after *Astronomy with an Opera-Glass* this hobby is still fascinating. The author proves that one can be an explorer of the skies without a large telescope.

**Norman, Michael. *These Good Men: Friendships Forged from War*.** Crown, 1990. ISBN: 0-517-55984-6. Eighteen years after the Vietnam War, Norman contacts the members of his squad. The resilience of the human spirit and the effects of war are portrayed in these personality sketches.

**Stern, Jerome. *Making Shapely Fiction*.** W. W. Norton, 1991. ISBN: 0-373-02929-8. A book with helpful advice and examples of the techniques needed by the serious writer. An essay entitled "Don't Do This" suggests ways to avoid common pitfalls in your writing. The author is director of the writing program at Florida State University. He brings a light touch to this topic and offers a book full of wisdom, technical advice, and examples.

**Trillin, Calvin. *American Stories*.** Ticknor and Fields, 1991. ISBN: 0-395-59367-0. True stories told masterfully. From the experiences of a reporter for *The New Yorker*. Many of the personalities will be familiar to today's teenagers.

**Van Doren, Charles. *The Joy of Reading*.** Harmony Books, 1985. ISBN: 0-517-55580-8. What makes a masterpiece? Van Doren discusses the elements found in his favorite books. An annotated bibliography is included which notes the best editions of the classics he discusses. He writes, "Life without books would be, for me, a vacant horror."

***Voices from the Attic*.** Video. Direct Cinema, 1988. A documentary about the Holocaust. Excellent for social studies discussion, portraying the endurance and courage of families hiding from the Nazis in Poland. Fifty-seven minutes.

# List 1–5.  Intellectually Challenging Resources: Reproducible List

### Grades K–5

Allen, Marjorie N. *Changes*. Macmillan, 1991.

dePaola, Tomie. *Bonjour, Mr. Satie*. Putnam, 1991.

*Dinosaurs!* Golden Book Video, 1987. (Video)

Kaye, M. M. *The Ordinary Princess*. Pocket Books, 1989.

Macaulay, David. *Black and White*. Houghton Mifflin, 1990.

Provensen, Alice. *The Buck Stops Here: The Presidents of the United States*. Harper, 1990.

*The Velveteen Rabbit*. Video. Random House, 1985.

Whitmore, Arvella. *The Bread Winner*. Houghton Mifflin, 1990.

### Grades 6–8

Avi. *The True Confessions of Charlotte Doyle*. Orchard, 1990.

Cormier, Robert. *Beyond the Chocolate War*. Knopf, 1985.

Dalton, Annie. *Out of the Ordinary*. HarperCollins, 1990.

Greenberg, Jan. *The Painter's Eye*. Delacorte, 1991.

Park, Ruth. *Things in Corners*. Viking, 1991.

*Pegasus*. Hi-Tops Video, 1990. (Video)

Stine, R. L. *Phone Calls*. Archway, 1990.

Tchudi, Susan J. *The Young Writer's Handbook*. Charles Scribner's Sons, 1984.

**Grades 9–12**

Adams, Douglas. *Last Chance to See.* Harmony Books, 1991.

*Center Stage: One-Act Plays for Teenage Readers and Actors.* HarperCollins, 1990.

Gilbar, Steven. *The Open Door: When Writers First Learned to Read.* David R. Godine, 1989.

Harrington, Philip. *Touring the Universe Through Binoculars.* John Wiley and Sons, 1990.

Norman, Michael. *These Good Men: Friendships Forged from War.* Crown, 1990.

Stern, Jerome. *Making Shapely Fiction.* W. W. Norton, 1991.

Trillin, Calvin. *American Stories.* Ticknor and Fields, 1991.

Van Doren, Charles. *The Joy of Reading.* Harmony Books, 1985.

*Voices from the Attic.* Direct Cinema, 1988. (Video)

**References**

ALA Youth Division. Lists and Awards: Printed annually in *Booklist: Best Books for Young Adults, Children's Notable Books, Newbery and Caldecott Showcase, Fiction for the Gifted,* and *Editor's Choice.*

Gallant, Jennifer Jung. *Best Videos for Children and Young Adults: A Core Collection for Libraries.* ABC-CLIO, 1990.

*Good Reading.* 22nd edition. R. R. Bowker, 1985.

Hauser, Paul and Gail A. Nelson. *Books for the Gifted Child.* Volume 2. R. R. Bowker, 1990.

Jarnow, Jill. *All Ears: How to Choose and Use Recorded Music for Children.* Penguin, 1991.

# POETRY

"The experience of each new age requires a new confession, and the world seems always waiting for its poet."

RALPH WALDO EMERSON
*Essays, Second Series: The Poet*

"We are the music-makers/And we are the dreamers of dreams," wrote the poet Arthur William Edgar O'Shaughnessy in *Ode*. Guiding your students to an appreciation of the music and the dreams of the poets is one of the finest gifts you can bestow. From the rhymes of their first picture books to contemporary free verse they may acquire a thirst that only poetry will quench.

Here are several references for your consideration as well as grade-level lists of titles to add to your poetry collections.

## List 1–6.   Poetry: Annotated List

Glazer, Joan I. and Linda Leonard Lamme. **"Poem Picture Books and Their Uses in the Classroom."** *The Reading Teacher,* **October 1990.** With an extensive bibliography.

Janeczko, Paul. *The Place My Words Are Looking For: What Poets Say About and Through Their Work.* **Bradbury, 1990. ISBN: 0-02-747671-5.** Insights into the craft of poetry and the lives of poets.

Spiegel, Dixie Lee. **"Materials to Introduce Children to Poetry."** *The Reading Teacher.* **February 1991.** Read about *Poetry Please!,* a part of a thirteen-tape video series.

*The World's Best Poetry for Children.* **Two volumes. Poetry Anthology Press, 1986. ISBN: 0-89609-260-7.** The format of this resource makes it easy to use. There are nine major sections with themes such as sorrow, love, home, and friendship. Five hundred poems are indexed by author, title, and first lines. Biographical dates are given for the authors, and a chronology of world poetry is included.

### Grades K–5

Adoff, Arnold. *In for Winter, Out for Spring.* **Illustrated by Jerry Pinkney. Harcourt Brace Jovanovich, 1991. ISBN: 0-15-238637-8.** The illustrator's dedication in this selection reads "In celebration of the family." The poems focus on the seasons and the life of a young black girl named Rebecca.

**Feldman, Jacqueline.** *The Lavender Box.* **Illustrated by Nannette Hoffman. Ellicott Press, 1990. ISBN: 0-9623903-0-5.** Ink drawings complement the poems in this collection. *School Library Journal* recommended this volume saying, "imagery reverberates on every page," and also suggested its value as a read-aloud.

*For Laughing Out Loud. Poems to Tickle Your Funny Bone.* **Selected by Jack Prelutsky. Illustrated by Marjorie Priceman. Knopf, 1991. ISBN: 0-394-82144-0.** One hundred thirty-two puns and poems, riddles, and rhymes.

**Hubbell, Patricia.** *A Grass Green Gallop.* **Illustrated by Ronald Himler. Atheneum, 1990. ISBN: 0-689-31604-6.** This is a collection that celebrates the horse in diverse poetry forms. The pictures are great for younger readers.

**Johnston, Tony.** *I'm Gonna Tell Mama I Want an Iguana.* **Illustrated by Lillian Hoban. Putnam, 1990. ISBN: 0-399-21934-X.** Humor, of course, in a happy picture book.

**Kennedy, X. J.** *The Kite That Braved Old Orchard Beach: Year-Round Poems for Young People.* **Illustrated by Marian Young. Margaret K. McElderry Books, 1991. ISBN: 0-689-50507-8.** *Kirkus* called this a solid collection, and *VOYA* said the poems capture particularly well the emotions of growing up.

**Lewis, Claudia.** *Up in the Mountains and Other Poems of Long Ago.* **Illustrated by Joel Fontaine. HarperCollins, 1991. ISBN: 0-06-023810-0.** Sixteen poems that tell of family life at the turn of the century. The feelings and emotions are universal and timeless.

**Prelutsky, Jack.** *Beneath a Blue Umbrella.* **Illustrated by Garth Williams. Greenwillow Books, 1990. ISBN: 0-688-06429-9.** A collection of short, humorous poems in which a hungry hippo raids a melon stand, a butterfly tickles a girl's nose, and children frolic in a Mardi Gras parade.

**Prelutsky, Jack.** *Something Big Has Been Here.* **Illustrated by James Stevenson. Greenwillow Books, 1990. ISBN: 0-688-06434-5.** Humorous poetry by a prize winner.

**Smith, William Jay.** *Birds and Beasts.* **Illustrated by Jacques Hnizdovsky. Godine, 1990. ISBN: 0-87923-865-8.** This collection combines twenty-nine poems with woodcuts and a joyful, breezy charm.

**Stevenson, Robert Louis.** *My Shadow.* **Illustrated by Ted Rand. Putnam, 1990. ISBN: 0-399-22216-2.** Children in different places in the world see their shadows in Rand's lively illustrations of Stevenson's famous poem.

*'Til All the Stars Have Fallen: A Collection of Poems for Children.* **Selected by David Booth and illustrated by Kady MacDonald Denton. Viking, 1991. ISBN: 0-670-83272-3.** A collection of seventy-six poems which *Kirkus* calls a "delightful gathering." *School Library Journal* starred their review of it.

***To the Moon and Back: A Collection of Poems*. Compiled by Nancy Larrick and illustrated by Catharine O'Neill. Delacorte, 1991. ISBN: 0-385-30159-6.** *Booklist* indicates that this is a good collection for reading aloud. The poets are mostly contemporary, and the poems are full of imagination. The illustrations are pen drawings; letterpress printing. A lighthearted collection with lovely artwork.

## Grades 6–8

***American Sports Poems*. Selected by R. R. Knudson and May Swenson. Orchard, 1988. ISBN: 0-531-08353-5.** From funny to sublime. You will be hard-pressed to find any sport unrepresented here—even wrestling and pumping-iron.

**Berry, James. *When I Dance*. Illustrated by Karen Barbour. Harcourt Brace Jovanovich, 1991. ISBN: 0-15-295568-2.** Berry's roots are Caribbean, and his poems reflect both that culture and his experiences in Great Britain.

***Gonna Bake Me a Rainbow Poem: A Student Guide to Writing Poetry*. Compiled by Peter Sears. Scholastic, 1990. ISBN: 0-590-43085-5.** A collection that will encourage young poets to write. These are the winners of the Scholastic writing contests. The poets offer comments about how they work, and Sears makes constructive and instructive suggestions.

**Hearne, Betsy. *Polaroid and Other Poems of View*. Photos by Peter Kiar. Atheneum, 1991. ISBN: 0-689-50530-2.** A collection of poems about adolescents and their reflections on their world.

***I Like You, If You Like Me: Poems of Friendship*. Selected by Myra Cohn Livingston. Macmillan, 1987. ISBN: 0-689-50408-X.** Ninety poems by both contemporary and traditional poets.

**Livingston, Myra Cohn. *Poem-Making: Ways to Begin Writing Poetry*. Harper-Collins, 1991. ISBN: 0-06-024020-2.** A solid technical guide to use with students to examine what makes a good poem. In addition the collection includes wonderful examples of many types of poetry that will interest and excite young readers and writers.

***A New Treasury of Poetry*. Selected by Neil Philip. Illustrated by John Lawrence. Workman, 1990. ISBN: 1-55670-145-4.** *Publishers Weekly* reports, "Young and old will find treasures to last a lifetime." Good selection for all the favorites. Two hundred eighty-eight poems in all.

***Preposterous: Poems of Youth*. Selected by Paul Janeczko. Orchard, 1991. ISBN: 0-531-08501-5.** About one hundred short poems by contemporary poets that illuminate the years of adolescence.

***Talking to the Sun: An Illustrated Anthology of Poems for Young People*. Selected by Kenneth Koch and Kate Farrell. The Metropolitan Museum of Art and Henry Holt and Company, 1985. ISBN: 0-87099-436-0.** The poems in this beautiful collection have been selected from various time periods and from many countries. The poems are arranged by theme and are illustrated with reproductions of artwork from The Metropolitan Museum of Art. A unique blend of the two arts.

***Who Do You Think You Are? Poems About People*. Edited by David Woolger. Oxford, 1990. ISBN: 0-19-276074-2.** Some of the poems in this collection are from non-Western cultures and have been translated into English. Hazel Rochman, *Booklist* (12/15/90) reviewer, suggests using these poems for booktalks and read-alouds. About one hundred poems in all.

***Wider Than the Sky: Poems to Grow Up With*. Collected by Scott Elledge. Harper and Row, 1990. ISBN: 0-06-021787-1.** In the preface the author offers advice about reading poetry. Explanatory notes are added at the end of the collection, which includes a range of poetry from Seuss to Shakespeare. There are two hundred poems in all. (The title is taken from Emily Dickinson's "The Brain Is Wider Than the Sky.")

**Willard, Nancy. *The Ballad of Biddy Early*. Illustrated by Barry Moser. Knopf, 1989. ISBN: 0-394-8814-0.** This selection was a notable children's trade book in the field of social studies. Willard draws upon the legend of Biddy Early, a nineteenth century Irish woman, for her inspiration. The watercolors complement the mysterious element of the woman's rather mystical powers.

## Grades 9–12

**Ackerman, Diane. *Jaguar of Sweet Laughter: New and Selected Poems*. Random House, 1991. ISBN: 0-679-40214-4.** The *Booklist* review (4/1/91) says Ackerman's words "chime, sing, and ring," and called this fine collection a "must for poetry collections of any size."

***Ain't I a Woman! A Book of Women's Poetry From Around the World*. Compiled by Illona Linthwaite. Peter Bedrick Books, 1988. ISBN: 0-87226-187-5.** Contributions by women from many ethnic groups, in many different styles, and about many different themes.

**Angelou, Maya. *I Shall Not Be Moved*. Random, 1990. ISBN: 0-394-47142-3.** "Angelou writes about love, beauty, the South, the struggle for freedom, and the dignity black people have maintained against all odds." (*School Library Journal*)

**Balaban, John. *Words for My Daughter*. Copper Canyon, 1991. ISBN: 1-55659-037-7.** A winner in the National Poetry Series. The poet was a conscientious objector in the Vietnam War and served in the medical corps. With his poems, recalling vivid memories, are the translations of other poets' works.

***Five Hundred Years of English Poetry. Chaucer to Arnold*. Compiled by Barbara Lloyd-Evans. Peter Bedrick Books, 1990. ISBN: 0-87226-215-4.** A comprehensive anthology, making available the works of the major English poets in one volume. *School Library Journal* recommended it for all libraries.

**Glenn, Mel. *My Friend's Got This Problem, Mr. Candler: High School Poems*. Photograph illustrations by Michael J. Bernstein. Clarion, 1991. ISBN: 0-89919-833-3.** This is Glenn's fourth book of poetry about high school students. Poems and photos ring true.

**Henderson-Holmes, Safiya.** *Madness and a Bit of Hope.* **Harlem River Press, 1991. ISBN: 0-86316-136-7.** *Booklist* (7/91) called this collection, "A vivid, visceral work that deserves a wide audience." The poems are tightly constructed, yet rhythmic.

*Life Doesn't Frighten Me at All.* **Compiled by John Agard. Holt, 1990. ISBN: 0-8050-1237-0.** On the ALA "Best" list for 1990, this collection features writers from many countries and from well-known to lesser known poets.

*The Rattle Bag.* **Selected by Seamus Heaney and Ted Hughes. Faber and Faber, 1990 (reprint). ISBN: 0-571-11966-2.** The *Times Literary Supplement* praised this anthology as exciting and splendid. The editors have chosen poems of great diversity. Some are selected from oral traditions, others are contemporary.

**Stewart, Mary.** *Frost on the Window and Other Poems.* **Morrow, 1991. ISBN: 0-688-10541-6.** Romantic rhymes from the well-known novelist.

**Strauss, Gwen.** *Trail of Stones.* **Illustrated by Anthony Browne. Knopf, 1990. ISBN: 0-679-80582-6.** This small collection of poems received a starred review in *Booklist.* The poems are based upon old fairy tales.

**Willard, Nancy.** *Water Walker.* **Knopf, 1989. ISBN: 0-394-57208-4.** Called a "miraculous and wonderful book" in a starred *Booklist* review, this small volume celebrates the wonders of our world.

# List 1–6.  Poetry: Reproducible List

## Grades K–5

Adoff, Arnold. *In for Winter, Out for Spring.* Harcourt Brace Jovanovich, 1991.

Feldman, Jacqueline. *The Lavender Box.* Ellicott Press, 1990.

*For Laughing Out Loud: Poems to Tickle Your Funny Bone.* Selected by Jack Prelutsky. Knopf, 1991.

Hubbell, Patricia. *A Grass Green Gallop.* Atheneum, 1990.

Johnston, Tony. *I'm Gonna Tell Mama I Want an Iguana.* Putnam, 1990.

Kennedy, X. J. *The Kite That Braved Old Orchard Beach: Year-Round Poems for Young People.* Margaret K. McElderry Books, 1991.

Lewis, Claudia. *Up in the Mountains and Other Poems of Long Ago.* HarperCollins, 1991.

Prelutsky, Jack. *Beneath a Blue Umbrella.* Greenwillow, 1990.

Prelutsky, Jack. *Something Big Has Been Here.* Greenwillow, 1990.

Smith, William Jay. *Birds and Beasts.* Godine, 1990.

Stevenson, Robert Louis. *My Shadow.* Illustrated by Ted Rand. Putnam, 1990.

*'Til All the Stars Have Fallen: A Collection of Poems for Children.* Selected by David Booth. Viking, 1991.

*To the Moon and Back: A Collection of Poems.* Compiled by Nancy Larrick. Delacorte, 1991.

## Grades 6–8

*American Sports Poems.* Selected by R. R. Knudson and May Swenson. Orchard, 1988.

Berry, James. *When I Dance.* Harcourt Brace Jovanovich, 1991.

*Gonna Bake Me a Rainbow Poem: A Student Guide to Writing Poetry.* Compiled by Peter Sears. Scholastic, 1990.

Hearne, Betsy. *Polaroid and Other Poems of View.* Atheneum, 1991.

*I Like You, If You Like Me: Poems of Friendship.* Selected by Myra Cohn Livingston. Macmillan, 1987.

Livingston, Myra Cohn. *Poem-Making: Ways to Begin Writing Poetry.* HarperCollins, 1991.

*A New Treasury of Poetry.* Selected by Neil Philip. Workman, 1990.

*Preposterous: Poems of Youth.* Selected by Paul Janeczko. Orchard, 1991.

*Talking to the Sun: An Illustrated Anthology of Poems for Young People.* Selected by Kenneth Koch. Henry Holt, 1985.

*Who Do You Think You Are? Poems About People.* Edited by David Woolger. Oxford, 1990.

*Wider Than the Sky: Poems to Grow Up With.* Collected by Scott Elledge. Harper and Row, 1990.

Willard, Nancy. *The Ballad of Biddy Early.* Knopf, 1989.

### Grades 9–12

Ackerman, Diane. *Jaguar of Sweet Laughter: New and Selected Poems.* Random House, 1991.

*Ain't I a Woman! A Book of Women's Poetry From Around the World.* Compiled by Illona Linthwaite. Peter Bedrick, 1988.

Angelou, Maya. *I Shall Not Be Moved.* Random, 1990.

Balaban, John. *Words for My Daughter.* Copper Canyon, 1991.

*Five Hundred Years of English Poetry.* Compiled by Barbara Lloyd-Evans. Peter Bedrick, 1990.

Glenn, Mel. *My Friend's Got This Problem, Mr. Candler: High School Poems.* Clarion, 1991.

Henderson-Holmes, Safiya. *Madness and a Bit of Hope.* Harlem River Press, 1991.

*Life Doesn't Frighten Me at All.* Compiled by John Agard. Holt, 1990.

*The Rattle Bag.* Selected by Seamus Heaney and Ted Hughes. Faber and Faber, 1990.

Stewart, Mary. *Frost on the Window and Other Poems.* Morrow, 1991.

Strauss, Gwen. *Trail of Stones.* Knopf, 1990.

Willard, Nancy. *Water Walker.* Knopf, 1989.

### References

Glazer, Joan I. and Linda Leonard Lamme. "Poem Picture Books and Their Uses in the Classroom." *The Reading Teacher,* October 1990.

Janeczko, Paul. *The Place My Words Are Looking for: What Poets Say About and Through Their Work.* Bradbury, 1990.

*The World's Best Poetry for Children.* Poetry Anthology Press, 1986.

# PICTURE BOOKS

> **"What is the use of a book,"** thought Alice,
> **"without pictures or conversations?"**
>
> LEWIS CARROLL
> *Alice's Adventures in Wonderland*

Often we select picture books for children with few criteria to guide us. The pictures may seem unique and appealing to us, while the theme may elude us. Thinking we should foster particular interests, we select with that in mind only to find out that the pictures are not at all inspiring. In addition to referring you to our standard selection tools, I call to your attention the following sources. The article by Jeffrey Hurt will afford new insights into the process of picture book selection and will offer criteria to help you establish your selection standards. *A to Zoo* is another acquisition tool from that vast R. R. Bowker database. While here I am suggesting only picture books for young beginning readers, the book by Patricia Cianciolo will guide you to the best illustrated books for all ages.

## List 1–7.  Picture Books: Annotated List

### Selection Resources

Cianciolo, Patricia J. *Picture Books for Children*. Third edition. ALA, 1990. ISBN: 0-8389-0527-7.

Hurt, Jeffrey. "A Preference Oriented Guide for Selecting Picture Books," *School Library Media Quarterly*. AASL, Spring 1991.

Lima, Carolyn and John A. Lima. *A to Zoo: Subject Access to Children's Picture Books*. Third edition. R. R. Bowker, 1989. ISBN: 0-8352-2599-2.

### Favorite Titles

Aliki. *Manners*. Greenwillow, 1990. ISBN: 0-688-09198-9. Aliki's illustrations add just the right lighthearted touch to interest little ones and teach them some basics in an appealing way.

Gibbons, Gail. *The Puffins Are Back!* HarperCollins, 1991. ISBN: 0-06-021603-4. A read-aloud, and a fine natural history lesson.

**Hadithi, Mwenye.** *Lazy Lion.* **Illustrated by Adrienne Kennaway. Little Brown, 1990. ISBN: 0-316-33725-0.** Nothing threatening about this lazy lion. Soft, water-washed pictures.

**Johnson, Angela.** *When I Am Old With You.* **Illustrated by David Soman. Orchard, 1990. ISBN: 0-531-05884-0.** This gentle story about the bond between a child (African-American) and his grandfather received a starred review in *School Library Journal*. Illustrated with watercolors. *Booklist* calls the sentiments expressed "universal."

**Macaulay, David.** *Black and White.* **Houghton Mifflin. 1990. ISBN: 0-395-52151-3.** A Caldecott winner; called a literary recreation, this imaginative book will keep everyone intrigued.

**Paterson, Katherine.** *The Tale of the Mandarin Ducks.* **Illustrated by Leo and Diane Dillon. Dutton, 1990. ISBN: 0-525-67283-4.** *Booklist* gave this Japanese fairy tale, with its lovely watercolor and pastel illustrations, a starred review.

**Ringgold, Faith.** *Tar Beach.* **Crown, 1991. ISBN: 0-517-58030-6.** The paintings "combine human warmth and ethereal beauty," as reviewed in *Booklist*.

**Rounds, Glen.** *Cowboys.* **Holiday House, 1991. ISBN: 0-8234-0867-1.** Wonderful sketches by the author show the cowboys rounding up cattle, playing cards in the bunkhouse, and killing a rattlesnake. Who can resist the mystique of the cowboy?

**San Souci, Robert D.** *The White Cat: An Old French Fairy Tale.* **Illustrated by Gennady Spirin. Orchard, 1990. ISBN: 0-531-05809-4.** A retelling of Madame D'Aulnoy's tale. *School Library Journal* (10/90) reviewed it favorably, commenting on the directness of this version and the "elaborate, detailed illustrations."

**Sis, Peter.** *Beach Ball.* **Greenwillow, 1990. ISBN: 0-688-09182-2.** A *New York Times* best illustrated book. Reviewed in *School Library Journal* (12/90).

**Van Allsburg, Chris.** *Just a Dream.* **Houghton Mifflin, 1990. ISBN: 0-395-53308-2.** A young litterbug who thinks recycling trash is a waste of time, Walter can't believe that his friend would give him "the stupidest" birthday present ever—a tree. Then he dreams a terrifying vision of what the future could be like.

**Wilson, Sarah.** *Three In a Balloon.* **Scholastic, 1990. ISBN: 0-688-09173-3.** *School Library Journal* called this a "resource to be treasured." These three are the first air passengers (truly!)—a sheep, a duck, and a rooster. *Booklist* says, "A delightful, high-flying trip."

**Wood, Don and Audrey.** *Piggies.* **Illustrated by Don Wood. Harcourt Brace Jovanovich, 1991. ISBN: 0-15-256341-5.** All about those ten little toes. Definitely primary.

**Yolen, Jane.** *Bird Watch.* **Illustrated by Ted Lewin. Putnam, 1990. ISBN: 0-399-21612-X.** Lovely watercolor illustrations introduce seventeen birds.

# List 1–7.  Picture Books: Reproducible List

Aliki. *Manners*. Greenwillow, 1990.

Gibbons, Gail. *The Puffins Are Back!* HarperCollins, 1991.

Hadithi, Mwenye. *Lazy Lion*. Illustrated by Adrienne Kennaway. Little Brown, 1990.

Johnson, Angela. *When I Am Old With You*. Illustrated by David Soman. Orchard, 1990.

Macaulay, David. *Black and White*. Houghton Mifflin, 1990.

Paterson, Katherine. *The Tale of the Mandarin Ducks*. Illustrated by Leo and Diane Dillon. Dutton, 1990.

Ringgold, Faith. *Tar Beach*. Crown, 1991.

Rounds, Glen. *Cowboys*. Holiday House, 1991.

San Souci, Robert D. *The White Cat: An Old French Fairy Tale*. Illustrated by Gennady Spirin. Orchard, 1990.

Sis, Peter. *Beach Ball*. Greenwillow, 1990.

Van Allsburg, Chris. *Just a Dream*. Houghton Mifflin, 1990.

Wilson, Sarah. *Three In a Balloon*. Scholastic, 1990.

Wood, Don and Audrey. *Piggies*. Illustrated by Don Wood. Harcourt Brace Jovanovich, 1991.

Yolen, Jane. *Bird Watch*. Illustrated by Ted Lewin. Putnam, 1990.

### Resource Materials

Cianciolo, Patricia J. *Picture Books for Children*. ALA, 1990.

Hurt, Jeffrey. "A Preference Oriented Guide for Selecting Picture Books," *School Library Media Quarterly*. AASL, Spring 1991.

Lima, Carolyn and John A. *A to Zoo: Subject Access to Children's Picture Books*. R. R. Bowker, 1989.

# FAMILY LIFE

> "The family is one of nature's masterpieces."
>
> GEORGE SANTAYANA
> *The Life of Reason*

Rudyard Kipling spent several years in a foster home, a grim environment in which there were few pleasures and in which reading became an escape for the young boy. He wrote in *Something of Myself* that reading was "a means to everything that would make me happy," and a story in a magazine was "a history of real people and real things." Other writers tell of reading as the gateway to understanding people and the door to self-realization.

Educators have always used literature to stimulate their students' thinking and to help those students to understand human behavior and relationships. In troubled times, with the number of students in family situations that are new and different, we are all challenged to gain greater social insight. This selection of stories about family life should prove useful to you and other teachers. They have been written by gifted writers who portray their characters clearly and interpret different situations with honesty.

## List 1–8.  Family Life: Annotated List

*Grades K–5*

**Alexander, Sally Hobart. *Mom Can't See Me*. Photos by George Ancona. Macmillan, 1990. ISBN: 0-02-700401-5.** True portrayal of an author's blindness from the point of view of her daughter, telling how the family copes.

**Anholt, Catherine. *Aren't You Lucky!* Little Brown, 1991. ISBN: 0-316-04264-1.** A child learns to accept a new baby brother. Sibling rivalry in a book for very small children.

**Booth, Barbara D. *Mandy*. Illustrated by Jim LaMarche. Lothrop, 1991. ISBN: 0-688-10339-1.** A poignant and beautiful story of a deaf child's love and attachment for her grandmother.

**Brooks, Bruce. *Everywhere*. HarperCollins, 1991. ISBN: 0-06-020729-9.** Two boys save a beloved grandfather.

**Bunting, Eve.** *Fly Away Home.* **Illustrated by Ronald Himler. Clarion, 1991. ISBN: 0-395-55962-6.** A boy and his father are among the homeless, living in airports. Should prompt sympathetic responses from students regarding this timely theme.

**Bunting, Eve.** *The Wall.* **Illustrated by Ronald Himler. Clarion, 1990. ISBN: 0-395-51588-2.** A boy visits the Vietnam War Memorial in Washington D.C. with his father for the purpose of finding his grandfather's name there. You will find the story, with the somber illustrations, moving, especially if you have visited this beautiful monument.

**Lyon, George Ella.** *Cecil's Story.* **Illustrated by Peter Catalanetto. Orchard, 1991. ISBN: 0-531-05912-X.** Father is called away to war.

**Munsch, Robert.** *Love You Forever.* **Illustrated by Sheila McGraw. Firefly Books, 1982. ISBN: 0-920668-36-4.** A touching story to be read aloud, about a young boy and his mother's strong love. It spans their lives from his infancy to her old age.

**Waddell, Martin.** *Grandma's Bill.* **Illustrated by Jane Johnson. Orchard, 1991. ISBN: 0-531-05923-5.** Bill visits Grandma every week. There she shares with him her photograph album with pictures of Grandpa Bill.

**Willhoite, Michael.** *Daddy's Roommate.* **Alyson, 1990. ISBN: 1-55583-178-8.** A story about daddy's gay relationship. This may fill a need in your collection.

### Grades 6–8

**Barrie, Barbara.** *Lone Star.* **Delacorte, 1990. ISBN: 0-385-30156-1.** Family life during war time, being a new kid in school, facing anti-Semitism.

**Clarke, J.** *Al Capsella and the Watchdogs.* **Henry Holt, 1991. ISBN: 0-8050-1598-1.** What do you do about strange parents? Tolerate them. The setting is Australian, but the parent-child relationships are universal.

**DeClements, Barthe.** *Monkey See. Monkey Do.* **Delacorte, 1990. ISBN: 0-385-30158-8.** Father is an embarrassment, so how can you make friends? A divorce, too.

**Doherty, Berlie.** *White Peak Farm.* **Orchard, 1990. ISBN: 0-531-0846-7.** On the 1991 ALA "best" list, this series of stories set in Great Britain depicts life in a family with an autocratic father.

**Hamilton, Virginia.** *Cousins.* **Philomel, 1990. ISBN: 0-399-22164-6.** Lots of cousins, complex plot. Grief and guilt, family love. A starred review in *Booklist* (10/1/90).

**Hathorn, Libby.** *Thunderwith.* **Little, 1991. ISBN: 0-316-35034-6.** This intriguing story is set in Australia. Lara must accept her mother's death and adjust to a step-family.

**Mazer, Harry.** *Someone's Mother Is Missing.* **Delacorte, 1990. ISBN: 0-385-30161-8.** Financial trouble after Father's death; Mother loses her grip on reality; Lisa learns to tolerate an unappealing cousin.

**Meryman, Richard.** *Andrew Wyeth.* **Abrams, 1991. ISBN: 0-8109-3956-8.** Biography of the painter. About growing up among gifted siblings in an artist's family.

**Schenker, Dona.** *Throw a Hungry Loop.* **Knopf, 1990. ISBN: 0-679-80332-7.** *School Library Journal* (10/90) reviewed this "realistic" story favorably. Strong family ties and values.

### Grades 9–12

**Conway, Jill Ker.** *The Road From Coorain.* **Knopf, 1989. ISBN: 0-394-57456-7.** An autobiography of an Australian girl who felt a strong commitment to family while striving to achieve her life ambitions. A Harvard graduate, she became the first woman president of Smith College. The book is beautifully written. *VOYA* recommended it highly.

**Gordimer, Nadine.** *My Son's Story.* **Farrar, 1990. ISBN: 0-374-21751-3.** The story of a young man in South Africa whose family is torn by political differences. An ALA editor's choice.

**Murdoch, Anna.** *Coming to Terms.* **HarperCollins, 1991. ISBN: 0-06-018303-9.** An unusual family moves from California to New York state to care for an aging uncle and overcomes the difficulties of resettlement.

**Porter, Connie.** *All-Bright Court.* **Houghton, 1991. ISBN: 0-395-53271-X.** A group of families are followed through years of change, upheaval, and hard times. Love survives.

**Schwartz, Steven.** *Lives of the Father.* **University of Illinois, 1991. ISBN: 0-252-01815-X.** This group of stories about men—uncles, sons, fathers—is given a starred review by *Booklist* (7/91). The stories are sensitive, understanding, and quite powerful.

**Strom, Yale.** *A Tree Still Stands: Jewish Youth in Eastern Europe Today.* **Putnam, 1990. ISBN: 0-399-22154-9.** The shadow of the Holocaust remains, still affecting young lives and family relationships. This photo-essay portrays the fears and the hopes of children growing up in several countries of eastern Europe.

**Thesman, Jean.** *The Rain Catchers.* **Houghton, 1991. ISBN: 0-395-55333-4.** It's an unusual family—a fourteen-year-old and a collection of older women. But there is love and understanding among the well-drawn characters, and important lessons in life.

**Yount, John.** *Thief of Dreams.* **Viking, 1991. ISBN: 0-670-83802-0.** In the 1940s, in the mountains of North Carolina, a fourteen-year-old comes of age in a family that is coming apart. Sensitively written.

# List 1–8.  Family Life: Reproducible List

### Grades K–5

Alexander, Sally Hobart. *Mom Can't See Me.* Macmillan, 1990.

Anholt, Catherine. *Aren't You Lucky!* Little Brown, 1991.

Booth, Barbara D. *Mandy.* Lothrop, 1991.

Brooks, Bruce. *Everywhere.* HarperCollins, 1991.

Bunting, Eve. *Fly Away Home.* Clarion, 1991.

Bunting, Eve. *The Wall.* Clarion, 1990.

Lyon, George Ella. *Cecil's Story.* Orchard, 1991.

Munsch, Robert. *Love You Forever.* Firefly Books, 1982.

Waddell, Martin. *Grandma's Bill.* Orchard, 1991.

Willhoite, Michael. *Daddy's Roommate.* Alyson, 1990.

### Grades 6–8

Barrie, Barbara. *Lone Star.* Delacorte, 1990.

Clarke, J. *Al Capsella and the Watchdogs.* Henry Holt, 1991.

DeClements, Barthe. *Monkey See, Monkey Do.* Delacorte, 1990.

Doherty, Berlie. *White Peak Farm.* Orchard, 1990.

Hamilton, Virginia. *Cousins.* Philomel, 1990.

Hathorn, Libby. *Thunderwith.* Little, 1991.

Mazer, Harry. *Someone's Mother Is Missing.* Delacorte, 1990.

Meryman, Richard. *Andrew Wyeth.* Abrams, 1991.

Schenker, Dona. *Throw a Hungry Loop.* Knopf, 1990.

### Grades 9–12

Conway, Jill Ker. *The Road From Coorain.* Knopf, 1989.

Gordimer, Nadine. *My Son's Story.* Farrar, 1990.

Murdoch, Anna. *Coming to Terms.* HarperCollins, 1991.

Porter, Connie. *All-Bright Court.* Houghton, 1991.

Schwartz, Steven. *Lives of the Father.* University of Illinois, 1991.

Strom, Yale. *A Tree Still Stands: Jewish Youth in Eastern Europe Today.* Putnam, 1990.

Thesman, Jean. *The Rain Catchers.* Houghton, 1991.

Yount, John. *Thief of Dreams.* Viking, 1991.

# Holidays

"The maid-servant, the sailor, and the schoolboy, are the three beings that enjoy a holiday beyond all the rest of the world," wrote Leigh Hunt in *The Maid-Servant* many years ago. And, since children may not have yet acquired those "secret anniversaries of the heart" that Longfellow felt were the "holiest of holidays," we note special days with happy celebrations in the schools.

Here is a list of materials about holidays worthy of your consideration. You will want to preview the many holiday videos and audiovisual materials offered by such producers as Pied Piper Media.

## List 1–9.  Holidays: Annotated List

Bauer, Caroline Feller. *Celebrations: Read-Aloud Holiday and Theme Book Programs.* H. W. Wilson, 1985. ISBN: 0-8242-0708-4. A teacher or media specialist's dream. Recipes, activities, readings, poems, games, and crafts for celebrating our ethnic heritage. Sixteen clever book programs are presented here. Each program includes a booklist for further readings of both classic and new selections.

*Chase's Annual Events: Special Days, Weeks and Months.* Annual. Contemporary Books. ISSN: 0740-5286. A chronological presentation of holidays and festivals. Interesting features are presidential proclamations, historic anniversaries, folklore, and the birthdates of celebrities.

Dunkling, Leslie. *A Dictionary of Days.* Facts On File, 1988. ISBN: 0-8160-1916-9. A reader's guide to all the named days in English-speaking countries. Named by *Library Journal* as one of the best reference books of 1988. Delightful to browse through.

*The Folklore of American Holidays.* Gale, 1987. ISBN: 0-8103-2126-2. "A compilation of more than four hundred beliefs, legends, superstitions, proverbs, riddles, poems, songs, dances, games, plays, pageants, fairs, foods, and processions associated with over a hundred American calendar customs and festivals." (From the title page, and, yes, they are all there!) This compilation is chronologically arranged with subject and ethnic group indexes. Editors are Hennig Cohen and Tristam Potter Coffin.

Shemanski, France. *A Guide to World Fairs and Festivals.* Greenwood, 1985. ISBN: 0-313-10786-0. Every celebration imaginable is here, even the most obscure, from the running of the bulls in Pamplona to running the Paris marathon. An appendix organizes the festivals by types, then one locates the description through the name index. A useful calendar of festivals is included.

van Straalin, Alice. *The Book of Holidays Around the World.* Dutton, 1986. ISBN: 0-525-44270-7. This is a full calendar of a year's events. According to the dust jacket, one can find a reason to celebrate on every day of the year. The festivals are illustrated by reproductions of artwork, and delicate decorations are added by Jaye Holme.

## Grades K–5

Barber, Antonia. *The Mousehole Cat.* Illustrated by Nicola Bayley. Macmillan, 1990. ISBN: 0-02-708331-4. On *Booklist's* 1991 "best" list: "exquisitely precise, imaginative illustrations . . . a gem of a book." Christmas in Cornwall.

*The Birthday Burglar and a Very Wicked Headmistress.* G. K. Hall. Two audiocassettes, 90 minutes. A reading of the novel by Margaret Mahy, which is a humorous adventure.

Bresnick-Perry, Rosyln. *Holiday Memories of a Shtetl Childhood.* Folkway Records. Audiocassette, 51 minutes. The memories of a wonderful childhood within an extended family in Russia.

Bunting, Eve. *How Many Days to America?* Illustrated by Beth Peck. Houghton Mifflin, 1990. ISBN: 0-395-54777-6. Brings new insights into the meaning of Thanksgiving.

Cuyler, Margery. *Daisy's Crazy Thanksgiving.* Illustrated by Robin Kramer. Holt, 1990. ISBN: 0-8050-0559-5. Thanksgiving is wild at Grandma and Grandpa's when Grandma forgets to cook the turkey and Grandpa wants pizza. There are animals and crazy relatives; all pretty wacky.

*Las Navidades: Popular Christmas Songs from Latin America.* Selected by Lulu Delacre and translated from the Spanish by Elena Paz. Scholastic, 1990. ISBN: 0-590-43548-5. This is a great selection since the traditions of the celebrations in various countries are explained and nicely illustrated.

Lindgren, Astrid. *Lotta's Easter Surprise.* Illustrated by Llon Wikland. R & S Books (Farrar), 1991. ISBN: 91-29-59862-1. The watercolor illustrations express the warmth and hope of spring. A book of family happiness, and a lovely surprise.

Livingston, Myra Cohen. *Celebrations.* Holiday House, 1985. ISBN: 0-8234-0550-8. Illustrated with paintings by Leonard Everett Fisher. A beautiful book of sixteen holidays celebrated in poetry. The watercolor illustrations perfectly complement each.

Lowry, Linda. *Martin Luther King Day.* Illustrated by Hetty Mitchell. Carolrhoda Books, 1987. ISBN: 0-87614-299-4. A portrait of this American hero in an inviting, easy-to-read book. Gives the background for the first annual celebration on January 20, 1986.

**Martin, Bill, Jr.** and **John Archambault.** *The Ghost-Eye Tree.* **Illustrated by Ted Rand. Holt, Rinehart and Winston, 1988. ISBN: 0-8050-0947-7.** A brother and sister's ghostly trip after dark to get milk. Good read-aloud for Halloween with primary grade children.

**Rosen, Mike.** *Winter Festivals.* **ISBN: 0-531-18353-X. 1990.** *Spring Festivals.* **ISBN: 0-531-18384-X. 1991.** *Summer Festivals.* **ISBN: 0-531-18383-1. 1991.** *Autumn Festivals.* **ISBN: 0-531-18352-1. 1990.** This series of books is published by Bookwright Press. They are illustrated with slick, contemporary photographs that will interest students immediately. Glossaries and bibliographies for further reading are included.

**Schotter, Roni.** *Hanukkah!* **Little Brown, 1989. ISBN: 0-316-77466-9.** Five young children and their family celebrate a magic, happy holiday in this lovely picture book.

**Stock, Catherine.** *Secret Valentine.* **Bradbury, 1991. ISBN: 0-02-788372-8.** This is one of a series of holiday picture books (*Birthday Surprise* and *Easter Surprise* are the others). The stories are simple and the watercolor illustrations are very appealing. This Valentine story is about intergenerational affection.

**Yolen, Jane.** *Hark! A Christmas Sampler.* **Illustrated by Tomie dePaola. Original arrangements by Adam Stemple. Putnam, 1991. ISBN: 0-399-21853-X.** Traditional folk tales, hymns, songs, and poems provide a delightful collection for celebrating the holiday. dePaola's illustrations complement beautifully.

### Grades 6–8

**Bradbury, Ray.** *The Halloween Tree.* **Illustrated by Joseph Mugnaini. Knopf, 1988 (reissue of the 1972 publication). ISBN: 0-394-82409-1.** *VOYA* called this a "gem." Eight boys travel back through the years to learn the meaning of Halloween and discover that many cultures celebrated the end of summer with ceremonies.

*A Christmas Gift.* **Video. Produced by Will Vinton. Billy Budd, 1980.** Clay animation of the ballad *Christmas Dinner.*

**Graham-Barber, Lynda.** *Mushy! The Complete Book of Valentine Words.* **Illustrated by Betsy Lewin. Bradbury Press, 1991. ISBN: 0-02-736941-2.** The title page quotes Thomas Carlyle: "If a book comes from the heart/It will continue to reach other hearts." If your students are intrigued by all the words we associate with Valentine's Day, here is the book for them. From *flirt* to *honeymoon*, they can learn about them here.

*It's No Crush, I'm In Love.* **Video. Produced by Elaine Halpert Sperber. Learning Corporation of America, 1983.** An ABC After-School Special that will stimulate discussion about what love is. The heroine falls in love with her teacher whose only interest in her is a selfish one.

**Limburg, Peter R.** *Weird! The Complete Book of Halloween Words.* **Illustrated by Betsy Lewin. Bradbury Press, 1989. ISBN: 0-02-759050-X.** More fun with words; lots of information about the origins of spooky words.

*Grades 9–12*

**Bannatyne, Lesley.** *Halloween: An American Holiday, An American History.* **Facts On File, 1990. ISBN: 0-8160-1846-4.** This volume traces the history of our Halloween customs through contemporary sources and oral history. Includes unusual facts and anecdotes.

**Kelly, Kate.** *Election Day: An American Holiday, An American History.* **Facts On File, 1991. ISBN: 0-8160-1871-5.** Traces the evolution of our voting processes and the history of our elections. The author's research offers a picture of how this holiday celebrates the democratic process in our country.

*Quasi Maestro.* **Video. Produced by Will Vinton and David Altschul. Will Vinton Productions, 1987.** Claymation in which the actors are the bells during a rendition of "Bell Ringers" in a cathedral. Lots of fun.

*Skeleton.* **Video. Produced by Seaton McLean and Atlantis Films. Beacon/ Altschul, 1988. From the** *Ray Bradbury Theatre Series.* Well done, with a chilling climax. Good for Halloween programming at the high school level or in writing classes studying the short story.

# List 1–9.  Holidays: Reproducible List

Bauer, Caroline Feller. *Celebrations: Read-Aloud Holiday and Theme Book Programs.* H. W. Wilson, 1985.

*Chase's Annual Events: Special Days, Weeks and Months.* Annual. Contemporary Books.

Dunkling, Leslie. *A Dictionary of Days.* Facts On File, 1988.

*The Folklore of American Holidays.* Gale, 1987.

Shemanski, France. *A Guide to World Fairs and Festivals.* Greenwood, 1985.

van Straalin, Alice. *The Book of Holidays Around the World.* Dutton, 1986.

### Grades K–5

Barber, Antonia. *The Mousehole Cat.* Macmillan, 1990.

*The Birthday Burglar and a Very Wicked Headmistress.* G. K. Hall. (Audiocassettes)

Bresnick-Perry, Rosyln. *Holiday Memories of a Shtetl Childhood.* Folkway Records. (Audiocassettes)

Bunting, Eve. *How Many Days to America?* Houghton Mifflin, 1990.

Cuyler, Margery. *Daisy's Crazy Thanksgiving.* Holt, 1990.

*Las Navidades: Popular Christmas Songs from Latin America.* Selected by Lulu Delacre. Scholastic, 1990.

Lindgren, Astrid. *Lotta's Easter Surprise.* R & S Books, 1991.

Livingston, Myra Cohen. *Celebrations.* Holiday House, 1985.

Lowry, Linda. *Martin Luther King Day.* Carolrhoda Books, 1987.

Martin, Bill, Jr. *The Ghost-Eye Tree.* Holt, Rinehart and Winston, 1985.

Rosen, Mike. *Winter Festivals.* Bookwright Press, 1990.

Rosen, Mike. *Spring Festivals.* Bookwright Press, 1991.

Rosen, Mike. *Summer Festivals.* Bookwright Press, 1991.

Rosen, Mike. *Autumn Festivals.* Bookwright Press, 1990.

Schotter, Roni. *Hanukkah!* Little Brown, 1989.

Stock, Catherine. *Secret Valentine.* Bradbury, 1991.

Yolen, Jane. *Hark! A Christmas Sampler.* Putnam, 1991.

### Grades 6–8

Bradbury, Ray. *The Halloween Tree.* Knopf, 1988.

*A Christmas Gift.* Billy Budd, 1980. (Video)

Graham-Barber, Lynda. *Mushy! The Complete Book of Valentine Words.* Bradbury Press, 1991.

*It's No Crush, I'm In Love.* Learning Corp. of America, 1983. (Video)

Limburg, Peter R. *Weird! The Complete Book of Halloween Words.* Bradbury Press, 1989.

### Grades 9–12

Bannatyne, Lesley. *Halloween: An American Holiday, An American History.* Facts On File, 1990.

Kelly, Kate. *Election Day: An American Holiday, An American History.* Facts On File, 1991.

*Quasi Maestro.* Will Vinton Productions, 1987. (Video)

*Skeleton.* Produced by Seaton McLean/Atlantis Films, 1988. (Video)

# SPORTS

By sports like these are all their cares beguil'd/
The sports of children satisfy the child.

GOLDSMITH
*The Traveler*

I hope you can load the bases with a few of the selections in the following lists. There are fiction and nonfiction titles featuring different recreational and competitive sports. Some should interest the spectator, others the participant. Consider them for your spring line-up or the first string. There may be a few bench warmers here, and certainly a pinch-hitter or two.

## List 1–10.  Sports: Annotated List

### Grades K–5

**Barrett, Norman. *Canoeing*. Watts, 1988. ISBN: 0-531-10349-8.** Team this one up with Barrett's *Windsurfing* (ISBN: 0-531-10354-4) for an attractive pair that present overviews of the sports and exciting color photos. The equipment used as well as a bit of history and records set in competition are included.

**Christopher, Matt. *Hit-Away Kid*. Little Brown, 1988. ISBN: 0-316-13995-5.** Barry learns about sportsmanship.

**Giff, Patricia. *Ronald Morgan Goes to Bat*. Viking, 1988. ISBN: 0-670-81457-1.** What it takes to succeed. A first reader that says hooray for enthusiasm and practice.

**Marzollo, Jean. *Red Ribbon Rosie*. Random, 1988. ISBN: 0-394-98406-4.** You might introduce this book to your elementary students just before field day. This story about Rosie portrays the temptation to win at any cost in the familiar setting of field day competitions.

**Miller, J. David. *The Super Book of Football*. Sports Illustrated, 1990. ISBN: 0-316-57370-1.** *School Library Journal* (3/91) reviewed this as a book sure to delight young football fans. Useful for middle school students as well. Charts of records and statistics will interest the older enthusiasts.

**Schmidt, Gerald D. *Let's Go Fishing: A Book for Beginners*. Illustrated by Brian Payne. Roberts Rinehart, 1990. ISBN: 0-911797-84-X.** Freshwater fishing in America, illustrated with line drawings. The instructions are clearly presented, and the diagrams that show how to tie knots and how to prepare the catch are sure to intrigue young readers.

**Slote, Alfred.** *Finding Buck McHenry.* **HarperCollins, 1991. ISBN: 0-06-021653-0.** Jason collects baseball cards and also plays the game. In pursuing his interests he discovers some information that may prove his friend, the school janitor, was really a great baseball player. The reader will learn something about old prejudices in the game, as well as being entertained by the story.

**Solomon, Chuck.** *Playing Hockey.* **Crown, 1990. ISBN: 0-517-57414-4.** A photo-essay book that features color photos and brief captions. The energy and spirit that are communicated will interest young readers in the game.

## Grades 6–8

*Baseball Cards: Questions and Answers.* **Edited by Jon Brecka. Krause Publications, 1990. ISBN: 0-87341-144-7.** Collecting baseball cards has become a popular hobby, particularly with middle school students. Older enthusiasts will like this book, also. A compilation of the most frequently asked questions with the answers, provided by *Sports Collectors Digest.*

**Berler, Ron.** *The Super Book of Baseball.* **Sports Illustrated, 1991. ISBN: 0-316-09240-1.** History, players, the American and National leagues, and record holders are the categories in this entertaining book. The statistics, trivia, and glossary of terminology will intrigue the middle school reader.

*A Century of Children's Baseball Stories.* **Edited by Debra Dagavarian. Stadium Books, 1990. ISBN: 0-9625132-0-2.** The selections included here appeared in magazines and offer a historical perspective of the game. The nine stories are arranged chronologically and thereby present a developmental view of the rules and social significance of the game.

**Gutman, Bill.** *Smitty.* **Turman Publishing Company, 1988. ISBN: 0-89872-301-9.** A girl on a boys' team!

*He Makes Me Feel Like Dancin'.* **Video. Produced by Emile Ardolino. Edgar J. Scherick Associates, 1984.** Jacques D'Amboise excites school children about dance in this lively video.

**Parker, Donald.** *Table Tennis.* **Ward Lock Limited, 1989. ISBN: 0-7063-6775-8.** One of the *Play the Game* series which is well worth your consideration for clear, precise technical information about games—from American football (this is a British publication) to volleyball. The action photographs are contemporary and many instructive diagrams and drawings are included.

**Sherman, Eric.** *365 Amazing Days in Sports: A Day-to-Day Look at Sports History.* **Sports Illustrated, 1990. ISBN: 0-316-78537-7.** This compendium of significant events in sports history is not indexed, but youngsters will find it fun to browse through. A lot of sports trivia here, mainly about the major sports.

**Weber, Bruce.** *Bruce Weber's Inside Pro Football League.* **Scholastic, 1988. ISBN: 0-590-41728-2.** Major teams of the NFL. Bibliographies for reluctant readers list this as a good choice.

**Weiner, Eric.** *The Kids' Complete Baseball Catalogue.* **Julian Messner, 1991. ISBN: 0-671-70196-7.** Everything a kid ever wanted to know about baseball, from where to get *free stuff* (!) to schedules and calendars, to league round-ups. Photographs and line drawings.

### Grades 9–12

**Banks, Carl and Michael Eisen.** *Carl Banks' Football Training Program: A Conditioning and Total Health Program for the Young Athlete.* **New American Library, 1991. ISBN: 0-452-26620-3.** Too often health, nutrition, and conditioning are forgotten by the young athlete enjoying the hype of the game. The tips offered in this off-season conditioning program could be useful for all athletes. A motivational book.

**Bissinger, H. G.** *Friday Night Lights: A Town, a Team, and a Dream.* **Addison Wesley, 1990. ISBN: 0-201-19677-8.** There are many facets to this book; it is not simply about high school football in a Texas town. People, from the players to the spectator, as well as teachers and coaches, are the important characters. This is a commentary on education and politics, football hype, and the Texas economy. Bissinger is a Pulitzer Prize winner and has given us a thought-provoking piece here.

**Dickey, Glenn.** *Just Win, Baby: Al Davis and His Raiders.* **Harcourt Brace Jovanovich, 1991. ISBN: 0-15-146580-0.** Here is one for mature readers with an intense interest in football. Dickey portrays this controversial coach as a man driven by success. Received a starred review in *Booklist* (9/15/91).

*Grass Roots and Schoolyards: A High School Basketball Anthology.* **Edited by Nelson Campbell. Stephen Greene, 1988. ISBN: 0-8289-0641-6.** Fifty years' worth of stories about high school basketball, compiled from newspapers, books, and magazines.

**James, Bill.** *Bill James' Historical Baseball Abstract.* **(Revised edition) Villard, 1988. ISBN: 0-394-75805-6.** The manner in which this reference tool is divided tells it all: The Game, The Players, The Records. A very readable, informative book. The statistics cover the 1870s to the present.

**McGurn, James.** *On Your Bicycle: An Illustrated History of Cycling.* **Facts On File, 1988. ISBN: 0-8160-1748-4.** Photographs and illustrations provide a great picture book that will intrigue cycling enthusiasts. It provides a social history of the cycle from its invention as a velocipede to the racers in the Tour de France.

**Mills, George R.** *Go Big Red! The Story of a Nebraska Football Player.* **University of Illinois, 1991. ISBN: 0-252-01825-7.** This should be recommended to those high school students considering a career in football. The author looks back to his experiences as a college player in the seventies. On balance, there are many positive elements in the sports environment regardless of the drawbacks.

***The Random House Book of Sports Stories.* Selected by L. M. Schulman. Illustrated by Thomas B. Allen. Random, 1990. ISBN: 0-394-82874-7.** Sixteen selections, excerpts and complete short stories, by well-known authors such as Hemingway, London, and Updike. The most popular sports are represented here. The styles range from serious to humorous; all are entertaining.

**Sherwonit, Bill. *To the Top of Denali: Climbing Adventures on North America's Highest Peak.* Alaska Northwest, 1990. ISBN: 0-88240-402-4.** These are stories of incredible achievement in scaling Alaska's Mt. McKinley over the years. They include the 1910 Sourdough Expedition, the first one-man ascent, and more. The author confronts the present-day question of how to preserve this marvel of nature.

***Sports in America: Paradise Lost?* Edited by Oliver Trager. Facts On File, 1990. ISBN: 0-8160-2412-X.** Issues in the sports arenas that have proved controversial in the last few years are considered in this collection of editorials and cartoons from United States and Canadian newspapers. The good indexes make this an excellent reference tool.

**Williams, Doug and Bruce Hunter. *Quarterblack: Shattering the NFL Myth.* Bonus Books, 1990. ISBN: 0-929387-47-3.** Autobiography of the first black quarterback in the NFL.

# List 1–10.    Sports: Reproducible List

**Grades K–5**

Barrett, Norman. *Canoeing*. Watts, 1988.

Christopher, Matt. *Hit-Away Kid*. Little Brown, 1988.

Giff, Patricia. *Ronald Morgan Goes to Bat*. Viking, 1988.

Marzollo, Jean. *Red Ribbon Rosie*. Random, 1988.

Miller, J. David. *The Super Book of Football*. Sports Illustrated, 1990.

Schmidt, Gerald D. *Let's Go Fishing: A Book for Beginners*. Robert Rinehart, 1990.

Slote, Alfred. *Finding Buck McHenry*. HarperCollins, 1991.

Solomon, Chuck. *Playing Hockey*. Crown, 1990.

**Grades 6–8**

*Baseball Cards: Questions and Answers*. Edited by Jon Brecka. Krause Publications, 1990.

Berler, Ron. *The Super Book of Baseball*. Sports Illustrated, 1991.

*A Century of Children's Baseball Stories*. Edited by Debra Dagavarian. Stadium Books, 1990.

Gutman, Bill. *Smitty*. Turman Publishing Company, 1988.

*He Makes Me Feel Like Dancin'*. Edgar J. Scherick Associates, 1984. (Video)

Parker, Donald. *Table Tennis*. Ward Lock Limited, 1989.

Sherman, Eric. *365 Amazing Days in Sports: A Day-to-Day Look at Sports History*. Sports Illustrated, 1990.

Weber, Bruce. *Bruce Weber's Inside Pro Football League*. Scholastic, 1988.

Weiner, Eric. *The Kids' Complete Baseball Catalogue*. Julian Messner, 1991.

**Grades 9–12**

Banks, Carl and Michael Eisen. *Carl Banks' Football Training Program*. New American Library, 1991.

Bissinger, H. G. *Friday Night Lights: A Town, a Team, and a Dream.* Addison Wesley, 1990.

Dickey, Glenn. *Just Win, Baby: Al Davis and His Raiders.* Harcourt Brace Jovanovich, 1991.

*Grass Roots and Schoolyards: A High School Basketball Anthology.* Edited by Nelson Campbell. Stephen Greene, 1988.

James, Bill. *Bill James' Historical Baseball Abstract.* Villard, 1988.

McGurn, James. *On Your Bicycle: An Illustrated History of Cycling.* Facts On File, 1988.

Mills, George R. *Go Big Red! The Story of a Nebraska Football Player.* University of Illinois, 1991.

*The Random House Book of Sports Stories.* Selected by L. M. Schulman. Random, 1990.

Sherwonit, Bill. *To the Top of Denali: Climbing Adventures on North America's Highest Peak.* Alaska Northwest, 1990.

*Sports in America: Paradise Lost?* Edited by Oliver Trager. Facts On File, 1990.

Williams, Doug and Bruce Hunter. *Quarterblack: Shattering the NFL Myth.* Bonus Books, 1990.

# MYSTERY AND DETECTIVE

> "I love to lose myself in a mystery,
> to pursue my Reason to an *O altitudo!*"
>
> SIR THOMAS BROWNE
> *1642*

The genre does captivate many of us; a mystery has the fascination of a marvelous puzzle to be solved. The following list is offered to those of you who would appreciate a few clues to interesting new titles. It's elementary—but secondary, too, of course!

## List 1–11.  Mystery and Detective: Annotated List

Barzun, Jacques and Wendell Hertig Taylor. *A Catalog of Crime.* Revised. HarperCollins, 1988. ISBN: 0-06-015796-8. A reader's guide to the genre.

Carr, John C. *The Craft of Crime.* Houghton Mifflin, 1983. ISBN: 0-395-33120-X. Interviews with twentieth-century authors of mystery and detective stories.

*Twentieth-Century Crime and Mystery Writers.* Third edition. Edited by Lesley Henderson. St. James Press, 1990. ISBN: 0-912289-17-1. *New York Times Book Review* said of this third edition: "The most comprehensive source available . . . a monumental piece of scholarship."

Waugh, Hillary. *Hillary Waugh's Guide to Mysteries and Mystery Writing.* Writer's Digest, 1991. ISBN: 0-89879-444-7. The list of recommended reading will interest young adult readers, as will the information about novelists. Can be a how-to manual for young authors.

### Grades K–5

Clifford, Eth. *Flatfoot Fox and the Case of the Missing Eye.* Illustrated by Brian Lies. Houghton, 1990. ISBN: 0-395-51945-4. At a birthday party, Fat Cat's beautiful glass eye is stolen. Flatfoot Fox must solve the mystery. The pen and ink drawings add to the appeal of this funny story.

Gilligan, Shannon. *The Locker Thief.* (Our Secret Gang Series) Bantam, 1991. ISBN: 0-553-15895-3. There is suspense and real dialogue in this mystery of the school locker thefts. Fourth grade sleuths must deduce who the culprits are.

Levy, Elizabeth. *Case of the Gobbling Squash.* Simon and Schuster, 1989. ISBN: 0-671-63655-3. A young detective and magician solve the case of a missing rabbit. Some magic tricks, too.

Markham, Marion M. *The April Fool's Day Mystery.* Illustrated by Pau Estrada. Houghton, 1991. ISBN: 0-395-56235-X. Who is the culprit in the April Fool's prank at school? Kate and Mickey Dixon, detective twins, are hired to prove the innocence of the accused. An attractive, appealing book for young readers; one in a series by Markham.

### Grades 6–8

Avi. *Wolf Rider: A Tale of Terror.* Bradbury, 1986. ISBN: 0-02-707760-8. Andy receives a crank call from a murderer, and he's off to solve a case.

Bellairs, John. *The Secret of the Underground Room.* Dial, 1990. ISBN: 0-8037-0863-7. This title was highly recommended in *VOYA* (2/91) as a story that will hold the reader's interest from the first page. Cryptic messages, evil spirits, and supernatural occurrences.

Brown, Rita Mae and Sneaky Pie Brown. *Wish You Were Here.* Illustrated by Wendy Wray. Bantam, 1990. ISBN: 0-553-05881-9. This title received a favorable review in *School Library Journal.* It's well written and witty, but with dogs as the detectives I would peg this for middle schoolers for sure. The drawings are great, and the plot is truly entertaining.

*Gold Bug.* Video. Produced by Doro Bachrach. Learning Corporation, 1979. An adaptation of the Edgar Allan Poe story. A boy searches for Captain Kidd's gold treasure.

Greenwood, L. B. *Sherlock Holmes and the Thistle of Scotland.* Pocket Books, 1990. ISBN: 0-671-70823-6. Victorian England is the setting, and the clues to the mystery of the missing jewel from Lady Caroline's hair clip pile up.

Howe, James. *Eat Your Poison, Dear.* Atheneum, 1988. ISBN: 0-689-31206-7. Something is rotten in the school cafeteria, and Sebastian Barth must solve the mystery. *Booklist* said "clever plotting." Look for *What Eric Knew* (ISBN: 0-689-31702-6) and *Stage Fright* (0-689-31160-5), also in the Sebastian Barth mystery series.

McFann, Jane. *One Step Short.* Avon, 1990. ISBN: 0-380-75805-9. Suspenseful, with added bonus of good characterizations. Mary's boyfriend dies and Mary is a suspect. Boy-girl relationships and teenage issues of peer pressure and self-esteem.

Roberts, Willo Davis. *Scared Stiff.* Atheneum, 1991. ISBN: 0-689-31692-5. A real thriller for middle school readers. *Publishers Weekly* says, "The clever sleuthing and intriguing setting will make readers want to ride this one to the finish." The setting is a scary cave in an amusement park.

**Shaw, Diana.** *Gone Hollywood.* **Little Brown, 1988. ISBN: 0-316-78343-9.** A TV actress disappears, and a teenager tries to solve the mystery.

## Grades 9–12

**Bradbury, Ray.** *A Graveyard for Lunatics; Another Tale of Two Cities.* **Knopf, 1990. ISBN: 0-394-57877-5.** Another title earning the highest recommendation in *VOYA* for expert writing. Many fascinating characters.

**Douglas, Carole Nelson.** *Good Night, Mr. Holmes.* **Tor, 1990. ISBN: 0-312-93210-3.** Should interest young adult readers in the Sherlock Holmes adventures. This is the mystery surrounding the only woman Holmes admired. She even has her own "Mr. Watson."

**Francis, Dick.** *The Edge.* **G. P. Putnam's Sons, 1989. ISBN: 0-399-13414-X.** It is easy to get hooked on Francis's mysteries. This is just one of many. He is British and an ex-jockey; his stories generally focus on the sport of horse-racing in some manner or another.

**Grimes, Martha.** *The Old Contemptibles.* **Little, 1991. ISBN: 0-316-32894-4.** *School Library Journal* (6/91) called this "a treat for all of Grimes's fans." Superintendent Richard Jury is a suspect in the murder of his friend Jane.

**Hardie, Sean.** *Table for Five.* **Simon and Schuster, 1991. ISBN: 0-671-72329-4.** Charlie is sent to Israel to direct a documentary. Once there he becomes entangled in Israeli politics, mystery, and romance.

**Hillerman, Tony.** *A Thief of Time.* **Harper and Row, 1988. ISBN: 0-06-015938-3.** Hillerman evokes the American Southwest in his mysteries that reveal his understanding of the Navajo culture. Your students will want to read more of the adventures of Lieutenant Joe Leaphorn and Officer Jim Chee. In this one the detectives are challenged by the connection between the mysterious disappearance of valuable Indian artifacts and a series of bizarre murders.

**Pullman, Philip.** *The Tiger in the Well.* **Knopf, 1990. ISBN: 0-679-90214-7.** A sequel to *The Ruby in the Smoke* and *The Shadow in the North,* this is a spellbinding tale. The year is 1881, and the place London. Sally finds herself and her small daughter in danger from an unknown enemy.

*The Screaming Woman.* **(Ray Bradbury Theatre Series) Video. Produced by Seaton McLean and Atlantis Films. Beacon/Altschul, 1989.** Drew Barrymore in a suspenseful tale. Good for short story unit or creative writing.

# List 1–11.   Mystery and Detective: Reproducible List

### Grades K–5

Clifford, Eth. *Flatfoot Fox and the Case of the Missing Eye.* Houghton, 1990.

Gilligan, Shannon. *The Locker Thief.* Bantam, 1991.

Levy, Elizabeth. *Case of the Gobbling Squash.* Simon and Schuster, 1989.

Markham, Marion M. *The April Fool's Day Mystery.* Houghton, 1991.

### Grades 6–8

Avi. *Wolf Rider: A Tale of Terror.* Bradbury, 1986.

Bellairs, John. *The Secret of the Underground Room.* Dial, 1990.

Brown, Rita Mae. *Wish You Were Here.* Bantam, 1990.

*Gold Bug.* Learning Corporation, 1979. (Video)

Greenwood, L. B. *Sherlock Holmes and the Thistle of Scotland.* Pocket Books, 1990.

Howe, James. *Eat Your Poison, Dear.* Atheneum, 1988.

McFann, Jane. *One Step Short.* Avon, 1990.

Robert, Willo Davis. *Scared Stiff.* Atheneum, 1991.

Shaw, Diana. *Gone Hollywood.* Little Brown, 1988.

### Grades 9–12

Bradbury, Ray. *A Graveyard for Lunatics; Another Tale of Two Cities.* Knopf, 1990.

Douglas, Carole Nelson. *Good Night, Mr. Holmes.* Tor, 1990.

Francis, Dick. *The Edge.* G. P. Putnam's Sons, 1989.

Grimes, Martha. *The Old Contemptibles.* Little Brown, 1991.

Hardie, Sam. *Table for Five.* Simon and Schuster, 1991.

Hillerman, Tony. *A Thief of Time.* Harper and Row, 1988.

Pullman, Philip. *The Tiger in the Well.* Knopf, 1990.

*The Screaming Woman.* Beacon/Altschul, 1989. (Video)

### Reference

Barzun, Jacques and Wendell Hertig Taylor. *A Catalog of Crime.* HarperCollins, 1988.

Carr, John C. *The Craft of Crime.* Houghton Mifflin, 1983.

*Twentieth-century Crime and Mystery Writers.* St. James Press, 1990.

Waugh, Hillary. *Hillary Waugh's Guide to Mysteries and Mystery Writing.* Writer's Digest, 1991.

# Personal Challenges

"Let him sing to the flute, who cannot sing to the harp."
—CICERO

Helping students to be all that they can be, isn't that our goal in education? In the media center we know better than to practice bibliotherapy. However, we join with other professionals in learning to identify at-risk students and whenever possible in referring them to the proper agents within the school. We do want children with problems, whether they be physical or emotional, to be able to find materials in our collections that will help them. Our goal is to avoid being intrusive and to respect our students' privacy, but to nevertheless be observant of and sympathetic to their needs. I often remind myself that each day many of our students live out Amelia Earhart's words: "Courage is the price that life exacts for granting peace."

Most adults can believe as Laurence Sterne wrote in *Tristam Shandy* that health is blessed and "above all gold and treasure." Many of our students have yet to learn that acquiring good health and maintaining it is a challenge, one worthy of their commitment.

Here, then, are a few current titles for your consideration.

## List 1–12.   Personal Challenges: Annotated List

*The American Medical Association Encyclopedia of Medicine.* **Edited by Charles B. Clayman, M.D. Random House, 1989. ISBN: 0-394-56528-2.** Authoritative information in a single volume, dictionary format. Esoteric terms are translated into lay language.

**Azarnoff, Pat.** *Health, Illness, and Disability: A Guide to Books for Children and Young Adults.* **R. R. Bowker, 1983. ISBN: 0-8352-1518-0.** Books in print as of 1983.

**Cline, Ruth, K. J.** *Focus on Families: A Reference Handbook.* **ABC-CLIO, 1989. ISBN: 0-87436-508-2.** This reference offers students resource material on such topics as stepfamilies, adoption, child abuse, and alcoholism and provides information on agencies to contact.

**Friedberg, Joan Brest, et al.** *Accept Me As I Am: Best Books of Juvenile Nonfiction on Impairment and Disabilities.* **R. R. Bowker, 1985. ISBN: 0-8352-1974-7.**

This title includes a bibliography of professional reading on the subject. Annotations indicate grade level, type of disability, and reading level. Ten percent of all school children, the authors tell us, have significant disabilities. The first part of the book discusses the evolution of attitudes about disabilities and includes an essay on the power of nonfiction.

Horner, Catherine Townsend. *The Single-Parent Family in Children's Books: An Annotated Bibliography.* Second edition. Scarecrow, 1988. ISBN: 0-8108-2065-X. Covers publications between 1965 and 1986. Considers divorce, separation, and death. A small number of nonfiction titles.

Wells, Shirley E. *At-Risk Youth: Identification, Programs, and Recommendations.* Libraries Unlimited, 1990. ISBN: 0-87287-812-0. *VOYA* (12/90) recommends this source for any educator looking for information on this topic.

## Grades K–5

Alexander, Sally Hobart. *Mom Can't See Me.* Illustrated by George Ancona. Macmillan, 1990. ISBN: 0-02-700401-5. The illustrations are black and white photographs; they depict Mom at her daily tasks. This is the true story of Alexander, as told through her daughter. Positive attitude, but not saccharine.

Arnold, Caroline. *A Guide Dog Puppy Grows Up.* Illustrated with photos by Richard Hewett. Harcourt, 1991. ISBN: 0-15-232657. The color photos take the reader through the selection and training of a guide dog.

Banks, Ann. *Hospital Journal: A Kid's Guide to a Strange Place.* Puffin, 1989. ISBN: 0-14-032688-X. An interactive notebook.

Cleary, Beverly. *Muggie Maggie.* Illustrated by Kay Life. Morrow, 1990. ISBN: 0-688-08553-9. Maggie sees no need to learn cursive. You will like the portrayals of teacher and principal.

Cooney, Barbara. *Hattie and the Wild Waves.* Viking, 1991. ISBN: 0-670-83056-9. Follow your passion! In Hattie's case that is painting.

Goldin, Barbara Diamond. *Cakes and Miracles: A Purim Tale.* Illustrated by Erika Weihs. Viking, 1991. ISBN: 0-670-83047-X. The tale is set in nineteenth-century Europe but the theme is universal. A young boy's indomitable spirit prevails over blindness. *School Library Journal* (8/91) labeled it "outstanding."

*Health Facts* (Series). Eight titles. Steck-Vaughn Company. ISBN: 589-2775-7. Concise text and full-color graphics. From overall health care to explanation of the major body systems.

Hines, Anna Grassnickle. *Remember the Butterflies.* Dutton, 1991. ISBN: 0-525-44679-6. The children learn about life from Grandfather shortly before his death.

**Krementz, Jill.** *How It Feels When a Parent Dies.* **Knopf, 1988. ISBN: 0-394-51911-6.** Children share their feelings.

**Lasky, Kathryn.** *The Fourth of July Bear.* **Illustrated by Helen Cogancherry. Morrow, 1991. ISBN: 0-688-08287-4.** Making friends in a new and unfamiliar place.

**Markle, Sandra.** *Outside and Inside You.* **Illustrated by Susan Kuklin. Bradbury, 1991. ISBN: 0-02-762311-4.** Strongly recommended in *Booklist* (3/15/91). Appealing photographs and graphics.

*McGruff's Self-Care Alert.* **Video. Aims, 1991.** Through the device of McGruff the crime dog, latchkey kids learn ways to stay safe when walking home alone and being home alone. Emergency procedures are illustrated.

**Stolz, Mary.** *King Emmett the Second.* **Pictures by Garth Williams. Greenwillow Books, 1991. ISBN: 0-688-09520-8.** A sequel to *Emmett's Pig,* in which the author deals with the concept of death and the challenge of moving to a new place. *Horn Book* called it "a restrained yet sensitive narrative."

*We're Just Like Crayons.* **Disc or audiocassette. Melody House, 1990.** Stephen Fite presents songs that deal with many personal challenges such as divorce, being handicapped, and friendship. Activities are suggested to accompany each song. Music and lyrics in a variety of styles.

### Grades 6–8

**Arter, Jim.** *Gruel and Unusual Punishment.* **Delacorte, 1991. ISBN: 0-385-30298-3.** A seventh-grader who is without friends acts out his pain with pranks. His association with a similarly bereft boy turns into a serious situation.

**Brooks, Martha.** *Paradise Cafe and Other Stories.* **Little Brown, 1990. ISBN: 0-316-10778-9.** Fourteen short stories deal with different kinds of love. The narrators of the stories are adolescents, growing up.

**Buckingham, Robert W. and Sandra K. Huggard.** *Coping with Grief.* **Rosen, 1991. ISBN: 0-8239-1271-X.** Personal stories reveal how grief is a by-product of many different kinds of loss. Practical suggestions for coping are offered as well as reading lists and support groups. One of the Rosen publisher's *Coping* series.

*Hidden Signs.* **Video. Pyramid Film & Video, 1988 (released in 1990).** "Sensitive dramatization reveals the intimate relationship that exists between the hearing fourth-grader and her deaf parents and depicts the effects on Amy of her peers' unmerciful teasing." (*Booklist,* 3/15/91)

**Hinton, S. E.** *Taming the Star Runner.* **Delacorte, 1988. ISBN: 0-440-50058-3.** Travis has trouble adjusting after time in a juvenile hall. He must tame his rage.

**Naylor, Phyllis Reynolds.** *Reluctantly Alice.* **Atheneum, 1991. ISBN: 0-689-31681-X.** Positive emphasis upon the problem of facing seventh grade.

**Nourse, Alan E.** *Teen Guide to Survival.* **Watts, 1990. ISBN: 0-531-10968-2.** A good reference to the topics of alcohol and substance abuse, depression, violence, and sex. There are bibliographies for further research.

**Nuwer, Hank.** *Steroids.* **Watts, 1990. ISBN: 0-531-10946-1.** Very topical in the 1990s. Easy reading and of interest to many students for reports.

**Terkel, Susan Neiburg.** *Understanding Child Custody.* **Watts, 1991. ISBN: 0-531-12521-1.** An instructive book for youngsters who may be involved in this situation. They need coping skills and solid information about their rights. A valuable tool for a large number of our students.

**Wersba, Barbara.** *Just Be Gorgeous.* **Harper, 1988. ISBN: 0-06-026360-1.** Two youngsters become friends and learn through their friendship to be true to themselves. The girl is sure she is unattractive; the boy is gay.

## Grades 9–12

*After the Tears: Teenagers Talk About Mental Illness in Their Families.* **Video. Produced by United Mental Health. HRM, 1990.** Teens and adults speak out about the ramifications of living with mental illness. The professional care-givers offer ways of coping and suggest specific agencies to contact.

**Arthur, Shirley.** *Surviving Teen Pregnancy: Your Choices, Dreams and Decisions.* **Morning Glory, 1991. ISBN: 0-930934-46.** *Kirkus* (6/15/91) called this title "a workbook in decision-making." The emphasis is on success stories in this book written by a teenage mother. Could be recommended for middle school students as well.

**Avi.** *Nothing But the Truth: A Documentary Novel.* **Watts, 1991. ISBN: 0-531-05959-6.** *Booklist* gave this title a starred review, saying it is sure to prompt debate on many issues—personal values, communication between parent and child, and the responsibility of the media. It challenges the reader to "reexamine our ethical standards."

**Bode, Janet.** *Beating the Odds: Stories of Unexpected Achievers.* **Illustrated by Stan Mack. Watts, 1991. ISBN: 0-531-15230-8.** Another winner among the *Booklist* starred reviews. The author offers first person stories by teens who have succeeded in spite of adversity. The advice of professionals is interwoven with the stories. Courageous teens.

*Choices.* **Video. Committee for Children. AIMS Media, 1989.** The young woman in the film runs away from an abusive parent, then faces new challenges on the street.

**Cooney, Caroline B.** *The Party's Over.* **Scholastic, 1991. ISBN: 0-590-42552-8.** Hallie feels like a misfit when her friends go off to college. Teens will be able to identify with Hallie. *Kirkus* called this story a "depiction of what it means to rethink basic values."

***Dear Lisa: A Letter to My Sister.*** **Video. Produced by J. Clements. New Day Films, 1990.** Girls growing up in our society face many issues. The life stories of thirteen contemporary women are juxtaposed with scenes from the Clements family.

**Kubler-Ross, Elisabeth, M.D.** ***AIDS: The Ultimate Challenge.*** **Macmillan, 1987. ISBN: 0-02-567170-7.** The author of *On Death and Dying* writes of the pandemic spread of AIDS. She has been working with people with AIDS since 1981, and she brings to them her special talent for helping patients and their families through the stages of dying.

**Miklowitz, Gloria D.** ***Standing Tall, Looking Good.*** **Delacorte, 1991. ISBN: 0-385-30162-6.** Portrays different motivations for three teens who enlist in the army and follows them through basic training.

**Nourse, Alan E.** ***Teen Guide to Survival.*** **Watts, 1990. ISBN: 0-531-10968-2.** Good reference to the topics of alcohol and substance abuse, depression, violence, and sex. Included are bibliographies for taking teens further in their research.

**Rench, Janice E.** ***Understanding Sexual Identity: A Book for Gay Teens and Their Friends.*** **Lerner, 1990. ISBN: 0-8225-0044-2.** *Horn Book* commended the author's straightforward, no-nonsense approach. Healthy sexuality is discussed; each chapter starts with a fictional account of a gay teenager dealing with conflict. Sexually transmitted diseases are discussed, focusing on AIDS.

***Scared Straight! Ten Years After.*** **Video. Arnold Shapiro. Pyramid Films, 1989.** This video updates the 1978 film in which seventeen juvenile offenders visited convicts at Rahway State Prison. This follow-up shows how their lives were changed by that encounter. *Scared Straight* can be a part of your purchase of the update.

# List 1–12.   Personal Challenges: Reproducible List

*The American Medical Association Encyclopedia of Medicine.* Edited by Charles B. Clayman, M.D. Random House, 1989.

Azarnoff, Pat. *Health, Illness and Disability.* R. R. Bowker, 1983.

Cline, Ruth  K. J. *Focuses on Families: A Reference Handbook.* ABC-CLIO, 1989.

Friedberg, Joan Brest, et al. *Accept Me As I Am.* R. R. Bowker, 1985.

Horner, Catherine Townsend. *The Single-Parent Family in Children's Books.* Scarecrow, 1988.

Wells, Shirley E. *At-Risk Youth: Identification, Programs, and Recommendations.* Libraries Unlimited, 1990.

### Grades K–5

Alexander, Sally Hobart. *Mom Can't See Me.* Macmillan, 1990.

Arnold, Caroline. *A Guide Dog Puppy Grows Up.* Harcourt, 1991.

Banks, Ann. *Hospital Journal: A Kid's Guide to a Strange Place.* Puffin, 1989.

Cleary, Beverly. *Muggie Maggie.* Morrow, 1990.

Cooney, Barbara. *Hattie and the Wild Waves.* Viking, 1991.

Goldin, Barbara. *Cakes and Miracles: A Purim Tale.* Viking, 1991.

*Health Facts.* Series. Steck-Vaughn.

Hines, Anna Grassnickle. *Remember the Butterflies.* Dutton, 1991.

Krementz, Jill. *How It Feels When a Parent Dies.* Knopf, 1988.

Lasky, Kathryn. *The Fourth of July Bear.* Morrow, 1991.

Markle, Sandra. *Outside and Inside You.* Bradbury, 1991.

*McGruff's Self-Care Alert.* AIMS Media, 1991. (Video)

Stolz, Mary. *King Emmett the Second.* Greenwillow, 1991.

*We're Just Like Crayons.* Melody House, 1990. (Audiocassette)

## List 1–12.   (Continued)

### Grades 6–8

Arter, Jim. *Gruel and Unusual Punishment.* Delacorte, 1991.

Brooks, Martha. *Paradise Cafe and Other Stories.* Little Brown, 1990.

Buckingham, Robert W. *Coping with Grief.* Rosen, 1991.

*Hidden Signs.* Pyramid Film and Video, 1990. (Video)

Hinton, S. E. *Taming the Star Runner.* Delacorte, 1988.

Naylor, Phyllis. *Reluctantly Alice.* Atheneum, 1991.

Nourse, Alan E. *Teen Guide to Survival.* Watts, 1990.

Nuwer, Hank. *Steroids.* Watts, 1990.

Terkel, Susan. *Understanding Child Custody.* Watts, 1991.

Wersba, Barbara. *Just Be Gorgeous.* Harper, 1988.

### Grades 9–12

*After the Tears: Teenagers Talk About Mental Illness in Their Families.* HRM, 1990. (Video)

Arthur, Shirley. *Surviving Teen Pregnancy: Your Choices, Dreams and Decisions.* Morning Glory, 1991.

Avi. *Nothing But the Truth: A Documentary Novel.* Watts, 1991.

Bode, Janet. *Beating the Odds: Stories of Unexpected Achievers.* Watts, 1991.

*Choices.* AIMS Media, 1989. (Video)

Cooney, Caroline B. *The Party's Over.* Scholastic, 1991.

*Dear Lisa: A Letter to My Sister.* New Day Films, 1990. (Video)

Kubler-Ross, Elisabeth, M.D. *AIDS: The Ultimate Challenge.* Macmillan, 1987.

Miklowitz, Gloria D. *Standing Tall, Looking Good.* Delacorte, 1991.

Nourse, Alan E. *Teen Guide to Survival.* Watts, 1990.

Rench, Janice. *Understanding Sexual Identity: A Book for Gay Teens and Their Friends.* Lerner, 1990.

*Scared Straight! Ten Years After.* Pyramid Films, 1989. (Video)

# HUMOR

Do you feel like Erma Bombeck who says "When humor goes, there goes civilization"? Here is a resource that may be new to you, and may be just the answer as you try for the light touch in your daily tasks and to make sure humor is represented in your collection.

> The Humor Project, Inc.
> 110 Spring Street
> Saratoga Springs, New York 12866

Dr. Joel Goodman is president of this project, and Margie Ingram is the director of HUMOResources. HUMOResources is a service of the project, offering access to the many materials they offer, including *Laughing Matter* magazine, workshops, conferences, and grants. Write for the *HUMOResources* catalog.

The March 1989 *Phi Delta Kappan* noted that humor from one's instructor is often appreciated. We often hear praise for the use of humor in instruction, but, regrettably, there is little to document humor as a useful tool in the education process. Avner Ziv of Tel Aviv University had, at the time of the article, conducted a limited empirical study of the effects of humor in an introductory course in statistics. His results showed that the humor group scored significantly higher on the final exam than the nonhumor group. It was noted that the study ought to be duplicated, but it is safe to say that humor works and, as the article mentioned here noted, there should be more training in its application in education.

Glen Walter, in *Teaching for Excellence* (April 1990), notes that "Education is too important to take seriously." Experience shows that laughter reduces stress, that it is good physical exercise, and that it elevates one's self-esteem. Walter offers nine ways to bring laughter into the classroom, and he quotes Dr. Joel Goodman's advice that laughter can help to prevent "hardening of the attitudes."

Here is a list of titles for different grade levels that should delight your students. After all, in the words of Horace, "Why may not one be telling truth while one laughs."

## List 1–13.  Humor: Annotated List

*Grades K–5*

**Ball, Duncan.** *Jeremy's Tail.* **Illustrated by Donna Rawlins. Orchard/Watts, 1991. ISBN: 0-531-05951-0.** *Kirkus* calls this an outrageous tall tale with "sumptuous illustrations." Jeremy is blindfolded while playing pin the tail on the donkey. He wanders from the house, onto a bus, and finally back to put the tail exactly in the right spot.

**Barrett, Judi.** *Cloudy With a Chance of Meatballs.* **Illustrated by Ron Barrett. Atheneum, 1985. ISBN: 0-689-70749-5.** Humorous cartoons illustrate Grandpa's story of the town of Chewandswallow, where precipitation is food.

**Blume, Judy.** *Fudge-A-Mania.* **Penguin, 1990. ISBN: 0-525-44672-9.** Five-year-old Fudge announces that he is marrying Sheila; this leads to a wonderful wedding scene. An update on Fudge that will thrill young readers.

**Charliet, Bernice and Grace Maccarone.** *Martin and the Tooth Fairy.* **Illustrated by G. Brian Karas. Scholastic, 1991. ISBN: 0-590-43305-9.** Martin has a scheme to get more money from the tooth fairy.

*Grownups Are Strange.* **Audiocassette. Round River Records, 1990.** Stories and guitar music. "Grandma vs. the Headless Man" and "The Claw." Bill Harley performs.

**Hawkes, Kevin.** *Then the Troll Heard the Squeak.* **Lothrop, 1991. ISBN: 0-688-09757-X.** All about cause and effect.

**Howe, James.** *Hot Fudge.* **Illustrated by Leslie Morrill. Morrow, 1990. ISBN: 0-688-08237-8.** The fudge disappears and Harold (the dog), Chester (the cat), and Howie (the puppy) try to find the culprit. Bunicula (the vampire rabbit) is the likely suspect.

**Park, Barbara.** *Maxie, Rosie, and Earl—Partners in Grime.* **Illustrated by Alexander Strogart. Knopf, 1990. ISBN: 0-679-80643-1.** Three middle graders are sent to the principal's office. Can friendship come from adversity?

*Ralph S. Mouse.* **Video. Directed by Thomas G. Smith. Churchill Films, 1990.** Adaptation of Beverly Cleary's novel. Three-dimensional animation and live-action footage. The winner of the first Andrew Carnegie Medal for Excellence in Children's Video, awarded by ALA. (*Booklist*, 3/15/91). ALA committee chair called it a "rollicking adventure" that will "captivate children of all ages."

**Smith, William Jay.** *Laughing Time: Collected Nonsense.* **Revised edition. Illustrated by Fernando Krahn. Farrar, 1990. ISBN: 0-374-34366-7.** First reader, or delightful for reading aloud to younger ones. Nonsense it is with a silly alphabet, goofy recipes, and wonderful limericks.

**Stadler, John.** *Cat Is Back at Bat.* **Dutton, 1991. ISBN: 0-525-44762-8.** The cat is at bat all right, using his tail as a bat. A captivating first reader.

***Talking on the Telephone.*** **Audiocassette. Kid Glove Productions, 1989.** A rollicking, wonderful collection by Deborah Dunleavy, a Canadian artist who wrote the songs she performs with backup singers and sounds. Sure to elicit happy participation.

**Willis, Jean.** ***Earth Hounds as Explained by Professor Xargle.*** **Translated into Human by Jean Willis. Illustrated by Tony Rass. Dutton, 1990. ISBN: 0-525-44600-1.** Looks at humans as they might be explained by an alien.

### *Grades 6–8*

**Haven, Susan.** ***Maybe I'll Move to the Lost & Found.*** **G. P. Putnam, 1990. ISBN: 0-399-21509-3.** Highly recommended by *VOYA* and starred by *School Library Journal*, this story has humor as well as good characterization and perspective on teenage concerns.

**Hunt, Joyce.** ***Eat Your Heart Out, Victoria Chubb.*** **Scholastic (An Apple Paperback), 1990. ISBN: 0-590-42554-4.** Although the reading level of this nifty little book is fifth grade, the characters and humor are decidedly middle school. Can these energetic kids get along with insufferable Victoria? Can they get along *without* her? Starting a summer luncheonette gives them an opportunity to learn that working can be fun, and one can get along with lots of different people.

**Hunt, Joyce.** ***The Four of Us and Victoria Chubb.*** **Scholastic (An Apple Paperback), 1991. ISBN: 0-590-42976-0.** Victoria is back to her old tricks—running everyone else's lives. Here the luncheonette kids return to school and enroll in a "creative" social studies class. Well, Victoria enrolls them, but they turn the situation to their advantage and begin to understand Victoria.

**Myers, Walter Dean.** ***The Mouse Rap.*** **Harper, 1990. ISBN: 0-06-024343-0.** This story of a hunt for treasure has rap and a light-hearted touch to recommend it. Family and relationships with friends make this a worthy selection.

**Phillips, Louis.** ***Loose Leaf: The Wackiest School Notebook Yet.*** **Illustrated by Joseph Farris. Atheneum, 1990. ISBN: 0-689-31437-X.** *School Library Journal* reviewed this as a special book that is fun, involves the reader, and challenges the mind. Cartoons are mixed with inventive wordplay, riddles, and palindromes. Recommended for children who like words and language.

**Pullman, Philip.** ***Spring-Heeled Jack: A Story of Bravery and Evil.*** **Illustrated by David Mostyn. Knopf, 1991. ISBN: 0-679-91057-3.** Dialogue, cartoon sequences, Dickensian text, delightful villains, and a thriller plot make this appealing. Reviewed in these terms by *Kirkus* (6/15/91).

***Ransom of Red Chief.*** **Video. Directed by Tony Bill. Learning Corporation of America, 1977.** The O. Henry story about the rotten kid whose parents will not take him back from the kidnappers.

**Taylor, William.** ***Agnes the Sheep.*** **Scholastic, 1991. ISBN: 0-590-43365-2.** *Bulletin of the Center for Children's Books* called this story "a catastrophic comedy," and *Booklist* gave it a star. Friends Belinda and Joe inherit a bad-tempered sheep.

## *Grades 9–12*

**Conford, Ellen.** *Loving Someone Else.* **Bantam, 1991. ISBN: 0-533-07353-2.** *Booklist* (7/91) reviewed this title favorably, mentioning Conford's "delicious flair for comedy." Holly becomes the live-in companion of the eccentric Brewster sisters.

**Dahl, Roald.** *Ah, Sweet Mystery of Life.* **Illustrated by John Lawrence. Knopf, 1990. ISBN: 0-394-58265-9.** A collection of seven of Dahl's stories that present a humorous view of life's foibles. Comic and wicked.

*Laughing Matters: A Celebration of American Humor.* **Selected and edited by Gene Shalit. Doubleday, 1987. ISBN: 0-385-18547-2.** Shalit states in his introduction: "Not everything funny is in this book, but everything in this book is funny." The introduction is called "Writing humor is a funny way to make a living." A great selection, which includes cartoons from Benchley to Larson.

**Oldham, June.** *Moving In.* **Delacorte, 1990. ISBN: 0-385-30047-6.** British farce and sophisticated wit, slapstick antics and a bit of romance.

**Salassi, Otto R.** *Jimmy D., Sidewinder, and Me.* **Knopf, 1990. ISBN: 0-679-80135-9.** *The New York Times Book Review* called this story of fifteen-year-old Dumas Monk "a fast-paced, well-told yarn." Dumas is in jail in Arkansas, arrested for murder. Off-beat humor.

**Thompson, Julian.** *Herb Seasoning.* **Scholastic, 1990. ISBN: 0-590-43023-8.** *Booklist* says "YAs are bound to chortle at Thompson's parody of familiar graduation woes."

**Waldman, Myron S.** *Forgive Us Our Press Passes: The Memoirs of a Veteran Washington Reporter.* **St. Martin's, 1991. ISBN: 0-312-05992-2.** An irreverent look at politics in America, by an insider.

**Watterson, Bill.** *The Authoritative Calvin and Hobbes: A Calvin and Hobbes Treasury.* **Illustrated. Andrews and McMeel, 1990. ISBN: 0-8362-1864-7.** Every third page is a full-color Sunday installment. Popular with high school students who grab the paper and turn to *Calvin and Hobbes* first.

# List 1–13.  Humor: Reproducible List

**Grades K–5**

Ball, Duncan. *Jeremy's Tail.* Orchard, 1991.

Barrett, Judi. *Cloudy With a Chance of Meatballs.* Atheneum, 1985.

Blume, Judy. *Fudge-A-Mania.* Penguin, 1990.

Charliet, Bernice. *Martin and the Tooth Fairy.* Scholastic, 1991.

*Grownups Are Strange.* Round River Records, 1990. (Audiocassette)

Hawkes, Kevin. *Then the Troll Heard the Squeak.* Lothrop, 1991.

Howe, James. *Hot Fudge.* Morrow, 1990.

Park, Barbara. *Maxie, Rosie, and Earl—Partners in Grime.* Knopf, 1990.

*Ralph S. Mouse.* Churchill Films, 1990. (Video)

Smith, William. *Laughing Time: Collected Nonsense.* Farrar, 1990.

Stadler, John. *Cat Is Back at Bat.* Dutton, 1991.

*Talking on the Telephone.* Kid Glove Productions, 1989. (Audiocassette)

Willis, Jean. *Earth Hounds As Explained by Professor Xargle.* Dutton, 1990.

**Grades 6–8**

Haven, Susan. *Maybe I'll Move to the Lost & Found.* Putnam, 1990.

Hunt, Joyce. *Eat Your Heart Out, Victoria Chubb.* Scholastic, 1990.

Hunt, Joyce. *The Four of Us and Victoria Chubb.* Scholastic, 1991.

Myers, Walter Dean. *The Mouse Rap.* Harper, 1990.

Phillips, Louis. *Loose Leaf: The Wackiest School Notebook Yet.* Atheneum, 1990.

Pullman, Philip. *Spring-Heeled Jack: A Story of Bravery and Evil.* Knopf, 1991.

*Ransom of Red Chief.* Learning Corporation, 1977. (Video)

Taylor, William. *Agnes the Sheep.* Scholastic, 1991.

**Grades 9–12**

Conford, Ellen. *Loving Someone Else.* Bantam, 1991.

Dahl, Roald. *Ah, Sweet Mystery of Life.* Knopf, 1990.

*Laughing Matters: A Celebration of American Humor.* Selected by Gene Shalit. Doubleday, 1987.

Oldham, June. *Moving In.* Delacorte, 1990.

Salassi, Otto R. *Jimmy D., Sidewinder, and Me.* Knopf, 1990.

Thompson, Julian. *Herb Seasoning.* Scholastic, 1990.

Waldman, Myron. *Forgive Us Our Press Passes: The Memoirs of a Veteran Washington Reporter.* St. Martin's, 1991.

Watterson, Bill. *The Authoritative Calvin and Hobbes: A Calvin and Hobbes Treasury.* Andrews and McMeel, 1990.

# About Words

Even before Dylan Thomas learned to read he loved the sound of words. As he became a reader his love "for the real life of words" increased. He wrote ("The Poetic Manifesto," *The Texas Quarterly*) that he knew he *had* to "know them most intimately."

Sometimes we need to be reminded of the proverb, "a word fitly spoken is like apples of gold in pictures of silver." Learning about words, their many meanings, and their proper usage provides a powerful tool for our students—the power of both the written and the spoken word.

The results of a successful research assignment for secondary pupils was published in the January 1990 issue of *English Journal*. This assignment was conceived by Gaylyn Karle Anderson and is presented in her article, "'I-Search a Word': Reclaiming the Library's Reference Section." We have added our newer sources of information to those the author suggests and have found this to be an ideal research task. A few of the additional sources are NewsBank (newspaper articles on microfiche), the *Readers' Guide to Periodical Literature* in CD-ROM format, DIALOG (online database searching) and our electronic card catalog. This assignment becomes a true treasure hunt, leading students from source to source. Students can achieve a little or a lot, but everyone finds information.

The following interesting titles should intrigue your avid word detectives.

## List 1–14.   About Words: Annotated List

### Grades K–5

Asher, Sandy. *Wild Words! How to Train Them to Tell Stories.* Walker and Co., 1989. ISBN: 0-8027-6887-3. Language arts in the elementary grades—creative writing.

MacCarthy, Patricia. *Herds of Words.* Dial, 1991. ISBN: 0-8037-0892. An entertaining book that introduces collective nouns and shows that they often sound like the things they describe. Illustrated.

*Mickey's Crossword Puzzle Maker.* **Disney Software, 1990. Apple II.** Fun in the language arts program for beginning readers.

*Stickybear Word Scramble.* **Computer software. Optimum Resource, 1990. IBM-PC, PS/2 and Tandy 1000.** Word games for the beginning computer user. *School Library Journal* (4/91) reviews this program thoroughly and labels it an enrichment tool.

**Terban, Marvin.** *Hey, Hay! A Wagonful of Funny Homonym Riddles.* **Clarion Books, 1991. ISBN: 0-395-54431-9.** *Booklist* says: "Terban makes vocabulary surprising, so that we stop and think about the words we use." Fun for middle schoolers, too.

## Grades 6–8

**Graham-Barber, Lynda.** *Mushy! The Complete Book of Valentine Words.* **Illustrated by Betsy Lewin. Bradbury, 1991. ISBN: 0-02-736941-2.** The origins of all those romantic words and phrases.

*The HBJ Student Thesaurus.* **Harcourt Brace Jovanovich, 1991. ISBN: 0-15-232880-7.** Eight hundred entries with two to five synonyms for each entry. Examples, in sentence form, show the differences among the words.

**Parnwell, E. C.** *The New Oxford Picture Dictionary.* **Oxford University Press, 1988. ISBN: 0-19-434199-2.** More than two thousand words are depicted in full-color illustrations.

**Klausner, Janet.** *Talk About English: How Words Travel and Change.* **Illustrated by Nancy Doniger. Crowell, 1990. ISBN: 0-690-04833-5.** *Kirkus* reviewed this a "a fascinating survey" with lively narrative that gives examples and anecdotes. *Horn Book* (3/4/91) says it is one book that provokes thought and entertains as well.

## Grades 9–12

*The Barnhart Dictionary of Etymology.* **Edited by Robert K. Barnhart. H. W. Wilson, 1988. ISBN: 0-8242-0745-9.** This resource was named one of the best reference books of 1988 by *Library Journal.* In the high school it is useful to the researcher, with clear explanations of the word's development—in meaning, spelling, pronunciation, and function.

**Bryson, Bill.** *The Mother Tongue: English and How It Got That Way.* **Morrow, 1990. ISBN: 0-688-07895-8.** A serious study of the development of languages. The author explores the manner in which languages developed at the same time in different places.

*Catch Phrases, Clichés, and Idioms: A Dictionary of Familiar Expressions.* **Compiled by Doris Craig. McFarland, 1990. ISBN: 0-89950-467-1.** Twenty thousand entries!

*The Facts On File Dictionary of New Words.* **Edited by Harold Lemay, Sid Lerner, and Marian Taylor. Facts On File, 1989. ISBN: 0-8160-2088.** Catch words, slogans, acronyms, etc., in an updated version of *Ballantine's New Words Dictionary.*

**Goldberg, Philip.** *The Babinski Reflex and 70 Other Useful and Amusing Metaphors From Science, Psychology, Business, Sports, and Everyday Life.* **Illustrated by Giorma Carmi. Jeremy P. Tarcher, 1990. ISBN: 0-87477-563-9.** The entries in this entertaining book include the origin of the metaphor with examples of its use and metaffect. *School Library Journal* warned that some entries are uninhibited.

**Limburg, Peter.** *Stories Behind Words: The Origins and Histories of 285 English Words.* **H. W. Wilson, 1986. ISBN: 0-8242-0718-1.** An entertaining reference that traces each word's evolution from coinage to present-day usage.

**Luta, William.** *Doublespeak.* **HarperCollins, 1989. ISBN: 0-06-016134-5.** How language is twisted by governments, advertising, educators, et al.

**Safire, William.** *Language Maven Strikes Again.* **Doubleday, 1990. ISBN: 0-385-41299-1.** Safire's columns from the Sunday *New York Times Magazine* are reprinted here, followed by his readers' reproaches.

**Shipman, Robert Oliver.** *A Pun My Word: A Humorously Enlightened Path to English Usage.* **Littlefield Adams, 1991. ISBN: 0-8226-3011-7.** Your students will have fun with this—sets of words that are misused, with examples of the proper usage.

# List 1–14.   About Words: Reproducible List

### Grades K–5

Asher, Sandy. *Wild Words! How to Train Them to Tell Stories.* Walker & Co., 1989.

MacCarthy, Patricia. *Herd of Words.* Dial, 1991.

*Mickey's Crossword Puzzle Maker.* Disney Software, 1990.

*Stickybear Word Scramble.* Optimum Resource, 1990.

Terban, Marvin. *Hey, Hay! A Wagonful of Funny Homonym Riddles.* Clarion Books, 1991.

### Grades 6–8

Graham-Barber, Lynda. *Mushy! The Complete Book of Valentine Words.* Bradbury, 1991.

*The HBJ Student Thesaurus.* Harcourt Brace Jovanovich, 1991.

Parnwell, E. C. *The New Oxford Picture Dictionary.* Oxford University Press, 1988.

Klausner, Janet. *Talk About English: How Words Travel and Change.* Crowell, 1990.

### Grades 9–12

*The Barnhart Dictionary of Etymology.* Edited by Robert K. Barnhart. H. W. Wilson, 1988.

Bryson, Bill. *The Mother Tongue: English and How It Got That Way.* Morrow, 1990.

*Catch Phrases, Clichés, and Idioms: A Dictionary of Familiar Expressions.* Compiled by Doris Craig. McFarland, 1990.

*The Facts On File Dictionary of New Words.* Edited by Harold Lemay, et al. Facts On File, 1988.

Goldberg, Philip. *The Babinski Reflex and 70 Other Useful and Amusing Metaphors from Science, Psychology, Business, Sports, and Everyday Life.* Jeremy P. Tarcher, 1990.

Limburg, Peter. *Stories Behind Words: The Origins and Histories of 285 English Words.* H. W. Wilson, 1986.

Luta, William. *Doublespeak.* HarperCollins, 1989.

Safire, William. *Language Maven Strikes Again.* Doubleday, 1990.

Shipman, Robert. *A Pun My Word.* Littlefield Adams, 1991.

# APPRECIATING CULTURES

> **Through our scientific genius we have made this world a neighborhood; and now we are challenged through our moral genius, to make it a brotherhood.**
>
> —MARTIN LUTHER KING, JR.

Carl A. Grant reported in his article "Race, Class, Gender, and Schooling" (*The Elementary School Journal,* May 1988) that demographic projections confirm one out of four students in our schools will soon be living in poverty, and as many as fifteen percent will be immigrants to this country. Furthermore, after the year 2000, projections show that one out of every three Americans will be non-white.

As educators, we deal daily with concerns that are related to the statistics just quoted. Grant tells us that reports over the past twenty-five years indicate that we have not addressed this problem in a meaningful way. "Multicultural and social-reconstructionist education prepares students to reconstruct society to better serve the interests of all citizens," he writes.

There are debates swirling about this issue, in state education departments, in governing agencies, in the media, in our own districts, and most definitely right in our own faculty rooms and professional meetings. Should there be national standards, should state mandates be initiated, should syllabi be rewritten?

Asa G. Hiliard III offers a good working definition of *culture* in "Cultural Style in Teaching and Learning" (*NEA Today,* January 1989): "Perhaps the best way to think about culture—or that aspect of culture we call 'style'—is to consider it the 'personality' of a group." He urges educators not to avoid addressing the question of style but to become sensitive to differing styles out of a "basic respect for our students, for their reality, and for their tremendous potential for learning."

Max Lerner warned in "We Teach What We Are" (*Actions and Passions*): "In the end, as any successful teacher will tell you, you can only teach the things you are. If we practice racism then it is racism that we teach."

We are a rich and diverse society, and the more we learn about different peoples the more we realize how much we have in common with one another. "Profound ignorance," wrote La Bruyère in *Characters,* "makes a man dogmatic."

The following lists were compiled with these thoughts in mind. The lists do not begin to encompass the many and diverse individual cultures represented among your students. However, each selection offers an appreciation of persons or groups with unique "styles."

# List 1–15.   Appreciating Cultures: Annotated List

"Book List." (Multicultural books.) *The Instructor,* February 1991. Curriculum connections, history and geography, problem-solving, and race relationships.

China in the Classroom: Resource Catalog. The Center for Teaching About China. USCPFA. A source for unusual and useful materials. The Center is a clearinghouse for teaching resources; dedicated to promoting friendship.

Cox, Susan and Lee Galda. "Multicultural Literature: Mirrors and Windows on a Global Community." *The Reading Teacher,* April 1990. Presents an interesting list of trade books.

*Folklore of World Holidays.* First edition. Edited by Margaret Read MacDonald. Gale, 1991. ISBN: 0-8103-7577-X. This source compiles the cultural beliefs and legends that are associated with over 375 holidays, celebrated in 150 countries. Pre-publication reviews were favorable.

Hayden, Carla D. *Venture Into Cultures: A Resource Book of Multicultural Materials and Programs.* ALA, 1991. ISBN: 0-8389-0579-X. This resource provides access to materials for planning educational programs that focus upon seven cultural groups.

Heltshe, Mary Ann and Audrey Burie Kirchner. *Multicultural Explorations: Joyous Journeys With Books.* Libraries Unlimited, 1990. ISBN: 0-87287-848-1. Units of study for introducing children to Japan, Italy, Hawaii, Kenya, Brazil, and Australia. The activities teach about family life, school, food, celebrations.

*Multicultural Review.* Serial. Greenwood Publishing Group, Inc. ISSN: 1058-9236. A quarterly "dedicated to a better understanding of ethnic, racial, and religious diversity." This journal targets a broad range of users from librarians and other educators to library patrons. This is an important tool for building a balanced collection of materials. Articles cover such issues as censorship and cultural literacy.

*School Library Journal.* January 1992. This issue celebrates diversity through books, software, and audiovisual reviews and recommendations.

Shemanski, Frances. *A Guide to World Fairs and Festivals.* Greenwood Press, 1985. ISBN: 0-313-20786-0. A useful resource for social studies which covers seventy-five countries. The celebrations are listed by topic or theme, with the country indicated. Information is provided on dates, origin, and purpose. A description of the event is included.

*Resource/Reading List 1990: Annotated Bibliography of Resources By and About Native People.* Compiled by Catherine Verrall and Patricia McDowell. Canadian Alliance in Solidarity with the Native Peoples, 1990. ISBN: 0-921425-03-1. Covers both print and nonprint materials. These materials were selected for accuracy, the background information they offer regarding current Native American concerns, and their sensitivity to the native point of view.

## Grades K–5

***America Is.*** **Video. Directed by Peter Rosen. Carousel, 1986.** The one-hundredth anniversary of the Statue of Liberty in song.

**Field, Rachel.** ***A Road Might Lead to Anywhere.*** **Illustrated by Giles Larouche. Little Brown, 1991. ISBN: 0-316-28178-6.** *Booklist* gave this reissue of the 1924 edition a starred review, saying the illustrations are "remarkably" suited to match the "sturdy simplicity of this verse."

**Godden, Rumer.** ***Fu-Dog.*** **Illustrated by Valerie Littlewood. Viking, 1989. ISBN: 0-6870-82300-7.** "Li-la can imagine anything," Malcolm says of his sister. Li-la and Malcolm learn about Chinese culture when Li-la receives a green satin Fu-Dog from a Chinese relative and the children go to London where they encounter many adventures.

**Hoyt-Goldsmith, Diane.** ***Pueblo Storyteller.*** **Photographs by Lawrence Migdale. Holiday, 1991. ISBN: 0-8234-0864-7.** How a Pueblo family lives today.

**Keegan, Marcia.** ***Pueblo Boy: Growing Up in Two Worlds.*** **Dutton, 1991. ISBN: 0-525-65060-1.** A photo essay about a ten-year-old Pueblo boy's way of life. Full color photographs.

**McLain, Gary.** ***The Indian Way: Learning to Communicate with Mother Earth.*** **Illustrated by the author and Michael Taylor. John Muir, 1990. ISBN: 0-945465-73-4.** Thirteen stories portray for the reader the Indian way of life. The strong affinity for nature comes through. Part of the book deals with applying these values to everyday life.

**Shannon, George.** ***More Stories to Solve: Fifteen Folktales From Around the World.*** **Illustrated by Peter Sis. Greenwillow, 1991. ISBN: 0-688-09161-X.** The theme is: The weak prevail over the strong. Simple international stories.

**Wall, Lina Mao.** ***Judge Rabbit and the Tree Spirit: A Folktale from Cambodia.*** **Illustrated by Nancy Horn. Children's Book Press, 1991. ISBN: 0-89239-071-9.** We learn a great deal about people from their legends and folklore. A note in this book tells us that the Judge Rabbit stories provide role models for Cambodian children.

## Grades 6–8

**Katz, William Loren.** ***Breaking the Chains: African-American Slave Resistance.*** **Atheneum, 1990. ISBN: 0-689-31493-0.** The material in this source includes diary entries and letters. Offers historical perspective on slavery in our country from the first importation to the Civil War. Describes the treatment of slaves that led to attempts by the slaves themselves to resist and end slavery.

**Lomas Garza, Carmen.** *Family Pictures/Cuadros de Familia.* **Children's Book Press, 1990. ISBN: 0-89239-050-6.** This is the story of the author's family and growing up in a Hispanic community in Texas. The text is bilingual. Illustrated with colorful paintings.

**Maartens, Maretha.** *Paper Bird: A Novel of South Africa.* **Translated from Afrikaans by Madeleine van Biljon. Clarion, 1991. ISBN: 0-395-56490-5.** There is a universality about the portrayal of poverty though the setting is a black community in South Africa. Given a starred review by *Booklist.*

*Made in China: A Search for Roots.* **Video. Directed by Lisa Hsia. Filmakers Library, 1986.** A very personal account of a young Chinese-American woman finding her cultural roots.

*Northern Tales: Traditional Stories of Eskimo and Indian Peoples.* **Selected by Howard Norman. (The Pantheon Fairy Tale and Folklore Library). Pantheon, 1990. ISBN: 0-394-54060-3.** One hundred sixteen tales that range widely in geographical origin. The stories include most all peoples who lived a hunting and fishing life.

**Thomson, Peggy.** *City Kids in China.* **Photographs by Paul S. Conklin. Harper-Collins, 1991. ISBN: 0-06-021655-7.** About children living in the Chinese city of Changsha. Schooling, single-parent situations, reading lessons. Black and white photos.

*When Night Comes: Vietnam Today.* **Video. CGI Productions, 1990.** The effects of thirty years of war. Sensitive portrayal of a proud people, living in a very poor country.

### Grades 9–12

**Alvarez, Julie.** *How the Garcia Girls Lost Their Accents.* **Algonquin, 1991. ISBN: 0-945575-57-2.** The difficulties of adapting to life in America for four sisters from the Dominican Republic. America through the eyes of young Hispanic women.

**Chestnut, J. L.** *Black in Selma: The Uncommon Life of J. L. Chestnut, Jr.* **Farrar, 1990. ISBN: 0-374-11404-8.** Backdrop is the civil rights movement in Selma.

*Children of the Dragon: The Story of Tiananmen Square.* **Macmillan, 1990. ISBN: 0-02-033520-2.** Photographs and the words of student activists.

*Cultures of the World.* **Series. Marshall Cavendish.** This series of books, with its emphasis on cultural diversity, is recommended in many reviewing sources. It is scheduled to be completed in 1994. *Asia, Latin America,* and *Asia/Australia* are currently available. These books are listed here for high school in response to the need for material for global studies. They also could be used successfully with middle school students. Nicely illustrated with photographs and maps, *Kirkus* (9/15/90) said this about the series: "Real knowledge of the human element of another country's culture: motivations, aspirations, behavior, goals."

**Friedman, Ina R.** *The Other Victims: First-Person Stories of Non-Jews Persecuted by the Nazis.* **Houghton, 1990. ISBN: 0-395-50212-8.** Narratives by those sometimes forgotten.

**Lord, Bette Bao.** *Legacies: A Chinese Mosaic.* **Knopf, 1990. ISBN: 0-394-58325-6.** Forty years in China before Tiananmen. An ALA "best book."

**Parks, Gordon.** *Voices in the Mirror: An Autobiography.* **Doubleday, 1990. ISBN: 0-385-26699-5.** Breaking racial barriers. An ALA "best book."

**Rylant, Cynthia.** *Soda Jerk.* **Illustrated by Peter Catalanotto. Watts, 1990. ISBN: 0-531-05864-6.** Observations about life in a small Virginia town.

*The Sky Is Gray.* **Video. Robert Geller/Learning in Focus, 1980. Coronet.** Based on the Ernest Gaines short story in which a black farm boy learns about coping with injustice from a remarkable mother.

**Smith, Hendrick.** *The New Russians.* **Random House, 1990. ISBN: 0-394-58190-3.** Hendrick is the former Moscow bureau chief of the *New York Times.* This is an update of his first book of observations (*Russians*), which was a Pulitzer Prize winner. In 1990, it was *au courant*—what next?

*Teatro!* **Video. Directed by Ruth Shapiro, et al. Filmakers Library, 1989.** A Blue Ribbon winner at the 1990 American Film and Video Festival. A Jesuit priest works to enlighten the rural population of Honduras regarding their rights.

**Thomas, Maria.** *African Visas: A Novella and Stories.* **Farrar, 1991. ISBN: 0-939149-54-0.** All but two of these stories are told by members of the Peace Corps. Seeing Africa through American eyes.

**Tifft, Wilton.** *Ellis Island.* **Contemporary, 1990. ISBN: 0-8092-4418-7.** Ellis Island is a part of family history for millions of Americans. The photographs from the archives document the strength and hope of the immigrants who passed through here; the text tells of the laws and the procedures that frame this perspective of our growth.

**Wang, Harvey.** *Harvey Wang's New York.* **Norton, 1990. ISBN: 0-393-02914-X.** Text and photographs are juxtaposed in an engaging manner. Most of the subjects are immigrants, shown at work.

**Ward, Clenyse.** *Wandering Girl.* **Holt, 1991. ISBN: 0-8050-1634-1.** The author is an Australian aborigine. In her job as a servant to a white family she first begins to recognize the differences between herself and her employers.

# List 1–15.   Appreciating Cultures: Reproducible List

"Book List." *The Instructor,* February 1991.

China in the Classroom: Resource Catalog. Center for Teaching About China.

Cox, Susan and Lee Galda. "Multicultural Literature: Mirrors and Windows on a Global Community." *The Reading Teacher,* April 1990.

*Folklore of World Holidays.* Edited by Margaret MacDonald. Gale, 1991.

Hayden, Carla D. *Venture Into Cultures: A Resource Book of Multicultural Materials and Programs.* ALA, 1991.

Heltshe, Mary Ann and Audrey Burie Kirchner. *Multicultural Explorations: Joyous Journeys With Books.* Libraries Unlimited, 1990.

*Multicultural Review.* Serial. Greenwood Publishing, Inc.

*Resource/Reading List 1990: Annotated Bibliography of Resources by and About Native People.* Compiled by Catherine Verrall and Patricia McDowell. Canadian Alliance in Solidarity with the Native Peoples, 1990.

Shemanski, Frances. *A Guide to World Fairs and Festivals.* Greenwood Press, 1985.

### Grades K–5

*America Is.* Directed by Peter Rosen. Carousel, 1986. (Video)

Field, Rachel. *A Road Might Lead to Anywhere.* Little Brown, 1991.

Godden, Rumer. *Fu-Dog.* Viking, 1989.

Hoyt-Goldsmith, Diane. *Pueblo Storyteller.* Holiday, 1991.

Keegan, Marcia. *Pueblo Boy: Growing Up in Two Worlds.* Dutton, 1991.

McLain, Gary. *The Indian Way: Learning to Communicate with Mother Earth.* John Muir, 1990.

Shannon, George. *More Stories to Solve: Fifteen Folktales From Around the World.* Greenwillow, 1991.

Wall, Lina Mao. *Judge Rabbit and the Tree Spirit: A Folktale From Cambodia.* Children's Book Press, 1991.

### Grades 6–8

Katz, William. *Breaking the Chains: African-American Slave Resistance.* Atheneum, 1990.

Lomas Garza, Carmen. *Family Pictures/Cuadros de Familia.* Children's Book Press, 1990.

Maartens, Maretha. *Paper Bird: A Novel of South Africa.* Clarion, 1991.

*Made in China: A Search for Roots.* Filmakers Library, 1986. (Video)

*Northern Tales: Traditional Stories of Eskimo and Indian Peoples.* Selected Howard Norman. Pantheon, 1990.

Thomson, Peggy. *City Kids in China.* HarperCollins, 1991.

*When Night Comes: Vietnam Today.* CGI Productions, 1990. (Video)

### Grades 9–12

Alvarez, Julie. *How the Garcia Girls Lost Their Accents.* Algonquin, 1991.

Chestnut, J. L. *Black in Selma: The Uncommon Life of J. L. Chestnut, Jr.* Farrar, 1990.

*Children of the Dragon: The Story of Tiananmen Square.* Macmillan, 1990.

*Cultures of the World.* Marshall Cavendish, series.

Friedman, Ina. *The Other Victims: First-Person Stories of Non-Jews Persecuted by the Nazis.* Houghton, 1990.

Lord, Bette Bao. *Legacies: A Chinese Mosaic.* Knopf, 1990.

Parks, Gordon. *Voices in the Mirror: An Autobiography.* Doubleday, 1990.

Rylant, Cynthia. *Soda Jerk.* Watts, 1990.

*The Sky Is Gray.* Video. Coronet, 1980.

Smith, Hendrick, *The New Russians.* Random House, 1990.

*Teatro!* Directed by Ruth Shapiro. Filmakers Library, 1989. (Video)

Thomas, Maria. *African Visas: A Novella and Stories.* Farrar, 1991.

Tifft, Wilton. *Ellis Island.* Contemporary, 1990.

Wang, Harvey. *Harvey Wang's New York.* Norton, 1990.

Ward, Clenyse. *Wandering Girl.* Holt, 1991.

# NONFICTION

Students will tell you they want to read a "true" story. The most successful nonfiction writing is detailed, carefully researched, and thoughtfully presented. It conveys facts and ideas that engage the reader and clarify the subject matter. Successful nonfiction writing for children will excite the reader and challenge his or her mind. It will be written precisely and will make the obscure clear. It will entice the student to go after more information on the topic. If the subject matter is controversial, the writer will present opposing views. The illustrations accompanying nonfictional materials will be accurate and complementary to the text. The words of Walter Savage Landor in *Imaginary Conversations* state it well:

"Elegance in prose composition is mainly this: a just admission of topics and of words; neither too many nor too few of either; enough of sweetness in the sound to induce us to enter and sit still; enough of illustration and reflection to change the posture of our minds when they would tire; and enough of sound matter in the complex to repay us for our attendance."

These qualities are reflected in the following nonfiction selections.

## List 1–16.   Nonfiction: Annotated List

### Grades K–5

**Bisel, Sara C. *The Secrets of Vesuvius: Exploring the Mysteries of an Ancient Buried City*. Scholastic, 1991. ISBN: 0-590-43850-6.** Not the easiest subject matter in which to generate interest, but this Time Quest Series book does it in a lively, fascinating style. The material brings personal stories from an anthropologist together with physical scientific evidence and social history. Color photographs and watercolors beautifully illustrate the artwork from excavations.

**Cole, Joanna. *The Magic School Bus Lost in the Solar System*. Illustrated by Bruce Degen. Scholastic, 1990. ISBN: 0-590-41428-3.** Ms. Frizzle and her class explore space to learn about the wonders of the universe.

***The Elements of Music.*** **Paul Anthony McRae and the Royal Philharmonic Orchestra of London. Produced by William Cole Hunter, SIRS, 1990. ISBN: (guide) 0-8977-748-4.** Six-part video which compares music elements to space. Stimulates interest in music. For all ages.

**Hirschi, Ron.** ***Loon Lake.*** **Photographs by Daniel J. Cox. Cobblehill Books, 1991. ISBN: 0-525-65046-6.** *Kirkus* called this "a beautifully composed photo-story." *Booklist* states: "simple words and splendid color photographs."

**Maestro, Betsy and Giulio.** ***The Discovery of the Americas.*** **Lothrop, 1991. ISBN: 0-688-06837-5.** The discovery from the Stone Age of both North and South America is presented here. Maps, chronology of dates, and facts about the people of pre-Columbian America.

**Markle, Sandra.** ***Outside and Inside You.*** **Illustrated by Susan Kuklin. Bradbury, 1991. ISBN: 0-02-762311-4.** *Booklist* (3/15/91) review calls attention to the "knock-out array of colorful computerized views, X-rays, stained slides, and photographs" in this tremendously appealing book about young bodies and keeping them healthy.

**McVey, Vicki.** ***The Sierra Club Book of Weatherwisdom.*** **Illustrated by Martha Weston. Little Brown, 1991. ISBN: 0-316-56341.** The writing is effective, easy to read and informal. Information about weather conditions and patterns is conveyed through examples of children in various parts of the world coping with its effects.

**Stanley, Fay.** ***The Last Princess: The Story of Princess Ka'iulani of Hawai'i.*** **Illustrated by Diane Stanley. Four Winds, 1991. ISBN: 0-02-786785-4.** A "bittersweet drama" that will "certainly capture the reader's imagination" (*Booklist*, 3/15/91). Not only a biography, this is the story of the annexation of the Hawaiian Islands by the United States in 1898.

### Grades 6–8

**Andersen, Yvonne.** ***Make Your Own Animated Movies and Videotapes.*** **Little, 1991. ISBN: 0-316-03941.** Film animation, videotape, and computer animation—both a how-to book for the beginner and information source for more advanced film makers. A very readable, usable title for those students turned on by this new art form.

**Cohen, Daniel.** ***Phantom Animals.*** **Putnam, 1991. ISBN: 0-399-22230-8.** This account of ghostly animals will fascinate middle schoolers. The author's stories are drawn from eyewitness accounts, newspaper articles, and folklore. Not terribly scientific, with no bibliographic references, but intriguing nevertheless.

**Conrad, Pam.** ***Prairie Visions.*** **Photographs by Solomon Butcher. HarperCollins, 1990. ISBN: 0-06-021375-2.** *Booklist* gave this fascinating book a starred review. The photos that Butcher spent fifteen years putting together are here combined with text which gives the reader a history of pioneer life in Nebraska, as well as a history of photography. "This is history that connects us and expands our vision," says *Booklist*.

**Devaney, John.** *America Goes to War: 1941.* **Walker, 1991. ISBN: 0-8027-6979-9.** The approach by the author is anecdotal, as he portrays the momentous decisions of the move towards war. Very readable and useful even to a student not well-versed in history. Maps and a chronology help to understand the progression of events.

**Giblin, James Cross.** *The Riddle of the Rosetta Stone: Key to Ancient Egypt.* **HarperCollins, 1990. ISBN: 0-690-04797-5.** *Kirkus* called this a "handsome and inspiring book" about the fascinating story of the relationship of the stone to history.

**Ventura, Piero.** *Great Composers.* **Putnam, 1989. ISBN: 0-399-21746-0.** The beautiful, color illustrations in this book would make it useful with younger children, but the concepts and reading level are for grades 6–9. The author's intent was to introduce the reader to the kind of music the composers created, and how it related to their time and place in history. Line drawings of musical instruments and brief biographies of composers complete this lovely book. A companion to *Great Painters.*

*Where the Forest Meets the Sea.* **Video. Animated by Jeannie Baker. Films, Inc., 1988.** Raising our consciousness regarding the need to preserve the rain forests.

### Grades 9–12

*America's Fascinating Indian Heritage: The First Americans: Their Customs, Art, History and How They Lived.* **Reader's Digest, 1990. ISBN: 0-89577-372-4.** *School Library Journal* (4/91) suggests the usefulness of this source in history, art, and the humanities. The information is presented by region and historical chronology and covers every major tribe in North America. Maps, photographs, and diagrams illustrate this easy-to-read resource.

*In and Out.* **Video. Directed by David Fine and Alison Snowden. Direct Cinema, 1989.** The fleeting nature of all life.

*Inventors and Discoverers: Changing Our World.* **National Geographic Society, 1988. ISBN: 0-87044-753-X.** Eleven authorities in the fields of science and social history contributed to this slick, well-illustrated book. The articles range from early discoveries through the technology of tomorrow.

*Journeys in New Worlds: Early American Women's Narratives.* **Edited by William L. Andrews. University of Wisconsin, 1991. ISBN: 0-299-12584-X.** These four stories are accounts told by women traveling on the American frontier. Each adventure gives us a picture of eighteenth-century life in the eastern United States. Introductions to each account put the story in historical and biographical context.

**Lichter, Linda.** *Watching America: What Television Tells Us About Our Lives.* **Prentice Hall, 1991. ISBN: 0-13-026824-0.** Television producers have evolved from promoters of the status quo to agents of change. The author, through an analysis of a random sampling of shows, deduces the effect of the medium on gender roles, family life, viewer reactions to violence, and more.

**Nichol, John.** *The Mighty Rain Forest.* **David and Charles, 1990. ISBN: 0-7153-9461-4.** This is a timely treatment of the fate of the vitally important rain forests. This nicely illustrated (photos) book shows the plants, animals and people who live in these beautiful areas; nontechnical.

**Sinyavsky, Andrei.** *Soviet Civilization: A Cultural History.* **Arcade, 1990. ISBN: 1-55970-034-3.** This is a timely account of the history of the Soviet Union, with personal stories and conversations that enliven our interest and inform. Language is explored through the inclusion of the works of poets and other writers. A book about a culture transformation.

*Teenage Soldiers, Adult Wars.* **Edited by Roger Rose and Patra McSharry. (Icarus World Issue Series). Rosen, 1991. ISBN: 0-8239-1305-8.** A fine group of short stories in which young soldiers from many countries of the world express their views of military conflict. Pressed into wars not of their own making, they face situations and decisions no young person should be called upon to make.

**Thompson, Dorothy.** *Queen Victoria; The Woman, the Monarchy and the People.* **Pantheon, 1990. ISBN: 0-394-53709-2.** This kind of resource is needed in high schools, where this period of English history is included in both English and social studies curricula. It is entertaining and yet highly informative about the woman and her times.

# List 1–16.  Nonfiction: Reproducible List

**Grades K–5**

Bisel, Sara C. *The Secrets of Vesuvius*. Scholastic, 1991.

Cole, Joanna. *The Magic School Bus Lost in the Solar System*. Scholastic, 1990.

*The Elements of Music*. Produced by William Cole Hunter. SIRS, 1990.

Hirschi, Ron. *Loon Lake*. Cobblehill Books, 1991.

Maestro, Betsy and Giulio. *The Discovery of the Americas*. Lothrop, 1990.

Markle, Sandra. *Outside and Inside You*. Bradbury, 1991.

McVey, Vicki. *The Sierra Club Book of Weatherwisdom*. Little Brown, 1991.

Stanley, Fay. *The Last Princess: The Story of Princess Ka'iulani of Hawai'i*. Four Winds, 1991.

**Grades 6–8**

Andersen, Yvonne. *Make Your Own Animated Movies and Videotapes*. Little, 1991.

Cohen, Daniel. *Phantom Animals*. Putnam, 1991.

Conrad, Pam. *Prairie Visions*. HarperCollins, 1990.

Devaney, John. *America Goes to War: 1941*. Walker, 1991.

Giblin, James Cross. *The Riddle of the Rosetta Stone*. HarperCollins, 1990.

Ventura, Piero. *Great Composers*. Putnam, 1989.

*Where the Forest Meets the Sea*. Films, Inc. 1988. (Video)

**Grades 9–12**

*America's Fascinating Indian Heritage*. Reader's Digest, 1990.

*In and Out*. Video. Direct Cinema, 1989.

*Inventors and Discoverers*. National Geographic Society, 1988.

*Journeys In New Worlds*. Edited by William L. Andrews. University of Wisconsin, 1991.

Lichter, Linda. *Watching America: What Television Tells Us About Our Lives*. Prentice Hall. 1991.

Nichol, John. *The Mighty Rain Forest*. David and Charles, 1990.

Sinyavsky, Andrei. *Soviet Civilization: A Cultural History*. Arcade, 1990.

*Teenage Soldiers, Adult Wars*. Edited by Roger Rose and Patra McSharry. Rosen, 1991.

Thompson, Dorothy. *Queen Victoria: The Woman, the Monarchy and the People*. Pantheon, 1990.

# HISTORICAL FICTION

> "Fiction carries a greater amount of truth in solution than the volume which purports to be all true."
>
> —WILLIAM THACKERAY
> *The English Humorists*

History can come alive for young people through historical fiction. As Willa Cather wrote in *O Pioneers,* "There are only two or three human stories, and they go on repeating themselves as fiercely as if they had never happened before." We are linked to our past and to our future.

Here is a list of some of the best new historical fiction in terms of appeal, accuracy, and literary quality.

## List 1–17.  Historical Fiction: Annotated List

*Grades K–5*

**Berleth, Richard. *Samuel's Choice.* Illustrated by James Watling. Whitman, 1990. ISBN: 0-8075-7218-7.** Two slaves play parts in Washington's historic escape from the British in the Battle of Long Island. A tribute to many people in Brooklyn in the early days of the Revolution.

**Christian, Mary Blount. *Goody Sherman's Pig.* Illustrated by Dirk Zimmer. Macmillan, 1991. ISBN: 0-02-718251-7.** The setting is Massachusetts (Boston) in 1636, and the story is based on a true event. Children will learn about the hardships of colonial life, the characteristics of dress, environment, livelihood, and daily activities as they read about "Goody" and her legal battle over her stolen pig.

**DeFelice, Cynthia. *Weasel.* Macmillan, 1990. ISBN: 0-02-726457-2.** Pioneer life in the Ohio territory where children must assume great responsibilities. Nathan learns that hate brings inner turmoil. Complex issues in a historical, thought-provoking context.

**Hodges, Margaret. *The Kitchen Knight: A Tale of King Arthur.* Illustrated by Trina Schart Hyman. Holiday, 1990. ISBN: 0-8234-0787-X.** Given a starred review by *Booklist,* this medieval story is dramatic and exciting. This rendition of the tale retains the emphasis on the heroism of the Kitchen Knight.

**Holland, Isabelle. *The Journey Home.* Scholastic, 1990. ISBN: 0-590-43110-2.** The themes treated in this story of the settlement of the West are unusual—the removal of orphans in the East to new homes there and the prejudice against

Catholics. The young orphans, sisters, have difficulty adapting to their new home in Kansas.

**Lyon, George Ella.** *Cecil's Story.* **Illustrated by Catalanotto. Orchard, 1991. ISBN: 0-531-05912-X.** What does a child feel when "Papa" goes off to war—then, now, anytime? Watercolor paintings illustrate the farm scenes from the Civil War period.

### Grades 6–8

**Avi.** *The True Confessions of Charlotte Doyle.* **Watts, 1991. ISBN: 0-531-05893-X.** Murder and intrigue on the high seas. What was it like to travel to America in 1832? A Newbery winner

**Keehn, Sally M.** *I Am Regina.* **Philomel, 1991. ISBN: 0-399-21797-5.** A dramatic story, based upon truth, about a young woman held by Indians from 1755 to 1763, told in the first person. Ten-year-old Regina is raised by Indians in an impoverished village, then reunited with her family as a woman.

**McClung, Robert.** *Hugh Glass, Mountain Man.* **Morrow, 1990. ISBN: 0-688-08092-8.** These are the true adventures of Hugh Glass, left to die in 1823 by companions on a venture for the Rocky Mountain Fur Company. In this fictionalized account of his survival, the reader gets an exciting and authentic picture of life in the West.

**Paterson, Katherine.** *Lyddie.* **Lodestar Books, 1991. ISBN: 0-525-67338-5.** The courage of working girls in the mid-1840s, the time of the industrial revolution. Lyddie is the girl of indomitable spirit in a workplace that the *New York Times* (5/19/91) reviewer says can be "heard, tasted, smelled, seen."

**Paulsen, Gary.** *The Cookcamp.* **Orchard, 1991. ISBN: 0-531-05927-8.** Family life is disrupted in World War II when father goes to war and mother must work. The five-year-old son is sent to stay with his grandmother who is a cook for a road construction crew in northern Minnesota.

**Sutcliff, Rosemary.** *The Shining Company.* **Farrar, 1990. ISBN: 0-374-36807-4.** This action story takes place in A.D. 600. Strong characterization and an authentic sense of early Britain.

**Taylor, Mildred D.** *Mississippi Bridge.* **Illustrated by Max Ginsburg. Dial, 1990. ISBN: 0-8037-0426-7.** From the Logan family saga, set in 1931. A ten-year-old white boy sees a bus accident. *Booklist* writes: "Taylor has shaped this episode into a haunting meditation . . . about segregation."

**Vos, Ida.** *Hide and Seek.* **Houghton, 1991. ISBN: 0-395-56470-0.** This narrative, written in the first person, is an authentic, detailed account of a Dutch family's survival in World War II. It takes the reader through antisemitism before the war, the occupation by the Nazis, the survival in hiding, and even the bitter sentiments following liberation.

**Westall, Robert.** *Echoes of War.* **Farrar, 1991. ISBN: 0-374-31964-2.** The author proposes that the effects of war linger well after the conflict is over. Each story is unique.

### Grades 9–12

**Courter, Gay.** *Flowers in the Blood.* **Dutton, 1990. ISBN: 0-525-24897-8.** The life of a wealthy Jewish family in nineteenth century India. The plot covers a half century and carries the reader from Calcutta to Darjeeling. Romantic and replete with insights into Indian culture.

**Denny, Robert.** *Aces: A Novel of World War II.* **Donald I. Fine, 1990. ISBN: 1-55611-225-4.** From this realistic story, young people learn of the awesome responsibility a pilot feels as he carries out a bombing mission.

**Hickey, James.** *Chrysanthemum in the Snow: The Novel of the Korean War.* **Crown, 1990. ISBN: 0-517-57402-0.** The author draws upon his experience as an infantryman in Korea. *School Library Journal* (12/90) called this a "moving tribute to the men and women who served their country in a far-off land."

**Hogan, Linda.** *Mean Spirit.* **Macmillan, 1990. ISBN: 0-689-12101-6.** Young people will be intrigued with the suspense of this novel, but will also learn of the prejudices and injustices suffered by Native Americans in the 1920s.

**Houston, James.** *Running West.* **Crown, 1990. ISBN: 0-517-57732-1.** This story, based on historical characters and events, is set in the Canadian north in the early eighteenth century. Portrays traditional cultures and the Canadian terrain.

**O'Brien, Tim.** *The Things They Carried.* **Houghton, 1990. ISBN: 0-395-51598-X.** Recollections of a tour of duty in Vietnam, told as stories about the soldiers and the talismans they carried into combat. Moving and deeply revealing of the effects of war.

**Slovo, Gillian.** *Ties of Blood.* **Morrow, 1990. ISBN: 0-688-08925-9.** Written in documentary fashion, this is a story of two families, one white and one black, and the history of South Africa during the twentieth century.

# List 1–17.  Historical Fiction: Reproducible List

### Grades K–5

Berleth, Richard. *Samuel's Choice*. Whitman, 1990.

Christian, Mary Blount. *Goody Sherman's Pig*. Macmillan, 1991.

DeFelice, Cynthia. *Weasel*. Macmillan, 1990.

Hodges, Margaret. *The Kitchen Knight: A Tale of King Arthur*. Holiday, 1990.

Holland, Isabelle. *The Journey Home*. Scholastic, 1990.

Lyon, George Ella. *Cecil's Story*. Orchard, 1991.

### Grades 6–8

Avi. *The True Confessions of Charlotte Doyle*. Watts, 1991.

Keehn, Sally M. *I Am Regina*. Philomel, 1991.

McClung, Robert. *Hugh Glass, Mountain Man*. Morrow, 1990.

Paterson, Katherine. *Lyddie*. Lodestar Books, 1991.

Sutcliff, Rosemary. *The Shining Company*. Farrar, 1990.

Taylor, Mildred. *Mississippi Bridge*. Dial, 1990.

Vos, Ida. *Hide and Seek*. Houghton, 1991.

Westall, Robert. *Echoes of War*. Farrar, 1991.

### Grades 9–12

Courter, Gay. *Flowers in the Blood*. Dutton, 1990.

Denny, Robert. *Aces: A Novel of World War II*. Donald I. Fine, 1990.

Hickey, James. *Chrysanthemum in the Snow: The Novel of the Korean War*. Crown, 1990.

Hogan, Linda. *Mean Spirit*. Macmillan, 1990.

Houston, James. *Running West*. Crown, 1990.

O'Brien, Tim. *The Things They Carried*. Houghton, 1990.

Slovo, Gillian. *Ties of Blood*. Morrow, 1990.

# FUNNY YOU SHOULD ASK! WHERE THE ANSWERS ARE

We all know about Rudyard Kipling's "six honest serving-men" (from the *Just So Stories*) who taught him all he knew: "What and Why and When/ And How and Where and Who."

From a reference log which we kept in our library throughout a recent school year I discovered that by far the most frequently asked reference questions were simply: What or who, was it? When or where, did it happen? How many were there? How does it work? Who said it?

Sometimes the answer to the reference question is an end to itself, and the quest stops there. More often, however, that question has to be addressed as part of a larger search. Before continuing with the research the student may need to identify a person, place, or thing; to place the person or object in a frame of reference; or quantify some aspect of the topic.

The idea for the following lists grew from experience with a reference question log. The first list is comprised of biographical resources, the second quotations, the third identification of unfamiliar objects and their purposes, the fourth locational sources, the fifth statistical, and the sixth places people and events in a historical context.

# WHO WAS IT?

People are curious about people. Librarians are faced constantly with a variation on the old theme: "I know I know him, but I just can't place him . . ." These references will help you to quickly put a name to the unknown, a face to the name.

## List 2–1.   Who Was It?: Annotated List

**Abrams, Irwin.** *The Nobel Peace Prize and the Laureates: An Illustrated Biographical History, 1901–1987.* **G. K. Hall, 1988. ISBN: 0-8161-8609-X.** Details the history of the Nobel Peace Prize and explains the selection process. Each biography is two pages in length and includes a photograph of the laureate. Charles Chatfield, a history professor and one of the reviewers of the book, said, "I will shelve it within easy reach . . . because it conveys that irrepressible, many-faceted commitment to peace and human welfare which should embolden us all."

*Almanac of Famous People:* **A Comprehensive Reference Guide to More Than 25,000 Famous and Infamous Newsmakers From Biblical Times to the Present. Three volumes. Fourth edition. Gale, 1989. ISBN: 0-8103-2784-8.** Serves as a biographical dictionary and an index to information about famous people.

*American Political Leaders.* **Edited by James McPherson and Gary Gerstle. ABC-CLIO, 1991. ISBN: 0-87436-570-8.** Profiles major U.S. political leaders from 1789 to the present. Includes the individual's contributions to history.

*Baker's Biographical Dictionary of Musicians.* **Eighth edition. Compiled by Nicolas Slonimsky. Macmillan, 1991. ISBN: 0-02-872415-1.** Brief biographical sketches of musicians up to the present.

**Barker-Benfield, G. J. and Clinton, Catherine.** *Portraits of American Women: From Settlement to the Present.* **St. Martin's Press, 1991. ISBN: 0-312-05789-8.** Profiles twenty-five influential women. The information offered includes overviews of the time periods represented, and the selection profiles women from very different walks of life. This resource was favorably reviewed in *Booklist* (4/15/91).

*Benet's Reader's Encyclopedia of American Literature.* **Edited by George Perkins, et al. HarperCollins, 1991. ISBN: 0-06-270027-8.** The newest edition of this wonderful, standard reference. I find this source and *Benet's Reader's Encyclopedia* to be the most frequently referenced books in my library. Extremely easy to use and informative. The new edition will include Canadian, Central and South American writers, and information about Native American oral history.

***Biography Index.*** **Serial. Quarterly with annual cumulations. H. W. Wilson. ISSN: 0006-3053.** Offers access to all types of biographical material, fiction and nonfiction books, magazines, and periodicals. This index is available online, on CD-ROM, and on tape, as well as in traditional print.

***Celebrity Register 1990.*** **Gale, 1989. ISBN: 0-8103-6875-7.** Notable personalities are featured. Over one thousand entries.

***Concise Dictionary of American Literary Biography.*** **Six volumes. Gale. ISBN: 0-8103-1818-0.** One may purchase individual volumes. This collection covers those American authors frequently studied in high school English classes. The concise set offers the chance to add useful sources to your library without acquiring the entire *Dictionary of Literary Biography.*

***Contemporary Heroes and Heroines.*** **Edited by Ray B. Browne. Gale, 1990. ISBN: 0-8103-4860-8.** Stories of more than one hundred twentieth-century men and women from diverse fields. The biographies are brief with contemporary, attractive black and white portraits of the persons profiled. Citations of sources will lead the student in his or her research. Brief essays on heroism expand the central theme.

***Contemporary Musicians.*** **Serial. Gale. (Vol. 5, 1991.)** This is a biographical/critical series. The musicians, from all genres, are the ones teens will be asking for according to *Reference Books Bulletin.*

***Current Biography.*** **Serial. H. W. Wilson.** Published monthly; cumulated in hardcover annually. Includes obituaries, cumulative indexes, and references to additional sources. Profiles are 2,500 to 3,000 words and include a portrait of the person. *American Reference Book Annual* cites this as a "durable resource."

***Current Leaders of Nations.*** **Edited by David C. Kursowski. Current Leaders Publishing Co. ISBN: 0-9624900-0-8.** Profiles every head of government alphabetically by country. Portraits and maps included. Compiled in a three-ring binder and updated regularly. Great for global studies.

***Encyclopedia of American Biography.*** **Edited by John A. Garraty. Harper and Row. 1974. ISBN: 0-06-011438-4.** Details more than one thousand lives with facts and dates. "A compendium of informed opinion" (from the introduction to the first edition) about significant figures in history. Criteria for selection: significance, fame, typicality (i.e. representing larger group), achievement. Very useful at both middle and high school levels.

***Encyclopedia of American Comics.*** **Edited by Ron Goulart. Facts On File, 1990. ISBN: 0-8160-1852-9.** Reviewed in *Booklist* (12/15/90). Six hundred fifty entries identify comic book characters. Fun for all ages.

*Giants of Philosophy.* Narrated by Charlton Heston. *Giants of Political Thought.* Narrated by Craig Deitschmann. *The Great Economic Thinkers.* Narrated by Louis Rukeyser. Three sets of audio cassettes. Knowledge Products. Learning about great thinkers through hearing their own words.

*The Illustrated Who's Who in Mythology.* Macmillan, 1985. ISBN: 0-02-923770-X. Profiles eleven hundred major mythological figures.

Jackson, Guida M. *Women Who Ruled.* ABC-CLIO, 1990. ISBN: 0-87463-560-0. *Library Journal* identifies this book as a "best reference book for 1990," "readable text, and recommended for school libraries." From queens in history to modern heads of state—over 360 women from "the obscure to the famous" who have ruled. Entries range from fifty to over five hundred words.

Kane, Joseph Nathan. *Facts About the Presidents.* Fifth edition. H. W. Wilson, 1989. ISBN: 0-8242-0774-2. From Washington to George Bush.

Marks, Claude. *World Artists, 1980-1990.* H. W. Wilson, 1990. ISBN: 0-8242-0802-1. (Also available is *World Artists, 1950-1980.* ISBN: 0-8242-0707-6.) Interesting, brief, biographical sketches identifying the artist's major work.

*NewsBank: Names in the News.* (Microfiche) NewsBank, Inc. One of the most popular sources in a secondary school library. Current news from over three hundred newspapers in the U.S. Student can acquire the full text of an article from your reader/printer.

*Newsmakers.* Quarterly serial cumulatd annually. Edited by Louise Mooney. Gale, 1992. ISBN: 8-8103-2245-5. Covers the "newsmakers" in many fields from around the world. Includes addresses and sources for additional information. Particularly useful for high school students.

*Reference Encyclopedia of the American Indian.* Fifth edition. Edited by Barry T. Klein. ABC-CLIO. ISBN: 0-915344-16-5. The 1990 edition is a revision and contains more biographical sketches and more listings in its Canadian section.

*Rock Movers and Shakers: An A–Z of People Who Made Rock Happen.* Edited by Barry Lazell, Dafydd Rees, and Luke Crampton. ABC-CLIO. 1991. ISBN: 0-87436-661-5. Profiles careers of 750 international rock artists and groups, listing tours, records, charts of successes. Anticipate popularity with all age groups.

*St. James Guide to Biography.* Edited by Paul E. Schellinger. St. James Press, 1991. ISBN: 1-55862-146-6. Each entry includes a bibliography of biographies with a critical review of those biographies. Seven hundred persons from ancient to modern times are included. Good for high school students.

Smith, Ronald. *Fascinating People and Astounding Events From the History of the Western World.* ABC-CLIO, 1990. ISBN: 0-87436-544-9. Amusing and informative anecdotes about people and events, principally from European history. Written for teachers, this resource offers ideas for classroom use. The author, formerly a European history teacher, includes suggestions for teachers and questions for discussion. Interesting browsing material.

**Tynan, Kenneth.** *Profiles.* HarperCollins, 1989. ISBN: 0-06-039123-5. Fifty portraits of leading actors and writers.

**Waldman, Carl.** *Who Was Who in Native American History: Indians and Non-Indians From First Contacts Through 1900.* Facts On File, 1990. ISBN: 0-8160-1797-2. Includes those who had an impact on Indian history. Over one thousand entries covering four centuries.

**Waldrup, Carole C.** *Presidents' Wives: The Lives of 44 American Women of Strength.* McFarland, 1989. ISBN: 0-89950-393-4. Women who helped shape Presidential careers. Includes photos and illustrations of forty-four women.

*Who's Who Among Black Americans.* Sixth edition. Gale, 1989. ISBN: 0-8103-2243-9. Personal and career facts regarding approximately seventeen thousand prominent African-Americans in all fields. Called "major, timely" by *American Library Book Review.*

*Who's Who Among Hispanic Americans.* Gale, 1991. ISBN: 0-8103-7451-X. Biographical information on six thousand notable contemporary Hispanic Americans from diverse occupations and professions. The three indexes offer access by occupation, geographic location, and country of descent.

*The Who's Who of Nobel Prize Winners.* Second edition. Edited by Bernard S. Schlessinger and June H. Schlessinger. Oryx, 1991. ISBN: 0-89774-599-X. A good ready-reference and bibliography. The indexes offer simple access by name, nationality or citizenship, religion, and educational institution.

*World of Winners.* Edited by Gita Siegman. Gale, 1989. ISBN: 0-8103-0474-0. More than 100,000 winners of 2,400 awards, honors and prizes in many fields.

# List 2–1. Who Was It (Biographical References): Reproducible List

Abrams, Irwin. *The Nobel Peace Prize and the Laureates.* G. K. Hall, 1988.

*Almanac of Famous People.* Gale, 1989.

*American Political Leaders.* ABC-CLIO, 1991.

*Baker's Biographical Dictionary of Musicians.* Macmillan, 1991.

Barker-Benfield, G. J. *Portraits of American Women.* St. Martin's Press, 1991.

*Benet's Reader's Encyclopedia of American Literature.* HarperCollins, 1991.

*Biography Index.* Serial. H. W. Wilson.

*Celebrity Register 1990.* Gale, 1989.

*Concise Dictionary of American Literary Biography.* Six volumes. Gale.

*Contemporary Heroes and Heroines.* Gale, 1990.

*Contemporary Musicians.* Serial. Gale.

*Current Biography.* Serial. H. W. Wilson.

*Current Leaders of Nations.* Current Leaders Publishing Co., Serial.

*Encyclopedia of American Biography.* Harper and Row, 1974.

*Encyclopedia of American Comics.* Facts On File, 1990.

*Giants of Philosophy.* Knowledge Products. (Audiocassettes)

*Giants of Political Thought.* Knowledge Products. (Audiocassettes)

*The Great Economic Thinkers.* Knowledge Products. (Audiocassettes)

*The Illustrated Who's Who in Mythology.* Macmillan, 1985.

Jackson, Guida M. *Women Who Ruled.* ABC-CLIO, 1990.

Kane, Joseph Nathan. *Facts About the Presidents.* H. W. Wilson, 1989.

Marks, Claude. *World Artists, 1980–1990.* H. W. Wilson, 1990.

*NewsBank: Names in the News.* NewsBank, Inc., Serial. (Microfiche)

*Newsmakers.* Serial. Gale.

*Reference Encyclopedia of the American Indian.* ABC-CLIO, 1990.

*Rock Movers and Shakers: An A–Z of People Who Made Rock Happen.* ABC-CLIO, 1991.

*St. James Guide to Biography.* St. James Press, 1991.

Smith, Ronald. *Fascinating People and Astounding Events From the History of the Western World.* ABC-CLIO, 1990.

Tynan, Kenneth. *Profiles.* HarperCollins, 1989.

Waldman, Carl. *Who Was Who in Native American History.* Facts On File, 1990.

Waldrup, Carole C. *Presidents' Wives: The Lives of 44 American Women of Strength.* McFarland, 1989.

*Who's Who Among Black Americans.* Sixth edition. Gale, 1989.

*Who's Who Among Hispanic Americans.* Gale, 1991.

*The Who's Who of Nobel Prize Winners.* Second edition. Oryx, 1991.

*World of Winners.* Gale, 1989.

# WHO SAID IT?

The basis for selecting quotations determined by John Bartlett for *Familiar Quotations* was "familiar or worthy of being familiar." Because the volume of communication, both spoken and written, has increased so dramatically over the years due to technologies and the proliferation of methods of mass communication, we hear and read many times each day phrases and expressions of thought which seem apt and memorable. In *The Art of Quotation*, Robert William Chapman warned that "a quotation, like a pun, should come unsought, and then be welcomed only for some propriety or felicity justifying the intrusion." Often times we need the "intrusion" of a quotation—to delight us or to confirm and enhance our thoughts. First we must identify the originator. Many students and teachers seek to discover what was said and by whom. Here, then, is a list of diverse sources of quotations.

## List 2–2.   Who Said It?: Annotated List

***The American Reader: Words That Moved a Nation*. Edited by Diane Ravitch. HarperCollins, 1989. ISBN: 0-06-016480-8.** E. D. Hirsch, author of *Cultural Literacy*, labeled this "a splendid collection of the words and sentiments that have shaped our nation." This book includes not only the classic contributions from our history but unusual selections not found elsewhere. Many pieces were written by representatives of the ethnic minorities in America. Albert Shanker calls it a "sourcebook of unity for our 'teeming nation of nations.'" Illustrations enhance this source of approximately two hundred speeches, documents, poems, and songs that trace our history.

***American Women: Their Lives in Their Words*. Edited by Doreen Rappaport. Crowell, 1990. ISBN: 0-690-04817-3.** The arrangement of this survey is chronological, beginning with "Women in the New World." What women have had to say about a myriad of experiences, from traditional roles to politics and contemporary struggles for equality, will provide the reader with rich material.

**Bartel, Pauline. *The Complete Gone With the Wind Trivia Book*. Taylor Publishing Company, 1989. ISBN: 0-87833-619-2.** Lots of fun, and an authoritative source for the quotations that have somehow become a part of our social history.

**Bartlett, John.** *Familiar Quotations: A Collection of Passages, Phrases and Proverbs Traced to Their Sources in Ancient and Modern Literature.* **Edited by Emily Morison Beck. The 15th and 125th anniversary edition. Little Brown, 1980. ISBN: 0-316-08275-9.** This is the premier book of quotations, offering the words of more than two thousand authors. The quotations are indexed by author and subject.

*Baseball's Greatest Quotations.* **Edited by Paul Dickson. HarperCollins, 1991. ISBN: 0-06-270001-4.** Naturally this will interest many baseball fans. Good choice for browsing. The publisher calls it "The Bartlett of Baseball."

**Lincoln, Abraham.** *Lincoln on Democracy.* **Edited by Mario Cuomo and Harold Holzer. State of New York/Lincoln on Democracy Project, 1990. ISBN: 0-06-039126-X.** This project was conceived by Governor Cuomo in response to questions about democracy from Polish visitors. A comprehensive review of Lincoln's ideas on the subject was undertaken and resulted in this useful collection.

*The Oxford Dictionary of Modern Quotations.* **Edited by Tony Augarde. Oxford University Press, 1991. ISBN: 0-19-866141-X.** Nineteenth and twentieth century quotations. The scope of the book is international; quotations from languages other than English are given in the original language with an English translation. Extensively indexed by keyword. About five thousand quotations.

*The Oxford Dictionary of Quotations.* **Third edition. Oxford University Press, 1979. ISBN: 0-19-211560-X.** The arrangement is alphabetical by author's name, then alphabetical by title of the works quoted. Thousands of quotations appear from the writings of well-known authors from around the world. The social and political memorabilia of this century appear. The index is by keyword.

**Partnow, Elaine.** *The Quotable Woman: From Eve to 1799.* **Facts On File, 1984. ISBN: 0-87196-307-8.** About six thousand quotations harvested from around the world and from many centuries. A wealth of disparate subjects are covered, from religion to woman's position in society.

**Partnow, Elaine.** *The Best of the Quotable Woman: From Eve to the Present.* **Facts On File, 1991. ISBN: 0-8160-2134-1.** Entries are chronological by the quoted person's birth date. The remarks of these outspoken women, from all ages, are meaningful to contemporary women.

*Political Quotations.* **Edited by Daniel B. Baker. Gale, 1990. ISBN: 0-8103-4920-5.** *Wilson Library Bulletin* says this collection "surpasses most specialized quotation dictionaries." Identifies over four thousand political quotations.

*A Teacher's Treasury of Quotations.* **Compiled by Bernard E. Farber. McFarland, 1985. ISBN: 0-89950-150-8.** The compiler states that his collection "attempts to present a balance between differing viewpoints." The quotations represent the works of authors from many different countries and cultures. Some have historical significance; many are witty and present insight into problems facing today's educators.

**Weiss, Irving and Anne D.** *Reflections of Childhood: A Quotations Dictionary.* **ABC-CLIO, 1991. ISBN: 0-87436-646-1.** From the publisher: "A wonderful collection of observations, reflections, and anecdotes about the life of children from ancient times to the present." The subject matter is unique and useful for teachers and media specialists.

*What They Said in* _____: *The Yearbook of Spoken Opinion.* **Edited by Alan F. Pater and Jason R. Pater. Monitor Book Co. Published annually.** Sources for quotations are given in full. Timely and well indexed and cross-indexed. The standard source book for the world's spoken opinion.

# List 2–2.  Who Said It (Quotation Sources): Reproducible List

*The American Reader: Words That Moved a Nation.* Edited by Diane Ravitch. HarperCollins, 1989.

*American Women: Their Lives In Their Words.* Edited by Doreen Rappaport. Crowell, 1990.

Bartlett, John. *Familiar Quotations.* Little Brown, 1980.

*Baseball's Greatest Quotations.* Edited by Paul Dickson. HarperCollins, 1991.

Lincoln, Abraham. *Lincoln On Democracy.* Edited by Mario Cuomo. NYState/Lincoln On Democracy Project, 1990.

*The Oxford Dictionary of Modern Quotations.* Edited by Tony Augarde. Oxford University Press, 1991.

*The Oxford Dictionary of Quotations.* Third edition. Oxford University Press, 1979.

Partnow, Elaine. *The Quotable Woman: From Eve to 1799.* Facts On File, 1984.

Partnow, Elaine. *The Best of the Quotable Woman: From Eve to the Present.* Facts On File, 1991.

*Political Quotations.* Edited by Daniel B. Baker. Gale, 1990.

*A Teacher's Treasury of Quotations.* Compiled by Bernard E. Farber. McFarland, 1985.

Weiss, Irving and Anne D. *Reflections of Childhood: A Quotations Dictionary.* ABC-CLIO, 1991.

*What They Said In _____: The Yearbook of Spoken Opinion.* Edited by Alan F. and Jason R. Pater. Monitor, Annual.

# WHAT IS IT?

> "Curiosity is one of the permanent and
> certain characteristics of a vigorous mind."
>
> —SAMUEL JOHNSON
> *The Rambler*

Anatole France wrote of curiosity in this way: "The whole art of teaching is only the art of awakening the natural curiosity of young minds for the purpose of satisfying it afterwards."

No need to call it a "whatchamacallit" or a "thingamabob" if you have references that are useful for identifying the unknown. The following list offers a few choices to supplement your standard encyclopedias and dictionaries.

## List 2–3.   What Is It?: Annotated List

Bortz, Fred. *Superstuff! Materials That Have Changed Our Lives*. Watts, 1990. ISBN: 0-531-10887-2. The materials of science and engineering are introduced, discussed, and illustrated. Everyday applications of materials are given.

Bragonier, Reginald and David Fisher. *What's What, A Visual Glossary of the Physical World*. Hammond, 1981. ISBN: 0-8437-3329-2. When this book first came out *The New York Times* said "every layout a dynamite visual." The illustrations are clear, detailed, and engaging. This resource provides a visual approach to finding a label for just about anything. The authors tell us they chose objects for inclusion based upon their usefulness to contemporary readers.

Cliffe, Roger W. *Woodworker's Handbook*. Sterling, 1990. ISBN: 0-8069-7238-6. Photos and diagrams, clear but detailed, help to identify tools and processes.

Corbeil, Jean-Claude. *The Facts On File Visual Dictionary*. Facts On File, 1986. ISBN: 0-8160-1544-9. "Look up the word from the picture and the picture from the word." Includes entries on scientific and technical information. Three indexes: thematic, general, and specialized; 25,000 terms; 3,000 illustrations. Everything from "A-frame" to "zipper pocket" graphically represented. Consider *The Facts On File Junior Visual Dictionary* (ISBN: 0-8160-2222-4) for middle school libraries.

*The Doubleday Children's Encyclopedia*. Four volumes. Edited by John Paton and Roberta Wiener. Doubleday, 1990. ISBN: 0-385-41210-X. More than 2,000 pictures for 1,300 entries. Favorably reviewed in *Booklist* (12/15/90).

***Earth Sciences on File.*** **Facts On File, 1988. ISBN: 0-8160-1625-9.** A guide to the earth and the universe. Seven sections cover astronomy, geology, meteorology, oceanography, energy, and environment. Tables, scales, and maps in line drawing format make these illustrations perfect for reproducing. Gathered in a three-ring loose-leaf binder. Teachers find them unequaled for worksheets, exams, and overhead projection masters.

**Hagerman, Paul S.** ***It's a Weird World.*** **Illustrated by Myron Miller. Sterling, 1990. ISBN: 0-8069-7412-5.** Weird but true answers to lots of trivial questions.

**Hawkes, Nigel.** ***Structures: The Way Things Are Built.*** **Macmillan, 1990. ISBN: 0-02-549105-9.** The author discusses forty structures, from the obelisk of Egypt to a nuclear power plant. With photographs and drawings he demonstrates the ingenuity and creativity behind each "monument."

***The Human Body on File.*** **Edited by Ruth Swan. Facts On File, 1983. ISBN: 0-87196-706-5.** An "atlas" of anatomy and a reference source for photocopying. Three hundred independent detachable plates. Three-ring binder format. Precise identifications of the where and the what of the human body.

***The Illustrated Encyclopedia of Technology.*** **Exeter Books, 1984. ISBN: 0-671-07040-1.** Covers consumer and service, building, transport, military and space, and other applied technologies. Color and black-and-white photos.

**Lambert, David and Jane Insley.** ***World of Science: Great Discoveries and Inventions.*** **Facts On File, 1985. ISBN: 0-8160-1062-5.** A science dictionary for eight- to twelve-year-olds. From the adding machine to the X-ray.

**Liungman, Carl G.** ***Dictionary of Symbols.*** **ABC-CLIO, 1991. ISBN: 0-87436-610-0.** Defines and illustrates symbols of western culture. The reader can locate a symbol by defining four of its visual characteristics. The cross-referenced index has entries for meanings, words, and names of systems and symbols.

**Macaulay, David.** ***The Way Things Work.*** **Houghton Mifflin, 1988. ISBN: 0-395-42857-2.** A guide to the workings of machines. Beautifully illustrated with detailed sepia drawings. A pleasure to peruse. Consider, also, Macaulay's *How Things Are Made.*

***Musical Instruments of the World: An Illustrated Encyclopedia.*** **By the Diagram Group. Facts On File, 1976. ISBN: 0-8467-0134-0.** Depicts "the vast range of man's inventiveness in his search for music-making objects." The illustrations show the designs and methods of creating sounds. The line drawings are beautiful, detailed, and informative. Musical groups, music makers, virtuosi, and writers are included in this fine book.

***The National Geographic Book of Mammals.*** **CD-ROM. National Geographic, 1990.** With this single source, the student can see and hear animals (two hundred of them in twenty different orders) in action, view maps, learn their classifications. Facts and essays equivalent to six hundred pages of text.

*The Oxford Illustrated Encyclopedia. Vol. 1. The Physical World.* **Edited by Sir Vivian Fuchs. Oxford University Press, 1985. ISBN: 0-19-869129-7.** Information is arranged alphabetically around the general them. Covers central concepts in mathematics, chemistry, physics, and earth sciences. Visuals and biographical information on the significant contributors to these sciences. Cross-referenced.

*The Oxford Illustrated Encyclopedia. Vol. 2. The Natural World.* **Edited by Malcolm Coe. Oxford University Press, 1985. ISBN: 0-19-869134-3.** Living organisms alone (we are told in the foreword) comprise over five million known species. Ninety percent are animals. This volume includes representatives from all major animal and plant groups. Cross-referenced for excellent access. Major contributors to the fields of natural science are included. Diagrams, photos, and line drawings. Colorful timelines and classification schemes on the endpapers.

**Parker, Steve.** *The Random House Book of How Things Work.* **Random House, 1991. ISBN: 0-697-90908-7.** The author describes for the reader how more than three hundred everyday objects and scientific devices work and what they are for. The illustrations are colorful and clear.

**Racinet, Albert.** *The Historical Encyclopedia of Costumes.* **Facts On File, 1989. ISBN: 0-8160-1976-2.** Includes garments from around the world, historical development, and costumes from all walks of life.

**Reader's Digest.** *How In the World?* **Reader's Digest, 1990. ISBN: 0-89577-353-8.** Many questions are answered and illustrated in color. Explorations, the Pyramids, curiosities of the world—twelve categories in this useful book.

**Reinfeld, Fred.** *Catalogue of the World's Most Popular Coins.* **Sterling, 1983. ISBN: 0-8069-6078-7.** Prices, dating techniques, photographs.

**Williams, Trevor I.** *The History of Invention: From Stone Axes to Silicon Chips.* **Facts On File, 1987. ISBN: 0-8160-1788-3.** Illustrations and diagrams identify the major inventions of the world, from agricultural tools to nuclear reactors.

# List 2–3.   What Is It?: Reproducible List

Bortz, Fred. *Superstuff! Materials That Have Changed Our Lives*. Watts, 1990.

Bragonier, Reginald. *What's What, A Visual Glossary of the Physical World*. Hammond, 1981.

Cliffe, Roger W. *Woodworker's Handbook*. Sterling, 1990.

Corbeil, Jean-Claude. *The Facts On File Visual Dictionary*. Facts On File, 1986.

*The Doubleday Children's Encyclopedia*. Edited by John Paton. Doubleday, 1990.

*Earth Sciences On File*. Facts On File, 1988.

Hagerman, Paul S. *It's a Weird World*. Sterling, 1990.

Hawkes, Nigel. *Structures: The Way Things Are Built*. Macmillan, 1990.

*The Human Body On File*. Facts On File, 1983.

*The Illustrated Encyclopedia of Technology*. Exeter Books, 1984.

Lambert, David and Jane Insley. *World of Science: Great Discoveries and Inventions*. Facts On File, 1985.

Liungman, Carl G. *Dictionary of Symbols*. ABC-CLIO, 1991.

Macaulay, David. *The Way Things Work*. Houghton Mifflin, 1988.

*Musical Instruments of the World: An Illustrated Encyclopedia*. Facts On File, 1976.

*The National Geographic Book of Mammals*. CD-ROM. National Geographic, 1990.

*The Oxford Illustrated Encyclopedia*. Vol. 1. *The Physical World*. Oxford University Press, 1985.

*The Oxford Illustrated Encyclopedia*. Vol. 2. *The Natural World*. Oxford University Press, 1985.

Parker, Steve. *The Random House Book of How Things Work*. Random House, 1991.

Racinet, Albert. *The Historical Encyclopedia of Costumes*. Facts On File, 1989.

Reader's Digest. *How In the World?* Reader's Digest, 1990.

Reinfeld, Fred. *Catalogue of the World's Most Popular Coins*. Sterling, 1983.

Williams, Trevor I. *The History of Invention: From Stone Axes to Silicon Chips*. Facts On File, 1987.

# WHERE IS IT?

Cervantes wrote in *Don Quixote,* "Journey over all the universe in a map, without the expense and fatigue of travelling, without suffering the inconveniences of heat, cold, hunger, and thirst." Beyond the pleasure of locating a place we are curious about, it has become a necessity to be knowledgeable about geography. The world seems smaller today than generations ago, culturally and geographically. From quick and clean locational sources to beautifully illustrated atlases, this list offers a few titles for your consideration.

## List 2–4.    Where Is It?: Annotated List

***Almanac of the 50 States.*** **Information Publications, 1991. ISBN: 0-931845-22-X.** About eight pages for each state, with comprehensive data profiles.

***Facts About the States: A Compendium of Information About the Fifty States, Including Puerto Rico and Washington D.C.*** **Compiled by Joseph Nathan Kane, Steven Anzovin, and Janet Podell. H. W. Wilson, 1989. ISBN: 0-8242-0407-7.** An encyclopedia ranking states in comparative tables. The facts presented are fascinating and informative.

***Goode's World Atlas.*** **Eighteenth edition. Edited by Edward Espenshade. Rand McNally, 1990. ISBN: 0-528-83128-3.** *Booklist* (12/1/90) recommended this atlas for all collections, saying its coverage is well balanced and it has a "proven track record." An essential for your school collection.

***Historical Atlas of the U. S.*** **National Geographic, 1988. ISBN: 0-87044-747-5.** Geographic perspectives are developed in six thematic sections: land, people, boundaries, economy, networks, communities. Pre-Columbian time to the present. Wonderfully illustrated with charts, graphs, maps, and period photographs.

***Illustrated Dictionary of Place Names, U. S. and Canada.*** **Edited by Kelsie B. Harder. Van Nostrand, 1976. ISBN: 0-442-23-069-9.** Start here for correct spellings and general locational information.

***The Illustrated Encyclopedia of World Geography.*** **Volumes 1 and 2.** *Earth's Natural Forces* **(ISBN: 0-19-520860-9) and** *World Government* **(ISBN: 0-19-520861-7). Oxford University Press, 1990.**

*NBC News Rand McNally World News Atlas, 1991.* **Rand McNally, 1990. ISBN: 0-528-83424-X.** This softcover atlas is an economical title to consider. World events are combined with maps providing excellent access to "where" it happened.

*Rand McNally Children's Atlas of the Universe.* **Edited by Elizabeth G. Fagan. Rand McNally, 1990. ISBN: 0-528-83408-8.** A travelogue that takes children to other planets. Color photographs, drawings, and easy-to-read text provide a wealth of information for younger children. A comprehensive index and a glossary add to the usefulness of this resource.

*The Times Atlas of the World.* **Eighth Comprehensive Edition. Times Books, 1990. ISBN: 0-8129-1874-6.** A fine atlas. The eighth edition supplements world maps with maps of the universe. It is the only eight-color atlas in the English language, and remains the most accurate available. *Booklist* recommends it as the "best world atlas in print."

*Webster's New Geographical Dictionary.* **Merriam-Webster, 1988. ISBN: 0-87779-446-4.** Entries for the U. S. and Canada are on a scale broader than for the rest of the world. Places are included if they have populations of 2,500 or more. Small maps prepared by Hammond are included with very brief entries which give precise locations, pronunciations, identifying information, area, population, economic data, and features of general interest or historical significance.

**Wright, David and Jill.** *The Facts On File Children's Atlas.* **Facts On File, 1991. ISBN: 0-8160-2703-X.** Consider this atlas for children over age seven. This atlas is designed to excite youngsters about geography. Includes topical quizzes and activity ideas.

# List 2–4.   Where Is It?: Reproducible List

*Almanac of the 50 States.* Information Publications, 1991.

*Facts About the States.* Compiled by Joseph Kane. H. W. Wilson, 1989.

*Goode's World Atlas.* Edited by Edward Espenshade. Rand McNally, 1990.

*Historical Atlas of the U. S.* National Geographic, 1988.

*Illustrated Dictionary of Place Names, U. S. and Canada.* Van Nostrand, 1976.

*The Illustrated Encyclopedia of World Geography,* Volumes 1 and 2. Oxford University Press, 1990.

*Rand McNally Children's Atlas of the Universe.* Edited by Elizabeth G. Fagan. Rand McNally, 1990.

*The Times Atlas of the World.* Times Books, 1990.

*Webster's New Geographical Dictionary.* Merriam-Webster, 1988.

Wright, David and Jill. *The Facts On File Children's Atlas.* Facts On File, 1991.

# HOW MANY?

Many important decisions are made daily in our society that are based on "the numbers." Domestic and foreign policies are often a result of "what the latest figures are" on a particular issue. In many secondary schools economics is a required course of study. Aside from that, however, it is just fun to know the statistics; sometimes they mean a little, sometimes a lot. In addition to your current almanac, a few of the resources in this list may help you and your students to win the numbers game.

## List 2–5.   How Many Are There?: Annotated List

*Atlas of the United States: A Thematic and Comparative Approach.* **Macmillan, 1986. ISBN: 0-02-922830-1.** The similarities and differences among the states. This beautiful, graphic atlas is fine for visual representation of statistical information about age, education, literacy, mobility, productivity, etc., of Americans. The second half of the atlas examines the United States in relation to the rest of the world. Very useful for developing correlations among many variables. The last illustrations are of "military might" worldwide.

*Census and You.* **Monthly serial. Superintendent of Documents, U. S. Government Printing Office.**

*The Economist Book of Vital World Statistics.* **By the editors of the** *Economist.* **Times Books, 1990. ISBN: 0-8129-1877-0.** The broad range of facts from diverse standard statistical sources will help students compare nations in a meaningful way. Many charts and tables grouped under fifteen broad headings. There are ranked lists which give a picture of the significant similarities and differences between the countries. Recommended for high schools.

*The Guinness Book of Records 1992.* **Edited by Donald McFarlan. Facts On File, 1991. ISBN: 0-8160-2643-2.** All records have been updated and many new ones added. Attractive new format, with an interesting preface about this amazing book's own record in publishing.

*Kaleidoscope.* **Current World Data. Edited by Timothy O'Donnell. Serial. ABC-CLIO.** Basic card file of information about the countries of the world is supplemented weekly. A useful resource for global studies. Statistics about each country are regularly updated. Find facts fast about a country's population, literacy rate, currency, economy. This source covers, besides other countries, each of the individual United States and the provinces of Canada. ABC-CLIO now offers a videotape for use in introducing *Kaleidoscope* to teachers and students.

**Kurian, George Thomas.** *The New Book of World Rankings.* **Third edition. Facts On File, 1991. ISBN: 0-8160-1931-2.** This revision of the 1984 edition includes sections which reflect our concerns over international relations, technological advances, the environment, and food and nutrition.

**Robbins, Michael.** *1991 Top Ten Almanac: The Best of Everything According to the Numbers.* **Workman, 1991. ISBN: 0-89480-854-0.** The best jobs, places to live, top-selling records. Full of facts, this resource is appealing to most students and meets their research needs.

*The Sports Fan's Ultimate Book of Sports Comparisons: A Visual, Statistical, and Factual Reference on Comparative Abilities, Records, Rules, and Equipment.* **By the Diagram Group. St. Martin's Press, 1982. ISBN: 0-312-75334-9.** Large colorful drawings, diagrams, and charts illustrate just what the title says. Includes both well-known and lesser-known sports.

*Statistical Abstract of the United States.* Buy the latest edition from the U.S. Government Printing Office or the regional distributors. Hundreds of tables reflect the demographic and cultural changes in the United States.

*World Economic Data: A Compendium of Current Economic Information for All Countries of the World.* **Third edition. ABC-CLIO, 1991. ISBN: 0-87436-658-5.** Excellent source for understanding our economy and our interdependence with other nations.

# List 2–5.   How Many Are There?
## (Statistical References): Reproducible List

*Atlas of the United States: A Thematic and Comparative Approach.* Macmillan, 1986.

*Census and You.* Serial. U. S. Government Printing Office.

*The Economist Book of Vital World Statistics.* Times Books, 1990.

*The Guinness Book of Records 1991.* Edited by Donald McFarlan. Facts On File, 1991.

*Kaleidoscope.* Serial ABC-CLIO.

Kurian, George Thomas. *The New Book of World Rankings.* Third edition. Facts On File, 1991.

Robbins, Michael. *1991 Top Ten Almanac: The Best of Everything According to the Numbers.* Workman, 1991.

*The Sports Fan's Ultimate Book of Sports Comparisons.* St. Martin's Press, 1982.

*Statistical Abstract of the United States.* U. S. Government Printing Office.

*World Economic Data.* Third edition. ABC-CLIO, 1991.

# WHEN DID IT HAPPEN?

One of the most fascinating results of any research project is to finally see events in relation to one another and to place people in the context of their times. A popular assignment with both language arts and social studies teachers is the construction of a time line. It is a unique process of discovery which allows a student to make correlations among the many forces that shape world events and effect social change. A number of the titles in the following list are time lines.

## List 2–6.   When Did It Happen?: Annotated List

*American Book of Days.* **Third edition. Compiled by Jane M. Hatch. H. W. Wilson, 1978. ISBN: 0-8242-0593-6.** The history of the United States as revealed through anniversaries, holidays, celebrations, and birthdays of important people.

**Asimov, Isaac.** *Asimov's Chronology of Science and Discovery: How Science Has Shaped the World and How the World Has Affected Science From 4,000,000 B.C. to the Present.* **HarperCollins, 1989. ISBN: 0-06-015612-0.** Useful at the secondary level, cleverly written and very readable. Does exactly what the title claims. Also recommended: *Asimov's Chronology of the World: The History of the World From the Big Bang to Modern Times,* also from HarperCollins.

*Calendar of Literary Facts.* **Edited by Samuel J. Rogal. Gale, 1991. ISBN: 0-8103-2943-3.** A ready-reference tool which gives easy access to major literary events from the fifteenth century to the present. A highly useful datebook which identifies books, authors, and events. The first part is a day-by-day chronology; this is followed by an arrangement by year. The scope is international; birth and death dates are given for approximately two thousand authors.

*Facts On File.* **Serial. Facts On File. Weekly World News Digest.** Reports the major international and national news in summary form. Print format prepared for three-ring binder. *The Facts On File News Digest CD-ROM 1980–1990* gives instant online access to events and dates. The indexes to your print version are excellent for quick reference to the date of a news event. Just enough information is supplied, in precise and concise language.

**Grun, Bernard.** *The Timetables of History: A Horizontal Linkage of People and Events.* **Simon and Schuster, 1975. ISBN: 0-317-63435-6.** Politics, literature, religion, philosophy, the arts, science, technology, and daily life from 5000 B.C. to A.D. 1974: how the events are related in time.

**Haglund, Elaine and Marcia L. Harris.** *On This Day.* **Libraries Unlimited, 1983. ISBN: 0-87287-345-5.** Chronological list of personalities, places, and events. There are reproducible activities and task cards for teachers to use.

**Hellemans, Alexander and Bryan Bunch.** *The Timetables of Science: A Chronology of the Most Important People and Events in the History of Science.* **Simon and Schuster, 1988. ISBN: 0-671-62130-0.** "Science before there was science" through 1988. Quick access to key events.

**Jarrett, William.** *Timetables of Sports History: Basketball.* **Facts On File, 1990. ISBN: 0-8160-1920-7.** Covers the period 1891–1989. Three-column format includes college season; professional basketball; and post-season tournaments, play-offs and the Olympic games. Chronological arrangement; a few black and white photographs. (There are Timetables of Baseball, Football, and Olympic Games in this series also.)

**Mann, William S.** *James Galway's Music in Time.* **Benzley Publishers, 1982. ISBN: 0-8109-1342-9.** Chronological development from "the beginnings" (music of nature and the first instruments) to "today and tomorrow." The concentration is on classical music. Attractive time line at the end. Thorough subject index. Color illustrations, portraits, anecdotes. Developed with the television series hosted by Galway.

*The Timetable of Technology.* **Hearst Books, 1982. ISBN: 0-87851-209-8.** Chronological listings of significant developments and discoveries in medicine, communication, transportation, and other areas of technology from 1900 through 1981. The headlines across the tops of pages are an interesting feature.

# List 2–6.  When Did It Happen?: Reproducible List

*American Book of Days.* Third edition. Compiled by Jane M. Hatch. H. W. Wilson, 1978.

Asimov, Isaac. *Asimov's Chronology of Science and Discovery.* HarperCollins, 1989.

*Calendar of Literary Facts.* Edited by Samuel J. Rogal. Gale, 1991.

*Facts On File.* Serial. Facts On File. Weekly World News Digest.

*The Facts On File News Digest CD-ROM 1980–1990.* Facts On File.

Grun, Bernard. *The Timetables of History: A Horizontal Linkage of People and Events.* Simon and Schuster, 1975.

Haglund, Elaine and Marcia L. Harris. *On This Day.* Libraries Unlimited, 1983.

Hellemans, Alexander and Bryan Bunch. *The Timetables of Science.* Simon and Schuster, 1988.

Jarrett, William. *Timetables of Sports History: Basketball.* Facts On File, 1990.

Mann, William S. *James Galway's Music In Time.* Benzley, 1982.

*The Timetable of Technology.* Hearst Books, 1982.

# section 3

# I WISH I'D SAID THAT!

How often we hear a word, a phrase, or a sentence that is so completely appropriate for the occasion that we earnestly wish we had been the originator. We know from our own experience that "A quotation, a chance word heard in an unexpected quarter, puts me on the trail of the book destined to achieve some intellectual advancement in me" (George Moore, *Confessions of a Young Man*). Emerson said (*Quotation and Originality*), "Next to the originator of a good sentence is the first quoter of it," and "By necessity, by proclivity, and by delight, we all quote." Therefore, the following list of quotations related to our work is offered for your use. Remember that "All words are pegs to hang ideas on" (Henry Ward Beecher, *Proverbs from Plymouth Pulpit: The Human Mind*).

## List 3–1.  Automation

"If it (automation) keeps up, man will atrophy all his limbs but the push-button finger."

FRANK LLOYD WRIGHT, *The New York Times* (11/27/55)

"The greatest task before civilization at present is to make machines what they ought to be, the slaves, instead of the masters of men."

HAVELOCK ELLIS, *The Task of Social Hygiene*

"Libraries that scorn information that is not in book form will play a declining role in the future."

EDWARD CORNISH, *The Futurist* (12/85)

"Information flies through the air with the 20th-century technologies . . . But ideas still travel best with a 15th-century technology—the printed page."

THOMAS SOBOL, *The Bookmark* (Winter 1991)

## List 3–2.  Books

"Man builds no structure which outlives a book."

EUGENE FITCH WARE, *The Book*

"He fed his spirit with the bread of books/And slaked his thirst at the wells of thought."

EDWIN MARKHAM, *Young Lincoln*

"No book is so bad but some profit may be gleaned from it."

PLINY THE YOUNGER, *Epistles*

"Books are the most mannerly of companions."

AMOS BRONSON ALCOTT, *Concord Days*

"The proper study of mankind is books."

ALDOUS HUXLEY, *Chrome Yellow*

"All books are either dreams or swords/You can cut, or you can drug, with words."

AMY LOWELL, *Sword Blades and Poppy Seed*

"You cannot open a book without learning something."

WILLIAM SCARBOROUGH, *Chinese Proverbs*

"The Love of Books, the Golden Key/That opens the Enchanted Door."

ANDREW LANG, *Ballade of the Bookworm*

"A fig for big books! We like only the little format which slips in to the pocket."

JULES JANIN, *Le Livre*

"The book and heart shall never part."

UNKNOWN, *The New England Primer*

"The good book is always a book of travel; it is about a life's journey."

H. M. TOMLINSON, *Out of Soundings*

"Books are ships which pass through the vast seas of time."

FRANCIS BACON, *Advancement of Learning*

"That is a good book which is opened with expectation and closed with profit."

JOSEPH ADDISON, *The Spectator*

"A room without books is a body without a soul."

CICERO, *Pleasures of Life*

"'Gracious heavens!' he cries out, leaping up and catching hold of his hair, 'What's this? Print!'"

CHARLES DICKENS, *Somebody's Luggage*

"A book that is shut is but a block."

THOMAS FULLER, *Gnomologia*

"It is with books as with men: a very small number play a great part, the rest are lost in the multitude."

VOLTAIRE, *Philosophical Dictionary: Books*

"The virtue of books is to be readable."

RALPH WALDO EMERSON, *Society and Solitude: Eloquence*

## List 3–3.   Censorship

"An act of vandalism, a fire now and then, is a tragedy, but we aren't going to lose much ground to cavemen. It's the censors we have to watch out for, and they are creeping back into the circle of our campfires."

JACK SMITH, *Los Angeles Times,* (4/21/82)

"There is no such thing as a moral or an immoral book. Books are well written, or badly written. That is all."

OSCAR WILDE, *The Picture of Dorian Gray*

"Only the suppressed word is dangerous."

LUDWIG BOERNE, *Ankündigung [der Waage]*

"Restriction of free thought and free speech is the most dangerous of all subversions. It is the one un-American act that could most easily defeat us."

WILLIAM O. DOUGLAS, address to the Authors' Guild, December 1952

"It is most unworthy to suppress books or silence teachers."

JUDAH LOEW, *Beer HaGola*

"Libraries seldom admit that they practice censorship. When hard-pressed, they call it 'a proper choice of books with a limited book fund.'"

EVELYN GELLER, *Forbidden Books in American Public Libraries, 1876–1939*

"The spirit of truth and the spirit of freedom—they are the pillars of society."

HENRIK IBSEN, *Pillars of Society*

"Of all the Tyrannies of human kind/The worst is that which Persecutes the mind."

JOHN DRYDEN, *The Indian Emperor*

"Books won't stay banned. They won't burn. Ideas won't go to jail. In the long run of history, the censor and the inquisitor have always lost."

A. WHITNEY GRISWOLD, *Essay on Education*

"Freedom is an indivisible word."

WENDELL LEWIS WILKIE, *One World*

"And so it criticized each flower/This supercilious seed;
Until it woke one summer hour/And found itself a weed."

MILDRED HOWELLS, *The Difficult Seed*

"Subject opinion to coercion: whom will you make your inquisitors?"

THOMAS JEFFERSON, *Notes on the State of Virginia, Query 17*

"Censorship, like charity, should begin at home; but, unlike charity, it should end there."

CLARE BOOTHE LUCE, *Nuggets*

"The problem of freedom in America is that of maintaining a competition of ideas, and you do not achieve that by silencing one brand of idea."

MAX LERNER, *Actions and Passions*

## List 3–4.   Education

"Our nation should use the institutions it has. It should insist that our libraries—academic and public, school library media centers and special— become full partners in a dynamic Learning Society."

*Alliance for Excellence*
(The Librarians' Response to *A Nation at Risk,*
Department of Education, 1984)

"You cannot put the same shoe on every foot."

PUBLIUS SYRUS, *Moral Sayings*

"Children should be led into the right paths, not by severity, but by persuasion."

TERENCE, *The Brothers*

"'Tis education forms the common mind/Just as the twig is bent the tree's inclined."

ALEXANDER POPE, *Moral Essays*

"The test and use of man's education is that he finds pleasure in the exercise of his mind."

JACQUES BARZUN, *Science vs. the Humanities: A Truce to the Nonsense on Both Sides*

"What sculpture is to a block of marble, education is to the soul."

JOSEPH ADDISON, *The Spectator*

"Better build schoolrooms for 'the boy,'/Than cells and gibbets for 'the man.'"

ELIZA COOK, *A Song for the Ragged Schools*

"All things I thought I knew; but now confess/The more I know I know, I know the less."

ROBERT OWEN, *Works*

"To know one's ignorance is the best part of knowledge."

LAO-TZY, *The Simple Way*

"You know, Percy, everybody is ignorant, only on different subjects."

WILL ROGERS, *The Illiterate Digest*

"Knowledge is power."

THOMAS HOBBES, *Leviathan*

"The fruits of the tree of knowledge are various."

MARY COLERIDGE, *Gathered Leaves*

"An investment in knowledge pays the best interest."

BENJAMIN FRANKLIN, *Poor Richard's Almanack*

"Nations have recently been led to borrow billions for war; no nation has ever borrowed largely for education."

ABRAHAM FLEXNER, *Universities*

"Public instruction should be the first object of government."

NAPOLEON BONAPARTE, *Sayings of Napoleon*

"They know enough who know how to learn."

HENRY ADAMS, *The Education of Henry Adams*

"The foundation of every state is the education of its youth."

DIOGENES. STOBEAEUS, *Florilegium*

"The roots of education are bitter, but the fruit is sweet."

ARISTOTLE. DIOGENES LAERTIUS, *Aristotle*

"Man is but a reed, the most feeble thing in nature; but he is a thinking reed."

BLAISE PASCAL, *Pensées*

## List 3–5.  Libraries

"My library was dukedom large enough."

WILLIAM SHAKESPEARE, *The Tempest*

"Libraries remain the meccas of self-help, the most open of open universities . . . where there are no entrance examinations and no diplomas, and where one can enter at any age."

DANIEL BOORSTEIN (Quoted in *Alliance for Excellence*)

"Libraries enable the past to talk to the future."

EDWARD CORNISH, *The Futurist* (12/85)

"Every library should try to complete on something, if it were only the history of pinheads."

OLIVER WENDELL HOLMES, *The Poet at the Breakfast Table*

"A library is thought in cold storage."

HERBERT SAMUEL, *A Book of Quotations*

"These are not books, lumps of lifeless paper, but *minds* alive on the shelves."

AUGUSTINE BIRRELL, *Obiter Dicta: Book-Buying*

"A library is not a shrine for the worship of books . . . A library, to modify the famous metaphor of Socrates, should be the delivery room for the birth of ideas—a place where history comes to life."

NORMAN COUSINS, *Saturday Review,* July 1, 1950

"[Libraries] are the home and refuge of our heritage. All that is good in our history is gathered in libraries."

WILL DURANT, Interview in *Modern Maturity,* August/September: 1982

"He that revels in a well-chosen library has innumerable dishes, and all of admirable flavour."

WILLIAM GODWIN, *The Enquirer: Early Taste for Reading*

"Libraries are an essential and 'civilizing element' of our democratic heritage, a birthright we must pass on enhanced and made more vibrant to the next generation and the next and all the generations ahead of us."

MARIO CUOMO, *The Bookmark* (Winter 1991)

## List 3–6. Teaching

"A teacher affects eternity; he can never tell where his influence stops."

HENRY ADAMS, *The Education of Henry Adams*

"The educator must above all understand how to wait; to reckon all effects in the light of the future, not of the present."

ELLEN KAY, *The Century of the Child*

"To teach is to learn twice over."

JOSEPH JOUBERT, *Pensées*

"Learning is like paddling a canoe against the current. It recedes if it does not advance."

CHINESE PROVERB, LIN YUTANG, *The Importance of Understanding*

"One laugh of a child will make the holiest day more sacred still."

ROBERT G. INGERSOLL, *The Liberty of Man, Woman and Child*

"Learning in old age is like writing on sand; learning in youth is like engraving on stone."

IBN GABITOL, *Choice of Pearls*

"I am glad to learn, in order that I may teach."

SENECA, *Letters to Lucilius*

"That is what learning is. You suddenly understand something you've understood all your life, but in a new way."

DORIS LESSING, *The Four-Gated City*

"Learning is discovering that something is possible."

FRITZ PERLS, *Omni* (11/79)

"Teaching is, in one of its aspects, a performing art."

JOSEPH EPSTEIN, *Quest* (9/81)

## List 3–7.   Youth

"For youthful faults ripe virtues shall atone."

WILLIAM WORDSWORTH, *Artegal and Elidure*

"A wild colt may become a sober horse."

THOMAS FULLER, *Gnomologia*

"The young are permanently in a state resembling intoxication; for youth is sweet and they are growing."

ARISTOTLE, *Nicomachean Ethics*

"Don't laugh at a youth for his affectations; he is only trying on one face after another to find a face of his own."

LOGAN PEARSALL SMITH, *Afterthoughts*

"Our youth we can have but to-day, we may always find time to grow old."

GEORGE BERKELEY, *Can Love Be Controlled by Advice?*

"Very young people are true but not resounding instruments."

ELIZABETH BOWEN, *The Death of the Heart*

"If youth is a fault, one soon gets rid of it."

JOHANN WOLFGANG VON GOETHE, *Proverbs in Prose*

"All children under nine or ten years of age are poets and philosophers."

ERNEST DIMNER, *The Art of Thinking*

"Those who love the young best stay young longest."

EDGAR Z. FRIEDENBERG, *The Vanishing Adolescent*

## section 4

# TRIVIA (NON-ESSENTIAL INFORMATION)

### List 4–1.  A Bit of Trivia

- The *Bay Psalm Book* was the first book printed in the American colonies, in 1640.
- The first library in North America was established at Harvard in 1638 with 380 books.
- The Library of Congress was established in 1800, and was burned by the British in 1814.
- Thomas Jefferson sold his personal library of 6,487 books to the Library of Congress for $23,950.
- Today, 6,487 books would cost about $80,000.
- The first public library in America was established in Peterboro, New Hampshire in 1833.
- Saint Jerome is the patron saint of librarians.
- The library scenes in the film *Goodbye Columbus* were shot in the Carnegie Library, Yonkers, New York; for the film *Ghostbusters,* in the New York Public Library; for *Ironwood,* in the Troy, New York Public Library.
- Queen Victoria donated books to the city of Chicago after the great fire of 1871.
- The American Library Association was founded in 1876.
- The first library school was established in 1887 at Columbia University.
- Andrew Carnegie began library philanthropy in 1901. In his lifetime he gave more than $43 million to establish libraries. Altogether his philanthropy built 1,679 libraries in 1,412 communities including 830 libraries overseas.
- The first children's reading room in the United States was established in Brookline, Massachusetts in 1890.
- In the nineteenth century it was common to prohibit children from public libraries.

- The first "library wagon" was put in use in 1905, in Washington County, Maryland. It was driven by a janitor, Joshua Thomas.

- In 1910, that "library wagon" was hit by a freight train. The driver and horses survived.

- In 1912, in Washington County, Maryland the first automobile book wagon made its rounds.

- It was 1849 when New Hampshire, leading the way, made it possible for local governments to tax for public libraries.

- The lions in front of the New York Public Library were nicknamed "fortitude" and "patience" by Mayor Fiorella LaGuardia in 1930—a tribute to the virtues of New Yorkers.

- Before those nicknames were applied, the lions were called Leo Astor and Leo Lenox, after the founders of the library, John Astor and James Lenox.

- By 1918, 42.6 percent of employed librarians still earned less than $900 per year.

- In its early days of publication, the *Library Journal* ran a "marriage column."

- In 1910, Gratia Countryman of the Minneapolis Public Library opened a reading room for the unemployed.

- Library projects of the WPA employed 27,000 people and used $18 million dollars of federal funds.

- ALA's Library War Service program in World War I set up thirty-six camp libraries and distributed ten million books and magazines.

- Membership in ALA during that war period grew to about three thousand.

- The ALA Council adopted the Library Bill of Rights in 1939, and the Freedom to Read in 1953.

- A contingent of librarians marched in Washington, D.C. in 1969 to protest the Vietnam War.

- Computerization replaced nine thousand card drawers at the New York Public Library.

- *The Lilliputian Magazine*, edited by John Newbery, book publisher, was the first children's magazine. It measured four inches by two-and-one-half inches, and was published in 1751.

- In 1990, the average American child watched thirty to forty thousand television commercials.

- One thousand basic words make up 90 percent of all writing.

- Walt Disney won twenty Oscars.

- During 1989, *Modern Maturity* magazine had a circulation more than nineteen times greater than *Seventeen* or *Boy's Life*.

- In 1989, 11,556 consumer and trade magazines were published.

- Five million of the twenty million books in the Library of Congress are crumbling due to the acid content of the paper.
- More than 50 percent of all U. S. capital investment is now in information technology.
- Of the 50,000 new books that appear each year in our country about twenty percent turn a profit.
- In 1949, approximately 3.4 percent of the nation's GNP was spent on education. By 1988, that figure had risen to 6.9 percent.
- In 1975, 90 million juvenile books were sold in the U.S. By 1988, that figure had increased to 264 million.
- In 1988, there were 59,311 public elementary and 20,758 secondary schools in the U.S. Add to those the number of combined elementary and secondary, and the alternative and special public schools, and the number is 83,248.
- Enrollment in those schools in the fall of 1990 was twenty-nine million elementary and eleven million secondary.
- The state spending the most per pupil in 1989–1990 spent $7571, and the state spending the least spent $2571.
- The Census Bureau reported in 1987 that 76 percent of U.S. adults had completed four years of high school.
- A survey conducted by the Census Bureau in 1982 and based on a literacy test given to 3400 adults indicated that thirteen percent of American adults are illiterate.
- A 1985 national survey of library media centers in public schools found the mean figure for number of books held was 7,386. Minnesota ranked highest, with an average of 12,048 books.
- Montana public school libraries had the most volumes per pupil: thirty-five. The mean was eighteen.
- Only 6 percent of elementary school libraries responding to a recent study hold six or more nonfiction items on the subject of AIDS.
- Recent research shows that a random sample of media specialists, conducting exemplary media programs in public schools, ranked considerably higher than the general public in abstract thinking and creativity.
- America leads the world in the percentage of high school students going on to college, 50 percent.
- Forty-one percent of the world's population live in urban areas. By 2020, this is expected to increase to 60 percent.
- There are now eleven cities in the world with populations over ten million. In 1950, there were only three cities with that many people.
- There were at least 244 reported attempts to censor books, programs, and other materials in public schools in the 1989–90 academic year.

- The national average per pupil expenditure for students in public elementary and secondary schools was $4,200 for the school year 1987–88.

- *The Guinness Book of Records* (excluding versions of the *Bible*) is the world's best selling book, having surpassed 65 million copies in 39 languages in 1990.

- W. & G. Foyle, Ltd. of London is the largest book store in the world, with 30 miles of shelving.

- Sweden has the greatest number of newspaper readers; 580 newspapers are sold for every 1,000 persons.

- *The New York Times* has won the greatest number of Pulitzer Prizes, sixty-three.

- In 1984, a survey of teachers showed 40 percent to be very satisfied with their profession. By 1988, that figure had risen to 50 percent.

- American students spend an average of 178 days a year in school. Among western nations, only Belgium has fewer days in its school year.

## List 4–2.   Trivia Sources

Christensen, Paul M. "Characteristics of Library Media Specialists Who Have Exemplary High School Media Programs." *School Library Media Quarterly,* Summer 1991.

Dickson, Paul. *The Library in America.* Facts On File, 1986.

*Education.* 1990 Edition. Information Plus, 1990.

Fraser, Greg. "The Big Deal," *Columbia,* Summer 1991.

*The Guinness Book of Records 1992.* Edited by Donald McFarlan. Facts On File, 1991.

Kennedy, William. "On Being Atavistic, Computerate, and a Literary Beach Bum: An Argument on Behalf of the Past." *The Bookmark,* Winter 1991.

Kernan, Alvin B. "The Death of Literature," *Princeton Alumni Weekly,* January 22, 1992.

*The New Book of American Rankings.* Edited by Clark S. Judge. Facts On File, Inc., 1984.

Shanker, Albert. "Where We Stand." *New York Times,* November 3, 1991.

*Thrust for Education Leadership.* Association of California School Administrators. November/ December, 1990.

*The Universal Almanac.* Edited by John W. Wright. Universal Press, 1991.

VanMeter, Vandelia L. "Sensitive Materials in U. S. Public Schools." *School Library Media Quarterly,* Summer 1991.

White, Howard D. "School Library Collections and Services: Ranking the States." *School Library Media Quarterly,* Fall 1990.

## List 4–3. Trivia Books

Bartel, Pauline. *The Complete Gone With the Wind Trivia Book.* Taylor Publishing, 1989. ISBN: 0-87833-619-2. You need not be a "Windie" to enjoy this fascinating and witty collection of trivia about the movie, the book, the movie industry, the stars, and more.

Ciardi, John. *A Browser's Dictionary: A Compendium of Curious Expressions and Intriguing Facts.* HarperCollins, 1979. ISBN: 0-06-0910766-9.

Gilbar, Steven. *The Book Book.* St. Martin's Press, 1981. ISBN: 0-312-08803-5. A compendium of lists, quizzes, and trivia about books.

Hendrickson, Robert. *American Literary Anecdotes* (ISBN: 0-8160-1599-6); *British Literary Anecdotes* (ISBN: 0-8160-2247-X); *World Literary Anecdotes* (ISBN: 0-8160-2248-8). Facts On File, 1990.

Panati, Charles. *Panati's Parade of Fads, Follies, and Manias;* the Origins of Our Most Cherished Obsessions. HarperPerennial, 1991. ISBN: 0-06-055191-7. Pop culture in America, from songs and media to all kinds of curiosities.

*The Whole Library Handbook. Current Data, Professional Advice, and Curiosa About Libraries and Library Services.* Compiled by George M. Eberhart. ALA, 1991. ISBN: 0-8389-0573-0.

## List 4–4. More Trivia

**From *Science News Books:***

Davis, Kenneth C. *Don't Know Much About History: Everything You Need to Know About American History But Never Learned.* 1990.

Feldman, David. *Do Penguins Have Knees?* 1991.

Feldman, David. *Why Do Dogs Have Wet Noses?* 1990.

Poundstone, William. *Big Secrets: The Book That Gives the Inside Story on Hundreds of Secrets of American Life.* 1983.

Poundstone, William. *Bigger Secrets: More Than 125 Things They Prayed You'd Never Find Out.* 1986.

Randall, Bernice. *When Is a Pig a Hog?* 1991.

# TOOLS OF THE TRADE

# SELECTION

Decisions regarding acquisitions are of primary importance. Your collection must be selective and meet the needs of your school. Since you cannot buy everything on the market you must make choices. This is an awesome responsibility. Therefore, you base selection upon predetermined criteria. You establish selection policies which you implement by means of appropriate "selection procedures."

In composing your selection policy and procedures statement you will want to confer with:

- The principal of your school
- The other school librarians in the district
- The department supervisors
- The district curriculum supervisor

Since your school board must defend and support acquisition policies, you may wish to have that agency represented, even before you present a suggested policy statement to them for approval.

Refer to the list of professional readings in this book for guidance in developing your selection policy. There are many model statements of policy and procedures to be found which can be adapted to your particular situation. If you doubt the efficacy of adopting a materials selection policy statement in your district, read "Factors Influencing the Outcome of Library Media Center Challenges at the Secondary Level," by Dianne McAfee Hopkins. This article was printed in the Summer 1990 issue of *School Library Media Quarterly* and is the report of the findings of an exploratory intellectual freedom study conducted in 1988 in Wisconsin. That study indicates that a positive relationship does exist between retention of challenged materials and the existence *and use* of a materials selection policy.

This brief list of titles will be informative and helpful if you embark upon the process of preparing a written materials selection policy.

## List 5–1A.  Selection Policy References

*Guide for Written Collection Policy Statements:* Collection Management and Development Guides, #3. Resources and Technical Services Division. ALA, 1989. ISBN: 0-8389-3371-8.

*Information, Freedom, and Censorship:* World Report 1991. Frances D'Souza, Director, Article 19, The International Centre on Censorship. ALA, 1991. ISBN: 0-8389-2156-6.

*Intellectual Freedom Manual,* Third edition. ALA Office for Intellectual Freedom and Intellectual Freedom Committee. ALA, 1989. ISBN: 0-8389-3368-8.

Reichman, Henry F. *Censorship and Selection: Issues and Answers for Schools.* ALA and the American Association of School Administrators, 1988. ISBN: 0-8389-3350-5.

*School Library and Media Center Acquisitions Policies and Procedures,* Second edition. Oryx, 1986. ISBN: 0-89774-160-9.

Streiff, Jane E. *Secondary School Librarian's Almanac.* Center for Applied Research in Education, 1989. ISBN: 0-87628-783-6.

There were at least 244 reported attempts to censor books, programs, and other materials in our public schools in the 1988–90 school year according to an article in *Thrust for Education Leadership,* November–December 1990. We may believe that it will never happen to us, and yet we are on the front line of any controversy over the materials that are available to students in schools. The best defense is preparation for a challenge. With multiculturalism now a topic of fierce debate among schools officials and the parents of our students, with economic conditions preventing a growing number of citizens from achieving the "American dream," and with increasing dissatisfaction at all levels of society with the academic achievement in our schools, we can expect a more critical view to be taken of our school library collections. Not only must we have a selection policy in place, but we must adhere to it, review it frequently, and publicize the fact that we have one.

Basically, your policy should set forth:

- The legal responsibility for the selection and approval of print and non-print materials
- The objectives of selection
- The criteria for selection of materials
- The methods used in selection procedures
- The procedures that will be used to meet challenges to materials purchased for student use

## List 5–1B.   Selection Tools

Besides reviewing materials at conferences and other professional meetings, studying the promotional literature from publishers, and haunting book stores, one should consult these valuable selection tools.

### *Periodicals*

***Book Links: Connecting Books, Libraries, and Classrooms.* ALA *Booklist.* Six issues annually. ISSN: 1055-4742.** Preschool through grade eight. This publication, a new venture by YASD in 1990, "reemphasizes" ALA's concern for literacy and the use of trade books in the classroom. "Bibliographies, thematic subject groupings, retrospective reviews, background information about authors and illustrators, and essays about using books with children." (*Journal of Youth Services in Libraries,* Fall 1990)

***Book Review Digest.* Ten issues per year. H. W. Wilson. ISSN: 0006-7326.** Covers English-language fiction and nonfiction titles that have been featured in one hundred U. S. and Canadian periodicals. Includes juvenile titles with recommendations for appropriate age groups. This resource is an excellent source for excerpts of reviews. I urge students to use it for access information on the full reviews. The full bibliographic information on each title makes this a great selection tool. Abridged Dewey Decimal numbers are here, thus making this a useful tool for cataloging, also. BRD is now available in CD-ROM format as well as online and on tape.

***Booklist and Reference Books Bulletin.* Serial: twice monthly, September–June; monthly July–August. American Library Association. ISSN: 0006-7385.** *Booklist* is your guide to print *and* nonprint materials. Its reviews are prepared for small and medium-sized libraries and school libraries. Each issue features professional news and comments, special lists of recommended purchases, and a section devoted to reference books. Bibliographic information includes Dewey Decimal classification and Library of Congress subject headings. The inclusion of a title in *Booklist* constitutes a recommendation for purchase. Outstanding titles are noted. In addition to the indexes in the monthly issues, semi-annual indexes are printed in the February 15 and the August issues. *Booklist* evaluators offer "Software's Greatest Hits" for the previous year in a January issue.

***Bulletin of the Center for Children's Books.* Eleven issues per year. University of Chicago Press, Journals Division. ISSN: 0008-9036.** The comprehensive reviews in the *Bulletin* include notations about grade level audience. Awards are listed here.

***English Journal.* Monthly, September–April. National Council of Teachers of English. ISSN: 0013-8274.** Professional articles and reviews, language study across the disciplines, research, lesson plans, and many book lists of value to the media specialist.

***The Horn Book Magazine.* Six issues per year. Horn Book, Inc. ISSN: 0018-5078.** Of special interest to children's librarians, *Horn Book* reviews outstanding books in the field. Articles about children's books are contributed by the authors, illustrators, and critics of children's literature. News of conferences, awards, tours, special events, and new products are all included in this handsome resource.

*InCider.* **The Apple II magazine. Monthly. IDG Communications. ISSN: 1054-6456.** Selects one program, an "editor's choice," which is a new product, each month. The old Apple IIe, which we now keep in our offices, is a workhorse. The Appleworks program is in use daily for preparing want lists and recording statistics on spread sheets.

*Kirkus Reviews.* **Twenty-four issues per year. Kirkus Service, Inc. ISSN: 0042-6598.** The reviews in *Kirkus* can be relied upon. They are forthright and thorough. Most useful for elementary librarians in the selection process.

*Library Hi Tech.* **Quarterly. Pierian Press. ISSN: 0737-8831.** The technology that is out there may overwhelm you, but this journal will direct you to the newest products. There are professional articles and reviews and notices of vendors' workshops and training sessions.

*Library Journal.* **Twenty-one issues per year. R. R. Bowker. ISSN: 0363-0277.** This journal features professional news and reviews of videos, magazines, audio products, and books. Includes a buyers guide. A regular feature is automation news.

*MacUser.* **Monthly. Ziff-Davis Publishing Co. ISSN: 0884-0997.** The evaluations in this magazine are used by the authors of *The Annual Guide to Highest Rated Educational Software: Only the Best,* which we have listed below.

*The Reading Teacher.* **Monthly, September–May. International Reading Association. ISSN: 0034-0561.** This is a wonderful journal, so sensible. Not only are the articles important to those of us seeking professional growth, but they are also extremely practical. Teaching strategies, lesson ideas, the latest research, and excellent reviews of professional and juvenile titles.

*School Library Journal.* **Monthly. R. R. Bowker. ISSN: 0362-8930.** *School Library Journal* is the "magazine of children's, young adult, and school libraries." Each monthly issue features three or four articles of interest to librarians in the targeted audience. The magazine carries regular columns on professional news of current interest about people, events, and research. The thoughtful, reliable reviews cover professional literature, and audiovisual materials, and software, as well as recommended books for young adults and children. The reviews are arranged by topic and indexed by author-title. Titles are rated for grade level, and full ordering information is provided.

### Books and Electronic Sources

*Books In Print.* **R. R. Bowker. Annual.** *American Reference Books Annual* calls this tool, combined with *Subject Guide to Books in Print* "indispensable" for acquisitions. Now the print versions of this resource, which keep you abreast of complete and current bibliographic information for ordering titles, are available in the *Plus* format (CD ROM products). If you have CD-ROM capability, these products allow fast searches, printing and displaying the information, and even electronic ordering.

**Cianciolo, Patricia J.** *Picture Books for Children.* **Third Edition. ALA, 1990. ISBN: 0-8389-0527-7.** *Booklist* (12/15/90): For teachers in nursery school through junior high. Discusses both text and artwork.

*Computer-Readable Databases.* **(Annual). Gale Research. ISBN: 0-8103-2945-X.** Six thousand databases and subfiles; available through DIALOG on magnetic tape or diskette.

**Dreyer, Sharon Spredemann.** *The Bookfinder, Volume 4: Annotations of Books Published 1983–1986.* **American Guidance Service, Inc., 1989. ISBN: 0-913476-50-1.** The added title to this resource is *A Guide to Children's Literature About the Needs and Problems of Youth Aged 2 and Up.* Each review runs 800–1,000 words. It indicates the target age group and the subject matter which is expressed in some 450 different psychological, behavioral, and developmental categories. First there is a synopsis of the story, with characters and plot. Then a commentary states the main message. Reading level is indicated as well as other forms of the publication (audio, film, etc.).

**Eaglen, Audrey.** *Buying Books: A How-to-Do-It Manual for Librarians.* **(A How-to-Do-It Manual for Libraries series title. Series editor: Bill Katz). Neal-Schuman Publishers, Inc., 1989. ISBN: 1-55570-013-6.** This series is designed to help librarians keep up with the ever-changing aspects and responsibilities of their profession. This book gives the reader an overview of the publishing industry and practical advice about purchasing books efficiently and effectively. The list of selected book wholesalers is helpful, as are the bibliography and the glossary. The publishing business changes daily, and the section on "merger mania" is most interesting, particularly as this trend affects librarians.

**Gallant, Jennifer Jung.** *Best Videos for Children and Young Adults: A Core Collection for Libraries.* **ABC-CLIO, 1990. ISBN: 0-87436-561-9.** This book indexes by audience/usage and subject/title. Its thoughtful annotations are quite helpful.

**Gillespie, John T. and Corinne J. Naden.** *Best Books For Children Preschool Through Grade 6.* **Fourth edition. R. R. Bowker; 1990. ISBN: 0-8352-2668-9.** List of quality books for recreational reading, and a bibliography of curriculum-related books for preschool through middle grades (*Booklist* 12/15/90).

*Guide to Popular U.S. Government Publications.* **Second edition. Libraries Unlimited, 1990. ISBN: 0-87287-796-5.** *Booklist* (11/1/90) calls this an excellent acquisition guide. Not only does it provide access to a wide variety of economically priced titles, but it also lists other publications catalogs from the government. These publications will be useful especially at the secondary level for building vertical files. There are title and subject indexes and brief annotations.

**Hansen, Paula and Gail Nelson.** *Books for the Gifted Child.* **R. R. Bowker, 1988. ISBN: 0-8352-2467-8.** K–5. Six categories here: picture books, fiction, nonfiction, poetry, folklore, biography. Each category is discussed thoroughly and is followed by guides for acquisition.

*High/Low Handbook: Encouraging Literacy in the 1900's.* **Third edition. Compiled by Ellen V. LiBretto. R. R. Bowker, 1990. ISBN: 0-8352-2804-5.** Called "an invaluable resource" in *School Library Journal.* Your source for materials of high interest that will intrigue the reluctant reader. All ages.

*Junior High School Library Catalog.* **Sixth edition. H. W. Wilson, 1990. ISBN: 0-8242-0799-8.** Four supplements, 3,300 titles. For grades 7–9. Valuable for collection planning.

**Katz, Bill and Linda Sternberg Katz.** *Magazines for Libraries.* **Sixth edition. R. R. Bowker, 1989. ISBN: 0-8352-2632-8.** *Wilson Library Bulletin* highly recommends this tool which profiles over 6,500 outstanding periodicals. The index, which is arranged by subject, is thorough and useful.

**Kennedy, DayAnn M., Stella S. Spangler, and Mary Ann Vanderwerf.** *Science and Technology in Fact and Fiction.* **R. R. Bowker, 1990. ISBN: 0-8352-2710-3.** Four indexes to the reviewed books offer comprehensive access by readability, author, title, and subject. From Bowker's tremendous database of titles.

**Lynn, Ruth Nadelman.** *Fantasy Literature for Children and Young Adults: An Annotated Bibliography.* **Third edition. R. R. Bowker, 1989. ISBN: 0-8352-2347-7.** For grades 3–6, ages 8–12. Titles are organized into ten categories of fantasy and five sub-categories. Entries have brief descriptions of the books, and reviews are cited. There are teaching resources and studies of the authors offered.

**Neill, Shirley Boes and George W. Neill.** *The Annual Guide to Highest Rated Educational Software: Only the Best.* **Education News Service, 1991. ISBN: 0-8352-2852-1.** This guide is produced annually, offering an authoritative resource for purchasing for preschool through grade 12. Evaluations are selected from groups in the United States and Canada. About 183 of the most highly rated programs are noted. The information offered is comprehensive and includes program, producer, area of curriculum, computers. Full descriptions of the programs are given, with hardware requirements, reviews, and evaluations. The titles are arranged by topic. Also worth a look: *Only the Best: The Cumulative Guide to Highest Rated Educational Software, 1985–1989, Pre-School–Grade 12.* The guides are compiled every three years.

*Senior High School Library Catalog.* **Thirteenth edition. H. W. Wilson, 1987. ISBN: 0-8242-0755-6.** Your guide in collection development, presenting the best for an ongoing selection plan.

**Spencer, Michael D. G.** *Free Publications from U. S. Government Agencies; A Guide.* **Libraries Unlimited, 1989. ISBN: 0-87287-622-5.** Provides access to entire publications programs. Divided into broad subject areas, for example, environment, education, crime. Agencies are explained.

**Truett, Carol.** *Microcomputer Software Sources: A Guide for Buyers, Librarians, Programmers, Businesspeople, and Educators.* **Libraries Unlimited, 1990.**

**ISBN: 0-87287-560-1.** This book covers software and its applications in education, business, libraries, and general use. It offers suggestions for obtaining free materials and guides. Each entry includes the ordering information you will need as well as an annotation.

***What Do I Read Next?* First edition. Edited by Neil Barron. Gale, 1990. ISBN: 0-8103-7555-9.** This is an annual guide to genre fiction which gives details on recent titles. Useful for selection and as a reader's advisor. From this source you can retrieve bibliographic information for ordering, and it can lead you to other titles by the same author, or to similar books by other authors.

***Young Adult Reader's Advisor.* General editor, Myra Immell. R. R. Bowker, 1991. ISBN: 0-8352-3068-6.** 2 volumes. Based on the curriculum of grades 6–12 and offers an overview of books that kids will *want* to read.

# List 5–1.  Selection: Reproducible List

*Book Links.* Serial. ALA/Booklist.

*Book Review Digest.* Serial. H. W. Wilson.

*Booklist and Reference Books Bulletin.* ALA.

*Books in Print.* Annual. R. R. Bowker.

*Bulletin of the Center for Children's Books.* Serial. University of Chicago Press.

Cianciolo, Patricia J. *Picture Books for Children.* ALA, 1990.

*Computer-Readable Databases.* Annual. Gale Research.

Dreyer, Sharon Spredemann. *The Bookfinder.* American Guidance Service, 1989.

Eaglen, Audrey. *Buying Books: A How-to-Do-It Manual for Librarians.* Neal-Schuman Publishers, Inc., 1989.

*English Journal.* Serial. NCTE.

Gallant, Jennifer Jung. *Best Videos for Children and Young Adults.* ABC-CLIO, 1990.

Gillespie, John T. and Corinne J. Naden. *Best Books for Children Preschool Through Grade 6.* R. R. Bowker, 1990.

*Guide for Written Collection Policy Statements.* ALA, 1989.

*Guide to Popular U.S. Government Publications.* Libraries Unlimited, 1990.

Hansen, Paula and Gail Nelson. *Books for the Gifted Child.* R. R. Bowker, 1988.

*High/Low Handbook: Encouraging Literacy in the 1990's.* R. R. Bowker, 1990.

*The Horn Book Magazine.* Serial. Horn Book, Inc.

*InCider.* The Apple Magazine. Serial. InCider, Inc.

*Information, Freedom, and Censorship.* ALA, 1991.

*Intellectual Freedom Manual.* ALA, 1989.

*Junior High School Library Catalog.* H. W. Wilson, 1990.

Katz, Bill and Linda Sternberg Katz. *Magazines for Libraries.* R. R. Bowker, 1989.

Kennedy, DayAnn M. *Science and Technology in Fact and Fiction.* R. R. Bowker, 1990.

*Kirkus Reviews.* Serial. Kirkus Services.

*Library Hi Tech.* Serial. Pierian Press.

*Library Journal.* Serial. R. R. Bowker.

Lynn, Ruth Nadelman. *Fantasy Literature for Children and Young Adults.* R. R. Bowker, 1989.

*MacUser.* Serial. Ziff-Davis Publishing Co.

Neill, Shirley and George W. Neill. *The Annual Guide to Highest Rated Educational Software.* Education News Service, 1991.

*The Reading Teacher.* Serial. International Reading Association.

Reichman, Henry F. *Censorship and Selection: Issues and Answers for Schools.* ALA and AASA, 1988.

*School Library and Media Center Acquisitions Policies and Procedures.* Oryx, 1986.

*School Library Journal.* Serial. R. R. Bowker.

Spencer, Michael D. G. *Free Publications from U. S. Government Agencies: A Guide.* Libraries Unlimited, 1989.

Truett, Carol. *Microcomputer Software Sources.* Libraries Unlimited, 1990.

*What Do I Read Next?* Edited by Neil Barron. Gale, 1990.

*Young Adult Reader's Advisor.* Edited by Myra Immell. R. R. Bowker, 1991.

# CATALOGING

Find a place to designate as your cataloging station. When new materials arrive, getting them out for circulation will be your primary objective. Whether they are "shelf ready" or not you will want to handle them and determine their appropriate accessible placement in your collection. If you are doing original cataloging, the first place to start is with the CIP information in the front of the book. Making decisions about classification, subject headings, and the records to be entered in the computer requires specific information.

The following is a list of useful cataloging tools:

## List 5–2.  Cataloging: Annotated List

*Abridged Dewey Decimal Classification.* **12th edition. Forest Press, 1990. ISBN: 0-910608-42-3.** Easier to use than previous editions and just right for small libraries, particularly in schools. There are substantial changes in the schedules which reflect new fields of endeavor.

*Anglo-American Cataloging Rules.* **Second edition, revised. American Library Association, 1988. ISBN: 0-8389-3346-7.** This new edition includes any changes authorized by the Joint Steering Committee for the Revision of AACR since 1978. Examples assist in interpreting the rules.

*The Booklist.* **American Library Association, 1905 to date. ISSN: 0006-7385.** Included with cataloging materials because many of the reviews in this publication carry the Dewey number. Noting this when preparing your orders facilitates original cataloging as materials arrive.

**Byrne, Deborah J.** *MARC Manual: Understanding and Using MARC Records.* **Libraries Unlimited, 1990. ISBN: 0-87287-813-9.** A useful tool for librarians automating their collections, in easy-to-understand language.

**Intner, Sheila S. and Jean Weihs.** *Standard Cataloging for School and Public Libraries.* **Libraries Unlimited, 1990. ISBN: 0-87287-737-X.** A technical manual for the media specialist who does original cataloging. The author guides one through the intricacies of cataloging from the first decisions to the last. The glossary and suggested readings are helpful. A good textbook for library science students, includes Canadian applications and examples of classification of AV materials.

***Junior High School Library Catalog.*** **Sixth edition. H. W. Wilson, 1990. ISBN: 0-8242-0799-8. Grades 7–9.** *VOYA* said, "Middle school and junior high school librarians should appreciate this essential, well-constructed tool." The format is the same as the *Senior High School Library Catalog.* From these two sources one can select a core collection for the library and find, too, the classification of materials. Purchase includes five-year supplement service.

***Library of Congress CD-MARC Bibliographic.*** **Library of Congress.** Six CD-ROM discs give you access to the Library of Congress MARC database. Records may be searched by LC or Dewey number, or through a variety of other access points. You can view the records or load them into other formats, and save them in print or on disks.

**Miller, Rosland E. and Jane Terwillegar.** ***Commonsense Cataloging.*** **H. W. Wilson, 1990. ISBN: 0-8242-0789-0.** General rules for cataloging both print and nonprint which reflect the impact of the new technologies.

***Sears List of Subject Headings.*** **Fourteenth edition. H. W. Wilson, 1991. ISBN: 0-8242-0803-X.** The best subject heading list for small libraries. This edition has been updated to reflect changing times and topics. The two thousand changes in Dewey numbers reflect the new *Abridged Dewey Decimal Classification* (twelfth edition). The introductory material offers advice about catalog revisions. There is now electronic access to *Sears* via H. W. Wilson's *Wilsonline.* Look for the *Sears List of Subject Headings: Canadian Companion,* third edition (ISBN: 0-8242-0754-8) which covers Canadian topics in depth.

***Senior High School Library Catalog.*** **Thirteenth edition. H. W. Wilson, 1987. ISBN: 0-8242-0755-6.** This edition of the standard source is in three parts: classified catalog, indexes to the catalog, directory of publishers and distributors. With this purchase you receive supplements for five years. Indispensable as a tool for cataloging, collection development, and purchasing. Subject headings are based on *Sears List of Subject Headings.*

# List 5–2.   Cataloging: Reproducible List

*Abridged Dewey Decimal Classification.* 12th edition. Forest Press, 1990.

*Anglo-American Cataloging Rules.* 2nd edition. ALA, 1988.

*The Booklist.* Serial. ALA.

Byrne, Deborah J. *MARC Manual: Understanding and Using MARC Records.* Libraries Unlimited, 1990.

Intner, Sheila S. and Jean Weihs. *Standard Cataloging for School and Public Libraries.* Libraries Unlimited, 1990.

*Junior High School Library Catalog.* 6th edition. H. W. Wilson, 1990.

*Library of Congress CD-MARC Bibliographic.* Library of Congress. (CD Software)

Miller, Rosland E. and Jane Terwillegar. *Commonsense Cataloging.* H. W. Wilson, 1990.

*Sears List of Subject Headings.* Fourteenth edition. H. W. Wilson, 1991.

*Senior High School Library Catalog.* Thirteenth edition. H. W. Wilson, 1987.

# AUTOMATION

The following list of professional reading will help you to acquire a good background on library automation. Be prepared with the right questions when you consider the new technologies in your media center.

## List 5–3.  Automation: Annotated List

*Apple Library Users Group Newsletter.* **ALUG, 10381 Bandley Drive, Cupertino, CA 95014.** "Published four times a year for people interested in using Apple computers in libraries or information centers." Strong emphasis on exchange of ideas.

**Aversa, Elizabeth and Jacqueline C. Mancall.** *Management of Online Search Services in Schools.* **ABC-CLIO, 1989. ISBN: 0-87436-513-9.** Highly recommended by *Online Searcher* (Spring 1989) for school library media specialists who already provide online services and for those who are planning them.

**Byrne, Deborah J.** *MARC Manual: Understanding and Using MARC Records.* **Libraries Unlimited, 1991. ISBN: 0-87287-813-9.** The applications of MARC in your professional cataloging; easier to comprehend than the documentation that arrives with your computers.

*Computers and the School Library.* **ABC-CLIO, 1990. ISBN: 0-87436-607-0.** A compilation of successful ideas first printed in *The Book Report.* Experienced users contributed the ideas for using computers in the school library. Budgets, the accessibility of appropriate hardware and software, and school policies are all considered.

**Dewey, Patrick R.** *Public Access Microcomputers: A Handbook for Librarians.* **Second edition. G. K. Hall, 1990. ISBN: 0-8161-1896-5.** A manual for starting an automated retrieval system. Also provides information on management of your service.

**Espinosa, Leonard J.** *Microcomputer Facilities in Schools.* **Libraries Unlimited, 1990. ISBN: 0-87287-639-X.** The practical illustrations in this resource will help you plan the placement of computers in your facility, taking into account factors such as traffic and supervision.

Holloway, Mary A. "Media Center Automation: The Way to Go." *School Library Journal,* **August 1988.** "A practical guide for planning, developing, and implementing a basic automated circulation system." Take note of this author's recommendations—they make sense.

Hooten, Patricia, ed. *Perspectives on School Library Automation.* **AASL, 1990. ISBN: 0-8389-7456-2.** Diverse viewpoints on the topic as presented at the AASL conference, "Automation and the Crystal Ball."

*Information Searcher,* **quarterly magazine. 14 Hadden Road, Scarsdale, NY 10583.**

Parisi, Lynn S. and Virginia L. Jones. *Directory of Online Databases and CD-ROM Resources for High Schools.* **ABC-CLIO, 1988. ISBN: 0-87436-515-5.** The relevant databases are described. This handbook may entice you into budgeting for more online services.

The list of recommended professional reading on the topic of automation of school libraries is short compared to the many materials that are available on this subject. There is a great deal of advice out there, and even with all of it you may find your path to automation of library services to be fraught with pitfalls.

*The Random House College Dictionary* defines automation as "the technique, method, or system of operating or controlling a mechanical or productive process by highly automatic means, as by electronic devices, reducing human intervention to a minimum." The last part of that definition is what we are all waiting for. As yet, in our third year of automated circulation and electronic catalog service, we have not seen the reduction of "human intervention to a minimum." Automation is a "hot topic." The aim of this book is to direct you to the best sources to guide you on your path to automation.

You *will* be automating your library services. There is no avoiding it if you want to remain in the business of information retrieval. *Webster's Collegiate Thesaurus* gives the following synonyms for *automatic:* impulsive, instinctive, involuntary, unmeditated, *unpremeditated* (italics mine). Nothing about automating a library system should be unpremeditated. The following tips, gleaned from our experience and research, will assist you on your path to computer-based library procedures:

1. *Before you start*
   A. Network with others as you start the process.
      — Start within your school by investigating programs that are already in place.
      — Plan with district colleagues for a cooperative endeavor.
      — Seek assistance from your local and state cooperative educational agencies.

— Visit exemplary systems in other schools. (Vendors and your state bureau of school libraries can put you in touch.)

— Attend appropriate conferences.

— Share your information and needs with your administration as you proceed.

**B.**  Select a modest objective—even the simplest one will become complicated. Possibilities are: "Need" determines software; not the reverse.

— Retrieval of information in reference activities (examples: periodical indexes on CD-ROM, DIALOG online services)

— Management of records (examples: circulation, electronic card catalog, computer software for printing catalog cards)

— Instructional programs (examples: access for students to word processing software, interactive laser discs)

**C.**  Analyze your situation. What are your resources?

— Funds?

— Expertise?

— Time?

— Staff?

**D.**  Define tasks: Who should do what?

**E.**  Select the software for the tasks first.

**F.**  Find the equipment to accommodate the software.

2. *Before you press "Enter"*

**A.**  Sell the supporting budget.

**B.**  Plan the installation.

**C.**  Provide for training.

3. *Design for the future*

**A.**  Consider additional applications and expanded services. Go slowly, determine need.

**B.**  Aim for *connectivity;* plan for a DOS-compatible network.

**C.**  Allow space. Machines take up space.

**D.**  Project staffing needs. Figure *more* as you increase services.

**E.**  Automation is time-intensive at first, so plan accordingly.

**F.**  Plan orientation of students and teachers.

4. *Avoid the pitfalls*

**A.**  Secure the information in your computer from pirates. Always store back-ups.

**B.**  Keep the documentation handy.

**C.**  Provide for repairs; know an expert in the school.

**D.** Buy locally from a reputable dealer.

**E.** Don't promise more than you can deliver.

**F.** Keep your manual system available.

**G.** Install surge protectors.

**H.** Accommodate requirements of your security system.

**I.** Include the appropriate furniture and electrical wiring.

## A Few Specifics

As you plan your future with automated, computerized information retrieval and management of data, try to determine what your real needs are.

1. Will the computer allow you to do something you cannot do now?

2. Will the automated process make a real difference in the amount of staff time devoted to direct service to students?

3. Can the cost be justified?

4. Do you have the support of the administration and the faculty?

## Automating Circulation and Catalog

With these procedures developed to the extent they are now, consider installing circulation and catalog programs simultaneously. There are three critical decisions to make before starting:

1. What software system do you prefer? Buy one that is expandable. Will it allow you to reserve materials? Will it generate bibliographies, overdues, student lists, inventory data?

2. What are the hardware requirements?

3. Who will enter the data?

As you prepare for this important installation:

1. Get your shelf list in shape. Add as much information as possible for the eventual uploading to the catalog. LC numbers and ISBNs are important.

2. Look at your collection with a critical eye. Weed out as much as possible. When data is collected, MARC records on old copyrights will be scarce. Consider purchasing a database of records (for example, *Bibliofile*) for use in the district.

3. Compare the cost of data entry by the software vendor you have selected to the cost of training staff and designating their time for data entry. We have found that the records entered by our own staff are more accurate than those entered by the software company.

4. All items to be included in your circulation/catalog system must be barcoded. Don't neglect to compute the cost of these materials and the time required to affix the labels. We prefer the uncoated barcodes which we then cover with a protective label. The coated barcodes are more easily removed.

5. Before the hardware arrives plan with the maintenance staff, with administrative approval, to have adequate wiring installed and furniture rearranged.

6. Keep your hard drive and security system secure on your computers. If your security system involves magnets (e.g., 3M), the computers must be about fifteen feet from both sensing gates and desensitizing equipment. Shields are available to cut down on this problem. Inquire of your security system vendor.

7. Once your circulation/catalog system is installed, you may purchase materials which are processed for the system, barcoded by the vendor, and recorded on a disk for uploading into your system. Verify these computer records after you load them into your system.

8. After your system is up and running, you may encounter these ongoing decisions:

   A. The records may not be completed. Completing them is a laborious but necessary task; use your main entry cards for information. Completing the note field is time well spent—the user should get the same information from the computer as he would from the manual card catalog.

   B. Your patron barcodes will need updating as students and faculty come and go.

   C. If you like your system, you will want to expand it by barcoding equipment items and keeping your delivery log on the computer. Keeping a record of textbooks may be a service you can offer the department supervisors.

   D. You will find the electronic catalog to be so popular that the problem of serving more than one patron at a time will be a critical concern. As you plan for additional terminals, consider equipping retrieval stations in remote places in the building. Possibilities are the faculty room, supervisors' offices, and study halls.

### CD-ROM and Online Information Retrieval

You may decide to start automating services in your media center with a student workstation, retrieving information from online databases or CD-ROM products. Keep in mind that:

1. One station serves one patron. Visualize the backup when classes are doing research in the media center.

2.  Online communication with databases requires dedicated phone lines, and costs are computed by time on line. You must factor in staff time for developing the search strategy ahead of time.

3.  Orientation to new services requires planning, with media staff as well as faculty and students. A good plan is to designate a media staff person to develop the overall utilization plan. That person should then keep current with the developments, keep the documentation up to date, and assume responsibility for evaluative procedures.

### Self-Directed Computer Use

A sensible way to start adding computers to your media services is to purchase a computer for your media center which you simply designate for self-directed student use. Startup disks can be kept at the circulation desk. A sign-on and sign-off log can be maintained. The student may use his own programs, or ones you may have in your collection. A quiet printer should be a part of the workstation so that word processing can be done.

### Evaluation of Automation of Services

Keeping accurate records of computer use is often neglected. Whatever kind of automated information retrieval system you install, keep accurate records of use. You may start with a modest project, but you will most likely need to expand it. Your records of the utilization of your software programs and the hardware will be the basis for requesting additional stations and new products.

### Looking Ahead

A brief piece in *Futurist* magazine, May/June, 1990, summed up the subject of automation very nicely. Mark Kibbey and Nancy H. Evans wrote that the electronic library of the future will have three essential characteristics:

- It will allow researchers to work anywhere.
- It will allow access to complete texts, not only bibliographic information.
- It will be easy for the nonspecialist to use.

—Three worthy goals to keep in mind as we automate.

# List 5–3. Automation: Reproducible List

*Apple Library Users Group Newsletter.* ALUG. Serial.

Aversa, Elizabeth. *Management of Online Search Services In Schools.* ABC-CLIO, 1989.

Byrne, Deborah J. *MARC Manual: Understanding and Using MARC Records.* Libraries Unlimited, 1991.

*Computers and the School Library.* ABC-CLIO, 1990.

Dewey, Patrick R. *Public Access Microcomputers: A Handbook For Librarians.* G. K. Hall, 1990.

Espinosa, Leonard J. *Microcomputer Facilities in Schools.* Libraries Unlimited, 1990.

Holloway, Mary A. "Media Center Automation: The Way to Go." *School Library Journal,* August 1988.

Hooten, Patricia, ed. *Perspectives on School Library Automation.* AASL, 1990.

*Information Searcher.* Serial.

Parisi, Lynn S. and Virginia L. Jones. *Directory of Online Databases and CD-ROM Resources for High Schools.* ABC-CLIO, 1988.

# PRESERVATION OF MATERIALS

An important aspect of the librarian's job is the protection of the library collection. The materials have been carefully selected and much time and energy expended in organizing them for access. We must conserve, preserve, and, in some instances, restore the materials for which we are responsible. With diminishing funds for school libraries, the development of collections becomes ever more critical. Preventive measures will alleviate many problems before they begin. Therefore:

- Keep the library clean.
- Store materials properly: vertically, loosely, adequately supported.
- Dust materials regularly.
- Control the temperature and the humidity.

## Is It Cost Effective?

When the materials become damaged decide whether you can repair them yourself, whether they need professional restoration, or whether they must be discarded. Is the title worth the time, the supplies, and the effort required to restore it?

The criteria you might apply to each item are:

- Is this title a unique item in the collection?
- Is it out of print, or readily available?
- Is it a duplicate copy?
- How useful has it proved to be?
- What is its circulation record?
- Were there restrictions upon withdrawal when it was acquired such as federal funds or a grant?

It can be satisfying to restore materials to good condition. Research the techniques before you start and practice on materials you are discarding.

If you are eager to try your hand at restoration, acquire this list of basic supplies:

- Liquid Paper® (different shades)
- Soft rubber eraser
- Fine grade sandpaper
- Rubber cement
- Small brushes
- Scissors
- Glue stick
- Putty knife
- Ink eradicator
- Cleaning fluid
- Soft rags
- Rice paper
- Transparent tape (never on book pages!)

A few common repair problems are listed here, with the recommended solutions:

- Pencil marks: soft eraser/Liquid Paper®
- Ink/marking pens: sandpaper/ink eradicator/Liquid Paper®
- Grease/dirt: cleaning fluid/sandpaper
- Spine markings: putty knife/cleaning fluid
- Holes/tears: rice paper/adhesive
- Stains: cleaning fluid/sandpaper

## List 5–4.   Preservation of Materials

DePew, John N. *A Library, Media, and Archival Preservation Handbook.* ABC-CLIO, 1991. ISBN: 0-87436-543-0.

Greenfield, Jane. *Books: Their Care and Repair.* H. W. Wilson, 1984. ISBN: 0-8242-0695-9. Also available: (video) *Basic Book Repair With Jane Greenfield.*

*How to Repair Books and Maintain Audiovisuals.* Floyd Simpson and Glynn Hill, eds. Broadman, 1984. ISBN: 0-8054-3708-8.

Johnson, Arthur. *The Practical Guide to Book Repair and Conservation.* Thames & Hudson, 1988. ISBN: 0-500-27518-1.

Kyle, Hedi. *Methods for Preserving Books, Pamphlets, and Other Printed Materials.* NY Botanical, 1983.

Lankford, Mary D. "Some Observations on Book Preservation." *School Library Journal,* November 1990.

Morrow, Carolyn and Carole Dyal. *Conservation Treatment Procedures: A Manual of Step-by-Step Procedures for the Maintenance and Repair of Library Materials.* Second edition. Libraries Unlimited, 1986. ISBN: 0-87287-294-7.

Shep, Robert L. *Cleaning and Caring for Books.* Seven Hills Books, 1987. ISBN: 0-946653-30-5.

Note: Library supply vendors, such as Demco and Brodart, offer inexpensive booklets about book repair and preservation.

# EQUIPMENT MAINTENANCE

Maintenance of equipment is a critical function of the media specialist's role in today's school libraries. Faced with "hold-the-line" or "roll-back" budgets, library media specialists find themselves keeping equipment in service that heretofore might have been retired. We are performing more repair calls on equipment in classroom use and learning the idiosyncrasies of obsolete models in an effort to continue service to our faculty. Though the newest technology in our libraries may be computers, LCD projectors, and laser disc players, we are still called upon to provide the traditional overhead projector, 16mm projector and record player to our classrooms.

A useful source:

Schroeder, Don and Gary Lare. *Audiovisual Equipment and Materials: A Basic Repair and Maintenance Manual.* Scarecrow Press, 1979. ISBN: 0-8108-1206-1. Still highly recommended. Also, by the same authors: *Audiovisual Equipment and Materials.* Volume 2. Scarecrow Press, 1989. ISBN: 0-8108-1165-2. Includes newer equipment such as VCRs, compact disc and laser disc technology. Illustrated extensively with diagrams and photographs.

As with many other library functions, prevention is the key to effective maintenance of equipment. Here are three lists. The first is a list of tips for prevention of equipment breakdown. The second is a list of basic tools for equipment maintenance and repair. The third is a list to be attached to equipment items before they are loaned from the media center.

## List 5–5A.   Preventive Maintenance

1. File warranties, manuals, schematics, and repair records for efficient retrieval.

2. Learn about each machine by testing and operating it yourself.

3. Train any media staff, including student volunteers, in the proper operation and care of equipment.

4. Provide in-service help so your faculty become proficient in the use of the particular equipment they request.

5. Check items for problems at the time of yearly inventory.
6. Schedule regular "tune-ups" with vendors of computers and video equipment.
7. Cover machines when they are not in use.
8. Keep a log of use, and rotate machines to prevent excessive wear and tear.
9. Store equipment in a climate-controlled area.
10. Secure equipment, particularly televisions and VCRs, on designated carts, which are kept as stationary as possible.
11. Do not allow students to move television equipment.
12. Check the condition of electrical cords on equipment and carts at the time of inventory.
13. Clean the heads of VCRs and audiocassette players.
14. Use anti-static wipes on monitors and screens of other audiovisual equipment to prevent dirt buildup.
15. Designate an area for equipment maintenance, equipped with the basic tools for minor repairs.
16. Attach appropriate "trouble-shooting" telephone numbers to computers, CD-players, micrographic readers, etc.
17. Provide charts and signs by your media center equipment, guiding students in their use.

## List 5–5B.   The Tool Box

1. A 16mm and 8mm film splicer.
2. Cotton swabs on six-inch sticks.
3. Anti-static wipes.
4. A drawer or box containing:
   - Screwdrivers of assorted sizes
   - Needle-nose pliers
   - Wrenches
   - Scissors
5. X-acto® knife
6. Head-cleaning tapes for VCRs and audiocassette players.
7. Computer disk for cleaning computer drives.

## List 5–5C.   For the User of This Equipment

1. If machine does not function properly check the instructions and the power source.

2. In case of a problem, call the media specialist before forcing parts or jamming the machine.

3. Rewind audio/videotapes after use.

4. Remove software materials from the machine after use.

5. Allow bulbs to cool before turning off machine fan.

6. Secure reels, electrical cords, other movable components.

7. Replace covers on machines.

8. Inform the media specialist of any problems you have had with this machine.

9. Do not allow students to move televisions.

# PROMOTING ACCEPTABLE STUDENT BEHAVIOR

Many factors have an impact on the environment the media specialist is able to establish and maintain in the library. Foremost is the ratio of library staff to students using the library at any one time. The support the administration provides for constructive use of the center, the scheduling of class use, and the budget provided for facilities and resources all have an impact on the instructional role of the media program. The cooperative relationship the media specialist is able to form with the classroom teachers will influence students' attitudes about the use of their school library. The media specialist is both a teacher and a librarian at all times, and promoting acceptable behavior in the media center requires knowledge of teaching techniques, behavior modification, child psychology and development, and the methodology that encourages students to become independent learners and responsible citizens.

This list of professional readings puts you in touch with new trends and proven methods of teaching and working with students in your capacity as a specialist. It is followed by a list of tips.

## List 5–6A. Promoting Acceptable Student Behavior

Adams, Helen R. *School Media Policy Development: A Practical Process for Small Districts.* Libraries Unlimited, 1986. ISBN: 0-87287-450-8. Stresses the need for flexibility and cooperation.

*Discipline.* Phi Delta Kappan. Center on Evaluation, Development and Research. Hot Topics Series, 1984–85.

Hart, Thomas L. *Behavior Management in the School Library Media Center.* ALA, 1985. ISBN: 0-8389-0429-7.

Heller, Dawn Hansen and Ann Montgomery. *Winning Ideas From Winning Schools: Recognizing Excellence.* ABC-CLIO, 1989. ISBN: 0-87436-527-9. Recommended for professional collections in *School Library Journal* (2/90).

Kohn, Rita and Krysta A. Tepper. *Have You Got What They Want? Public Relations Strategies for the School Librarian/Media Specialist: A Reference Tool.* 2nd edition. Scarecrow Press, 1990. ISBN: 0-8108-2359-4.

Kohut, Sylvester. *Classroom Discipline.* Second edition. National Education Association of the United States, 1986. ISBN: 0-8106-1486-3.

Rivers, L. Wendell. *The Disruptive Student and the Teacher.* NEA, 1983. Stock No. 1614-9.

Seeman, Howard, PhD. *Preventing Classroom Discipline Problems: A Guide for Educators.* Technomic Publishing Co., 1988. ISBN: 0-87762-533-6.

## List 5–6B.  Discipline Guidelines

Here is a list of guidelines which will help establish and maintain acceptable behavior in your media center. As the library/media specialist, you work with students in varied ways, from supervising individual and classroom projects to monitoring large groups using library resources, studying, or engaging in social activities. Remember that you are an important and integral part of the educational process.

- Learn to identify developmentally appropriate behavior.
- Reduce your personal stress.
- Recognize and modify your feelings of hostility and personal biases.
- Modify any need you may have to be liked by everyone.
- Practice listening.
- Modulate your voice to an agreeable tone.
- Model appropriate behavior and responses.
- Make no arbitrary rules.
- Insure that media center rules are consistent with school policies.
- Avoid confrontations.
- Avoid empty threats.

- Learn students' names.
- Recognize when behavior is out of your jurisdiction.

You will prevent many behavior problems if you:

- Shape the learning environment.
- Stress the removal of graffiti.
- Have materials students need.
- Provide adequate trash receptacles.
- Avoid clutter.
- Provide an efficient traffic pattern.
- Allow adequate space between seats.
- Provide fresh air and proper lighting.

When presenting a media skills lesson:

- Be well prepared.
- Convey your interest in your subject.
- Tell students what you expect of them.
- Start with an overview.
- Vary your techniques.
- Allow for questions.
- Personalize the assignment.
- Relate your presentation to a content area assignment.
- Organize complicated procedures into manageable tasks.
- Provide positive feedback.
- Provide practice time for the skills presented.

When a student is disruptive:

- Identify the source of the disruption.
- If possible, respond nonverbally to disruptions.
- Do not take disruptions personally; remain objective.
- Talk privately with the student, never in front of his/her peers.
- Do not lecture.
- Avoid personality references; talk about the behavior.
- Be brief.
- Provide warnings; be clear about the follow-up.
- Never hold a grudge.

- Admit your own errors; be willing to apologize.
- Give positive reinforcement of acceptable responses.
- Recognize the necessity for referral of the problem.
- Continuously evaluate your rules and be ready to revise.

A last word or two on this important facet of the role of the media specialist: Set a personal goal to maximize learning and student self-reliance in your center, minimize disruptions to learning, and think of discipline as a positive. Remind yourself of the advice of Pope John XXIII in his diary, *Journey of a Soul:*

> "See everything
> Overlook a lot
> Correct a little."

# TEACHING LIBRARY SKILLS

What is the matter with most library skills lessons? Why do they generally turn students off and prompt comments such as "boring," "not this again," "I'll go to the public library"? Unfortunately, such comments often hit the mark. "Teaching library skills" is often a euphemism for "redundancy," and too often it is carried out simply to comply with a state mandate or the expectations of an administrator, or to provide prep time for classroom teachers. Too often our lessons *are* boring and repetitive. I have found the public library, with the "teaching" component absent, allows the student to explore his skills as an independent learner. Our goal must be to make the skills lessons we are obligated to offer—and which we know are needed—meet the following objectives:

1. The lessons should be relevant to a specific content area assignment. To achieve this we must first be in communication with the teachers in our building. We must be curriculum generalists. I have found that teachers want to prepare assignments that encourage library research, but they need direction and assistance. This primary objective suggests reforms in the kind of preparation media specialists, administrators, and teachers receive. It assumes, also, an atmosphere and organization in the school that is conducive to cooperative planning and to effective communications among staff.

2. Our skills lessons should be models of effective teaching. Their preparation deserves the recognition of the school community in terms of planning time, resources, in-service training, facilities, and evaluation.

3. The administration of the media center must incorporate flexible rules, freedom of access, and involvement in the total educational program.

4. Students using the media center and its resources should experience success. They should learn to retrieve information independently and to evaluate its worth. Their mastery of library media skills should be applicable to the pursuit of lifetime learning.

The following two lists of resources will help media specialists attain these worthy objectives. The first directs the reader to information regarding the professional task of teaching media skills. The second offers resources which contain model lesson plans. These lists are followed by a "how-to" list that will help you prepare an effective lesson.

## List 5–7A.  Teaching Media Skills

**Caissey, Gail A. "Skills for the Information Age."** *Educational Horizons,* **Fall 1989. ISSN: 0013-175X.** The author proposes that schools must formally teach information-processing skills and offer opportunities for the reinforcement of those skills from kindergarten through the twelfth grade. These skills include learning to use the computer, and they can be integrated into all parts of the curriculum.

*A Casebook for Helping Teachers Teach.* **Edited by Philip M. Turner. Libraries Unlimited, 1988. ISBN: 0-87287-615-2.** Thirteen case studies, drawn from all grade levels, illustrate the ways in which media specialists and teachers can cooperate on units of instruction. A good companion to *Helping Teachers Teach* by the same author.

**Cutlip, Glen W.** *Learning and Information: Skills for the Secondary Classroom and Library Media Program.* **Libraries Unlimited, 1988. ISBN: 0-87287-580-6.** Presents a model based on the cognitive learning theory, stressing the role of the media center in the process. Highly recommended by *VOYA* (8/89).

**Eisenberg, Michael B. and Robert E. Berkowitz.** *Curriculum Initiative: An Agenda and Strategy for Library Media Programs.* **Ablex, 1988. ISBN: 0-89391-486-X.** Focuses on the role media specialists play in curriculum development and support. Emphasizes the interdependence of the classroom teacher and the media specialist. Provides the conceptual framework for a curriculum-based, integrated media program.

**Krimmelbein, Cindy Jeffrey.** *The Choice to Change: Establishing an Integrated School Library Program.* **Libraries Unlimited, 1989. ISBN: 0-87287-638-1.** This book describes the processes necessary for meeting our goal of integration of the media program into the total school curriculum. Recommended by *Wilson Library Bulletin* (6/89).

**MacDonald, Linda Brew, et al.** *Teaching Technologies in Libraries: A Practical Guide.* **G. K. Hall, 1991. ISBN: 0-8161-1906-6.** This title meets the needs of media specialists whose instruction and reference services include end-user searching of online and local CD-ROM databases. Focuses on using the technology to teach the technology.

**Pellowski, Anne.** *The World of Storytelling: A Guide to the Origins, Development, and Applications of Storytelling.* **H. W. Wilson, 1990. ISBN: 0-8242-0788-2.** Storytelling is an essential skill in promoting use of the library and in integrating library resources into the curriculum. The author provides the media specialist with historical details and the multi-ethnic aspects of stories. The bibliography includes nonprint materials.

Stripling, Barbara K. and Judy M. Pitts. *Brainstorms and Blueprints: Teaching Library Research as a Thinking Process.* Libraries Unlimited, 1988. ISBN: 0-87287-638-1. This book is useful for its model plans and discussion of theory. *VOYA* (2/89) recommended it as "innovative." High school level.

Turner, Philip M. *Helping Teachers Teach: A School Library/Media Specialist's Role.* Libraries Unlimited, 1985. ISBN: 0-87287-456-7. This book can help you become a curriculum expert and instructional design consultant. Focuses on our role in helping teachers to become more effective.

Turner, Philip M. "Information Skills and Instructional Consulting: A Synergy?" *School Library Media Quarterly,* Fall 1991. ISSN: 0278-4823. In order for us to be effective in teaching information skills we must be in on the planning of the curriculum and we must identify a logical method for choosing the appropriate skills. The teacher's instructional design, the cognitive requirements of the lesson, and the students' learning styles must be considered.

Zingher, Gary. *At the Pirate Academy: Adventures With Language in the Library Media Center.* ALA, 1990. ISBN: 0-8389-3384-X. This is the tenth volume of the series *School Library Media Programs: Focus on Issues and Trends.* The author focuses on the collaborative efforts of media specialists and teachers in integrating classroom activities and library use. Probably most useful to librarians in grades K–6. Includes bibliographies.

## List 5–7B.  Library Media Skills Lessons

*Activities Almanac: Daily Ideas for Library Media Lessons.* ABC-CLIO, 1990. ISBN: 0-87436-569-4. The historical and cultural events which are celebrated during the year form the theme for the many activities in this book. The lessons are gleaned from *School Library Media Activities Monthly.*

Bannister, Barbara Farley. *Library Media Center Activities for Every Month of the School Year.* Center for Applied Research in Education, 1986. ISBN: 0-87628-536-1. Designed for K–8 use. Many reproducible student activity pages provide immediate accessibility to lessons that are keyed to special events during the school year. The emphasis is on practice in research and appreciation of literature.

Blass, Rosanne J. and Nancy E. Allen Jurenka. *Responding to Literature: Activities for Grades 6, 7, and 8.* Libraries Unlimited, 1989. ISBN: 0-87287-465-6. Three hundred selections from various genres are summarized. Includes several activities for each book. Focus is on higher-level thinking skills.

Butzow, Carol M. and John W. *Science Through Children's Literature: An Integrated Approach.* Libraries Unlimited, 1989. ISBN: 0-87287-465-6. An excellent sourcebook for elementary science teachers (K–3) and librarians. Thirty outstanding children's fiction books are presented as instructional units. These books are strong in scientific concepts and have popular story lines. Whole language approach to teaching science.

*Finding It Fast in the Library.* **Sound Filmstrips. Words, Inc., Cheshire Corp., 1991.** This thirty-minute program depicts students on an information search in an attractive media center, using some new technologies and employing correct research strategies. For grades 6–8.

**Heltshe, Mary Ann and Audrey Burie Kirchner.** *Multicultural Explorations: Joyous Journeys With Books.* **Libraries Unlimited, 1991. ISBN: 0-87287-848-1.** The use of literature to introduce elementary children to six areas of the world. The activities reinforce the whole language approach to learning.

**Hunter, Beverly and Erica K. Lodish.** *Online Searching in the Curriculum: A Teaching Guide for Library/Media Specialists and Teachers.* **ABC-CLIO, 1988. ISBN: 0-87436-516-3.** *Online Searcher* (Winter 1989) recommended this resource saying the topics chosen are challenging and relevant to teenagers. There are lessons and activity sheets.

*Into the Curriculum: Lesson Plans for Library Media Skills.* **ABC-CLIO, 1990. ISBN: 0-87436-567-8.** The activities in lesson-plan format that comprise this collection are taken from *School Library Media Activities Monthly.*

**Irving, Jan.** *Fanfares: Programs for Classrooms and Libraries.* **Libraries Unlimited, 1990. ISBN: 0-87287-792-2.** Called a "valuable resource" in *Library Talk* (2/91), these twelve programs for grades K–5 include systematic plans for art projects, theatre scripts, etc., related to themes children love. Included are plans for using the media center.

**Jweid, Rosann and Margaret Rizzo.** *The Library-Classroom Partnership: Teaching Library Media Skills in Middle and Junior High Schools.* **Scarecrow Press, 1988. ISBN: 0-8108-2191-5.** *VOYA* said, "Rich with ideas." Covers eleven disciplines taught at the middle school level. Includes activity sheets, bibliographies, and presentation ideas.

**Kelly, Joanne.** *The Battle of Books: K–8.* **Libraries Unlimited, 1990. ISBN: 0-87287-792-2.** Here is a game about books that is available in print form or as software for IBM, Apple, or Mac. Thinking and writing skills are encouraged by the game, and the disk versions can be adapted for different groups.

**Lewis, Marguerite.** *Hooked on Independent Study! A Programmed Approach to Library Skills for Grades 3–8.* **Illustrated by Pamela J. Kudla. The Center for Applied Research in Education, 1990. ISBN: 0-87628-405-5.** Designed to promote those retrieval skills that involve and engage students in their own learning. From learning the parts of the book to using an index, these are the skills media specialists concentrate on in the elementary grades.

**Lewis, Marguerite.** *Remarkable People! Ready-to-Use Biography Activities for Grades 4–8.* **Illustrated by Pamela J. Kudla. The Center for Applied Research in Education, 1991. ISBN: 0-87628-792-5.** The "remarkable" people included in this useful book were carefully selected by the author. They are persons about whom the media specialist can provide additional material, and they are people who can be suitable role models. The biographical sketches are brief and are followed by fun discovery activities. Nicely illustrated with line drawings.

**McElmeel, Sharron L.** *Adventures With Social Studies (Through Literature).* **Libraries Unlimited, 1991. ISBN: 0-87287-465-6.** Introduces basic concepts in the social sciences through literature. Middle school teachers and librarians will find this resource useful for stimulating writing and thinking skills.

*Media Production and Computer Activities.* **ABC-CLIO, 1990. ISBN: 0-87436-568-6.** A collection of lessons from *School Library Media Activities Monthly* which integrate research skills and computer production techniques.

**Streiff, Jane E.** *The Secondary School Librarian's Almanac.* **The Center for Applied Research in Education, 1989. ISBN: 0-87628-783-6.** Primarily a book about school library management. This resource includes lesson plans for integrating library research skills with the content areas of the middle and high school curricula.

**Sullivan, Emilie P.** *Starting With Books: An Activities Approach to Children's Literature.* **Libraries Unlimited, 1990. ISBN: 0-87287-792-2.** Designed for preschool and primary grade teachers and media specialists who are developing literature-based lessons. There are lists of books to read and activities that involve children with books.

## List 5–7C. Tips for Presenting Skills Lessons

1. Plan well in advance of the library visit.
2. Plan with the classroom teacher.
3. Structure your presentation around an actual assignment.
4. Try for simplicity and brevity.
5. Vary your teaching techniques.
6. Agree with the classroom teacher on behavior expectations and the handling of disruptive incidents.
7. Allow the students time for practice of the skills presented.
8. Practice your presentation ahead of time.
9. Prepare handouts or visuals carefully; make sure they are clear.
10. Prepare the area for the presentation.
11. Allow space between chairs; avoid congestion.
12. Plan the traffic pattern.
13. Provide fresh air and adequate lighting.
14. Test the equipment you will be using; have a spare bulb at hand.
15. Introduce your presentation with an overview.

16. Make sure the students know what you expect from them.
17. Draw the students into the presentation.
18. Allow students to question or digress.
19. Convey your interest in the topic to the students.
20. Follow up with evaluation.

# List 5–7A. Teaching Media Skills

Caissey, Gail A. "Skills for the Information Age." *Educational Horizons,* Fall 1989.

*A Casebook for Helping Teachers Teach.* Edited by Philip M. Turner. Libraries Unlimited, 1988.

Cutlip, Glen W. *Learning and Information: Skills for the Secondary Classroom and Library Media Program.* Libraries Unlimited, 1988.

Eisenberg, Michael B. *Curriculum Initiative: An Agenda and Strategy for Library Media Programs.* Libraries Unlimited, 1988.

Krimmelbein, Cindy Jeffrey. *The Choice to Change: Establishing an Integrated School Library Program.* Libraries Unlimited, 1989.

MacDonald, Linda Brew, et al. *Teaching Technologies in Libraries: A Practical Guide.* G. K. Hall, 1991.

Pellowski, Anne. *The World of Storytelling: A Guide to the Origins, Development, and Applications of Storytelling.* H. W. Wilson, 1990.

Stripling, Barbara K. *Brainstorms and Blueprints: Teaching Library Research as a Thinking Process.* Libraries Unlimited, 1988.

Turner, Philip M. *Helping Teachers Teach: A School Library/Media Specialist's Role.* Libraries Unlimited, 1985.

Turner, Philip M. "Information Skills and Instructional Consulting: A Synergy?" *School Library Media Quarterly,* Fall 1991.

Zingher, Gary. *At the Pirate Academy: Adventures with Language in the Media Center.* ALA, 1990.

# List 5–7B.  Library Media Skills Lessons

*Activities Almanac: Daily Ideas for Library Media Lessons.* ABC-CLIO, 1990.

Bannister, Barbara Farley. *Library Media Center Activities for Every Month of the School Year.* Center for Applied Research in Education, 1986.

Blass, Rosanne J. *Responding to Literature: Activities for Grades 6, 7, and 8.* Libraries Unlimited, 1989.

Butzow, Carol M. *Science Through Children's Literature: An Integrated Approach.* Libraries Unlimited, 1989.

*Finding It Fast in the Library.* Sound Filmstrips. Cheshire, Corp., 1991.

Heltshe, Mary Ann. *Multicultural Explorations: Joyous Journeys With Books.* Libraries Unlimited, 1991.

Hunter, Beverly. *Online Searching in the Curriculum.* ABC-CLIO, 1988.

*Into the Curriculum: Lesson Plans for Library Media Skills.* ABC-CLIO, 1990.

Irving, Jan. *Fanfares: Programs for Classrooms and Libraries.* Libraries Unlimited, 1990.

Jweid, Rosann and Margaret Rizzo. *The Library-Classroom Partnership: Teaching Library Media Skills in Middle and Junior High Schools.* Scarecrow Press, 1988.

Kelley, Joanne. *The Battle of Books: K–6.* Print or computer disks. Libraries Unlimited, 1990.

Lewis, Marguerite. *Hooked On Independent Study!* Center for Applied Research in Education, 1990.

Lewis, Marguerite. *Remarkable People!* Center for Applied Research in Education, 1991.

McElmeel, Sharron L. *Adventures with Social Studies Through Literature.* Libraries Unlimited, 1991.

*Media Production and Computer Activities.* ABC-CLIO, 1990.

Streiff, Jane E. *The Secondary School Librarian's Almanac.* Center for Applied Research in Education, 1989.

Sullivan, Emilie P. *Starting With Books: An Activities Approach to Children's Literature.* Libraries Unlimited, 1990.

# Awards and Contests

As media specialists selecting materials for our collections, we are interested in buying the best. It is often necessary to rely on the judgment of the many groups that offer awards when selecting materials in different genres and formats, and for different age levels.

We are also interested in advising teachers and students about contests and awards that are available to them. The materials in the following list will be useful in selecting and providing information about awards, contests, grants, and prizes that are available to you, your students, and the professionals in your building.

## List 5–8.   Awards and Contests: Annotated List

*The Awards Almanac 1992.* **Edited by Noelle Watson. St. James Press, 1992. ISBN: 1-55862-082-6.** This source is international in scope, providing comprehensive information on grants, awards, scholarships, fellowships, and funding for research. Good source of information for teachers doing graduate work.

*Awards, Honors and Prizes.* **Volume 1: U.S. and Canada. Gale, 1991. ISBN: 0-8103-5090-4.** An alphabetical directory of 4,779 organizations that sponsor awards in many categories, from academics to sports. Volume 2: International and Foreign. ISBN: 0-8103-5089-0.

**Comfort, Claudette Hegel.** *Distinguished Children's Literature (The Newbery and Caldecott Winners, The Books and Their Creators).* **T. S. Denison, 1990. ISBN: 0-513-01965-0.** Brief histories of the awards with reviews of the winners for each year. Brief plot summaries and biographical sketches of the authors and illustrators.

*Contests for Students: All You Need to Know to Enter and Win 600 Contests.* **Edited by Mary Ellen Snodgrass. Gale, 1991. ISBN: 0-8103-7731-4.** The detailed entries provide all the information necessary to enter these contests. Purpose, eligibility, description, awards, and contacts are here. Five indexes give quick access to the right choice, from greeting cards, to stories, to posters.

**Corry, Emmett.** *Grants for Libraries: A Guide to Public and Private Funding Programs and Proposal Writing Techniques.* **Second edition. Libraries Unlimited, 1986. ISBN: 0-87287-534-2.** *VOYA* (6/87) called this title a "must" for all libraries.

**Criscoe, Betty L.** *Award-Winning Books for Children and Young Adults: An Annual Guide, 1989.* **Scarecrow Press, 1989. ISBN: 0-8108-2336-5.** Information about the backgrounds of the awards, a historical review of the year, and bibliographic information on the awards. The winning titles are listed in an appendix, as are the publishers of the winners. Age and grade level are given for those materials that are included.

*The International Reading Association Awards.* Information about these awards is carried each year in spring issues of *The Reading Teacher, Reading Research Quarterly, Journal of Reading, Lectura y Vida,* and *Reading Today.*

**Long, Kim.** *Contests, Prizes, and Awards for Students.* **ABC-CLIO, 1991. ISBN: 0-87436-586-4.** National, regional, and statewide academic competitions for students.

*Media and Methods. Awards Portfolio.* **May/June issue.** An annual evaluation of instructional materials organized by subject areas. The evaluators consider these criteria: "clarity of educational objectives, range of methods and strategies, quality of graphics and documentation, flexibility of curricular uses, extent of support materials, degree of interest level, and special strengths and weaknesses." Educational materials in all formats are considered.

**Park, Karin R. and Beth Luey.** *Publication Grants for Writers and Publishers: How to Find Them, Win Them, and Manage Them.* **Oryx, 1990. ISBN: 0-89774-557-4.** Written for persons writing proposals for the first time. The authors' premise is that grant-writing is worth the extensive time and effort necessary. Sample application forms and advice on preparation are included.

*School Library Journal.* **April issue, annually.**

*The Submission Sourcebook for Creative Classroom Publishing: A Teacher's Handbook.* **Edited by June A. Austin. Greenplace Books, 1989. ISBN: 0-932881-01-7.** Produced in cooperation with *Young Author's Magazine.* Excellent source for access to literary magazines, contests and awards, book publishing companies, and creative literary conferences. Sample agreements and other how-to information.

# List 5–8.  Awards and Contests: Reproducible List

*The Awards Almanac 1991.* St. James Press, 1991.

*Awards, Honors and Prizes.* Gale, 1991.

Comfort, Claudette. *Distinguished Children's Literature,* T. S. Denison, 1990.

*Contests for Students: All You Need to Know to Enter and Win 600 Contests.* Gale, 1991.

Corry, Emmett. *Grants for Libraries: A Guide to Public and Private Funding Programs and Proposal Writing Techniques.* Libraries Unlimited, 1986.

Criscoe, Betty L. *Award-Winning Books for Children and Young Adults: An Annual Guide.* Scarecrow Press, 1989.

Long, Kim. *Contests, Prizes and Awards for Students.* ABC-CLIO, 1991.

Park, Karin R. *Publication Grants for Writers and Publishers.* Oryx, 1990.

*The Submission Sourcebook for Creative Classroom Publishing: A Teacher's Handbook.* Greenplace, 1989.

# LIBRARY-RELATED OBSERVANCES AND THEMES

An ongoing task for media specialists is finding themes for promotional activities, bulletins, etc. Here is a list of sources for finding ideas, followed by a monthly calendar of national holidays you might choose to observe.

## List 5–9A.   Library-Related Observances and Themes

Bauer, Caroline Feller. *Celebrations: Read-Aloud Holiday and Theme Book Programs.* H. W. Wilson, 1985. ISBN: 0-8242-0708-4.

*Bulletin Boards, Displays and Special Events for School Libraries.* ABC-CLIO, 1990. ISBN: 0-87436-606-2.

Canoles, Marian L. *The Creative Copycat II.* Illustrated by Betty Ferguson Willcox. Libraries Unlimited, 1985. ISBN: 0-87287-436-2.

*Folklore of American Holidays.* Second edition. Edited by Hennig Cohen and Tristram Potter Coffin. Gale, 1991. ISBN: 0-8103-7602-4.

Haglund, Elaine and Marcia L. Harris. *On This Day.* Libraries Unlimited, 1983. ISBN: 0-87287-345-5.

*Holidays.* ABC-CLIO, 1990. ISBN: 0-87436-592-9.

*Holidays and Anniversaries of the World.* Second edition. Edited by Jennifer Mossman. Gale, 1990. ISBN: 0-8103-4870-5.

Schaeffer, Mark. *Library Displays Handbook.* H. W. Wilson, 1991. ISBN: 0-8242-0801-3.

## List 5–9B.   Select List of Holidays and Observances

*September*

       Labor Day   First Monday
       National Anthem Day   September 14

Citizenship Day   September 17
Harvest Moon Day   September 20
World Peace Day   September 21
Good Neighbor Day   Fourth Sunday
American Indian Day   Fourth Friday

## October

Child Health Day   October 7
Canadian Thanksgiving Day   Second Monday
Columbus Day   October 12
White Cane Safety Day   October 15
World Poetry Day   October 15
Black Poetry Day   October 17
United Nations Day   October 24
International Red Cross Day   October 26
Halloween   October 31
National Magic Day   October 31

## November

National Author Day   November 1
UNESCO Anniversary   November 4
Guy Fawkes Day   November 5
Election Day   First Tuesday after First Monday
American Education Week   Second Week
National Children's Book Week   Second Week
Veterans' Day   November 11
Canadian Remembrance Day   November 11
Dunce Day   November 11
World Fellowship Day   November 18
Thanksgiving Day   Fourth Thursday

## December

Pan American Health Day   December 2
Pearl Harbor Day   December 7
Human Rights Day   December 10
Nobel Prize Presentation Day   December 10
Bill of Rights Day   December 15

Winter Solstice    December 21
International Arbor Day    December 22
Canadian Boxing Day    December 26
Watch Night    December 31
New Year's Eve    December 31

## January

New Year's Day    January 1
World Literacy Day    January 8
Martin Luther King, Jr. Day    January 15
Inauguration Day    January 20
Vietnam Day    January 27

## February

American Music Month
Black History Month
American Heart Month
National Freedom Day    February 1
Groundhog Day    February 2
Lincoln's Birthday    February 12
Valentine's Day    February 14
Washington's Birthday    February 22
Sadie Hawkins Day    First Saturday

## March

International Women's History Month
United States Constitution Day    March 4
Ides of March    March 15
National Library Week Anniversary    March 16
St. Patrick's Day    March 17
Earth Day    March 21
Agriculture Day    March 24

## April

April Fool's Day    April 1
International Children's Book Day    April 2
World Health Day    April 7

       Humane Day   April 10
       Pan American Day   April 14
       Earth Day   April 22
       National Arbor Day   April 26

## May

       Law Day   May 1
       May Day   May 1
       Loyalty Day   May 1
       World Red Cross Day   May 8
       V-E Day   May 8
       Mother's Day   Second Sunday
       Armed Forces Day   Third Saturday
       Canadian Victoria Day   First Monday Preceding May 29
       Memorial Day   May 30

## June

       World Environment Day   June 5
       Flag Day   June 14
       Magna Carta Day   June 15
       Father's Day   Third Sunday
       Library Bill of Rights Day   June 18
       Newbery Award Anniversary   June 27
       United Nations Charter Day   June 28

*section* **6**

# WHO IS OUT THERE?

# PROFESSIONAL ORGANIZATIONS, FOUNDATIONS, AND ASSOCIATIONS

Making connections with people and organizations and maintaining professional contacts are vital to advancing your career and enhancing your growth as an effective library media specialist in the educational field. Whether you are interested in networking for purposes of resource-sharing, tapping into electronic bulletin boards, sharing ideas, engaging in a fuller social life, or contributing to policy-making at local, state, or national levels, membership in select organizations will offer the opportunities you need. You are a team member with the faculty of your school and district and you will want to support the appropriate teacher organizations. Join the school's parent-faculty organization as well as worthy student organizations. Local and state historical societies can provide you with excellent resources for your collection and an appreciation for the community in which you work.

If you have the option of purchasing institutional memberships to organizations, you may want to do so.

Here is a broad selection of library- and education-related organizations. Write to the address provided, requesting literature about the organization and the schedule of membership fees. Ask for free materials!

## List 6–1.  Professional Organizations, Foundations, and Associations

ACCESS: The Information Clearinghouse About Public Schools, National Committee for Citizens in Education
10840 Little Patuxent Parkway, Suite 301
Columbia, Maryland 21044

American Library Association
50 East Huron Street
Chicago, Illinois 60611

American Association of School Administrators
1801 North Moore Street
Arlington, Virginia 22209

American Association of School Librarians
50 East Huron Street
Chicago, Illinois 60611

ANTI-DEFAMATION LEAGUE OF
  B'NAI BRITH
823 United Nations Plaza
New York, New York 10017

ASSOCIATION FOR EDUCATIONAL
  COMMUNICATIONS AND
  TECHNOLOGY
1126 Sixteenth St., NW
Washington, D.C. 20036

ASSOCIATION FOR LIBRARY SERVICE
  TO CHILDREN, ALA
50 East Huron Street
Chicago, Illinois 60611

ASSOCIATION FOR THE PROMOTION OF
  CHILDREN'S BOOKS
22, Crets-de-Chambel
CH-1206 Geneva, Switzerland

CANADIAN LIBRARY ASSOCIATION
200 Elgin Street, Suite 602
Ottawa, Ontario, Canada K2P 1T5

THE CATHOLIC LIBRARY
  ASSOCIATION
461 West Lancaster Avenue
Haverford, Pennsylvania 19041

THE CENTER FOR TEACHING ABOUT
  CHINA
1214 W. Schwartz
Carbondale, Illinois 62901

CHILDREN'S ART FOUNDATION
915 Cedar Street
Santa Cruz, California 95060

CHILDREN'S BOOK CENTRE
229 College Street, Fifth Floor
Toronto, Ontario, Canada M5T 1R4

CHILDREN'S BOOK COUNCIL
67 Irving Place
New York, New York 10003

CHILDREN'S BOOK COUNCIL OF
  AUSTRALIA, INC.
P. O. Box 202
Sandy Bay, Tasmania, 7005 Australia

CHILDREN'S LITERATURE
  ASSOCIATION
210 Education, Purdue University
West Lafayette, Indiana 47907

CHILDREN'S READING ROUND TABLE
  OF CHICAGO
1321 East Fifty-sixth Street
Chicago, Illinois 60637

THE CHRISTOPHERS
12 East Forty-eighth Street
New York, New York 10017

CINE COUNCIL ON INTERNATIONAL
  NONTHEATRICAL EVENTS
1201 Sixteenth Street, NW
Washington, D.C. 20036

COUNCIL ON INTERRACIAL BOOKS
  FOR CHILDREN, INC.
1841 Broadway
New York, New York 10023

EDUCATIONAL PAPERBACK
  ASSOCIATION (EPA)
P. O. Box 1399
East Hampton, New York 11937

EPIE INSTITUTE, STERLING HARBOR
  PRESS
146 Sterling Avenue
P. O. Box 28
Greenport, New York 11944

FILM LIBRARY INFORMATION
  COUNCIL
Box 348, Radio City Station
New York, New York 10019

FRIENDS OF THE CHICAGO PUBLIC
LIBRARY
78 East Washington Street
Chicago, Illinois 60602

GREAT BOOKS FOUNDATION
35 East Wacker Drive, Suite 2300
Chicago, Illinois 60601-2298

GREENPEACE USA
1436 U Street, NW
Washington, D.C. 20009

HIGH/SCOPE EDUCATION RESEARCH
FOUNDATION
600 N. River Street
Ypsilanti, Michigan 48198

INTERNATIONAL READING
ASSOCIATION
800 Barksdale Road, Box 8139
Newark, Delaware 19714-8139

JANE ADDAMS PEACE ASSOCIATION,
INC.
777 United Nations Plaza
New York, New York 10017

THE LIBRARY ASSOCIATION
7 Ridgemount Street
London, England WCIE 7AE

NATIONAL ASSOCIATION FOR THE
EDUCATION OF YOUNG CHILDREN
1834 Connecticut Avenue, NW
Washington, D.C. 20009-5786

NATIONAL COALITION AGAINST
CENSORSHIP
132 West Forty-third Street
New York, New York 10109

NATIONAL COUNCIL FOR THE SOCIAL
STUDIES
3501 Newark Street, NW
Washington, D.C. 20016

NATIONAL COUNCIL OF TEACHERS OF
ENGLISH
111 Kenyon Road
Urbana, Illinois 61801

NATIONAL COUNCIL OF TEACHERS OF
MATHEMATICS
1906 Association Drive
Reston, Virginia 22091

NATIONAL STORY LEAGUE
3508 Russell #6
St. Louis, Missouri 63104

NEW YORK ACADEMY OF SCIENCES
2 East Sixty-third Street
New York, New York 10021

PARENTS CHOICE FOUNDATION
Box 185
Waban, Massachusetts 02168

READING IS FUNDAMENTAL
600 Maryland Avenue, SW
Room 500, Smithsonian
Washington, D.C. 20560

SEED PROJECT (SOFTWARE
EVALUATION EXCHANGE
DISSEMINATION)
P. O. Box 12748
200 Park Offices, Suite 200
Research Triangle Park,
North Carolina 27709

SEX INFORMATION AND EDUCATION
COUNCIL OF THE U.S.
715 Broadway, Room 213
New York, New York 10003

SIERRA CLUB
P.O. Box 7959
San Francisco, California 94120-9943

SOFTWARE PUBLISHERS ASSOCIATION
1101 Connecticut Avenue, Suite 901
Washington, D.C. 20036

STEPS, NATIONAL COALITION OF
  ADVOCATES FOR STUDENTS
100 Boylston Street, Suite 737
Boston, Massachusetts 02116

TEACHERS USA
Box 519, Baldwin Place
New York, New York 10505-0519

UNICEF
331 East Thirty-eighth Street
New York, New York 10016

UNITED STATES BOARD ON BOOKS
  FOR YOUNG PEOPLE (USBBY)
800 Barksdale Road
P. O. Box 8139
Newark, Delaware 19714-8139

U.S.-CHINA PEOPLES FRIENDSHIP
  ASSOCIATION
306 W. 38th Street, Room 603
New York, New York 10018

VOYA: VOICE OF YOUTH ADVOCATES,
  SCARECROW PRESS
52 Liberty Street
Metuchen, New Jersey 08840

YOUNG ADULT SERVICES DIVISION
  (YASD), ALA
50 East Huron Street
Chicago, Illinois 60611

YOUNG MEN'S CHRISTIAN
  ASSOCIATION OF THE U.S.
101 N. Wacker Drive
Chicago, Illinois 60606

YOUNG WOMEN'S CHRISTIAN
  ASSOCIATION OF THE U.S.
726 Broadway
New York, New York 10003

# PROFESSIONAL MATERIALS

As specialists in the school setting it is important that we stay informed about our profession. We must pay particular attention to the changing aspects and responsibilities of our jobs and to the vast innovations in products available for teaching and learning. The following professional materials will keep you up to date, provide for professional growth, and, in some cases, provide a few light moments.

## List 6-2. Professional Materials: Annotated List

*Apple Library Users Group Newsletter.* **Edited by Monica Ertel. (ALUG Newsletter). Apple Computer, Inc.**

**Aversa, Elizabeth S. and Jacqueline C. Mancall.** *Management of Online Search Services in School.* **ABC-CLIO, 1989. ISBN: 0-87436-513-9.**

*The Book Report. The Journal for Junior and Senior High School Librarians.* **5 issues per year. Linworth Publishing Co.**

*Booklist and Reference Books Bulletin.* **Serial. American Library Association. ISSN: 0006-7385.**

**Breivik, Patricia and E. Gordon Gee.** *Information Literacy: Revolution in the Library.* **Macmillan, 1989. ISBN: 0-02-911440-3.**

*Choice.* **Serial. Association of College and Research Libraries. ISSN: 0009-4978.** Reviews for upper level and adult collection development.

*EPIEgram: The Newsletter About Educational Materials and Technology.* **Serial. Sterling Harbor Press.** This newsletter provides the latest news and research results on educational materials and technology. The EPIE Institute is a not-for-profit organization and provides an unbiased evaluation of materials, hardware, curriculum, and educational programs.

*Horn Book Magazine.* **Serial. Horn Book, Inc. Six issues per year. ISSN: 0018-5078.** Useful reviews, professional articles, and news for elementary librarians.

*Information Power.* **Guidelines for School Library Media Programs. Prepared by AASL and AECT. ALA, 1988.**

*Information Searcher.* **Quarterly serial. Datasearch Group, Inc.** A newsletter for teaching online/CD-ROM searching in schools. Essential for the library/media specialist just getting started with these new technologies as well as for those who are already in the thick of it. The reviews of the literature and the tips for managing services are very useful. Puts you in touch with sources of information about the latest developments, conferences, and networking. Tips for searching databases and ideas for integrating online and CD-ROM services into the curriculum.

*Journal of Youth Services in Libraries.* **Serial. Association for Library Service to Children and the Young Adult Services Division of ALA. Quarterly ISSN: 0894-2498.** Reviews professional literature and features articles of professional interest.

**Klasing, Jane P.** *Designing and Renovating School Library Media Centers.* **ALA, 1991. ISBN: 0-8389-0560-9.** From the Trends and Issues series. Checklists, templates, and a wealth of information relieves the stress of renovating. Applications of new technologies.

**Kurzweil, Raymond.** *The Age of Intelligent Machines.* **Massachusetts Institute of Technology, 1990. ISBN: 0-262-11121-7.** Behind-the-scenes look at machine intelligence. *School Library Journal* (12/90) called it a "tour de force."

*Library Hotline.* **Weekly newsletter. Library Hotline.** A summary of news for librarians about personnel changes, conferences, grant monies, technology, and new programs.

*Library Talk, The Magazine for Elementary School Librarians.* **5 issues per year. Linworth Publishing Co.** Innovative ideas in both magazines. Information from regular columns is compiled in handbooks which are available from ABC-CLIO.

**Lurie, Alison.** *Don't Tell the Grownups: Subversive Children's Literature.* **Little Brown, 1990. ISBN: 0-316-53722-5.** Is there a revolutionary side to childhood, and why have the classics survived? Sixteen essays.

*The New York Times Book Review.* **Sundays.** We owe it to ourselves to read these book reviews. We are better librarians for it, and enjoy our work more fully.

*Online and CD-ROM Databases in School Libraries: Readings.* **Compiled by Ann Lathrop. Libraries Unlimited, 1989. ISBN: 0-87287-756-6.** Most of the articles in this book were contributed by school librarians working with online and CD-ROM research tools. Especially helpful are the thorough index, the glossary, the list of resources, and the bibliographies that follow each reading. Useful advice from media specialists in the trenches.

**Ravitch, Diane and Chester E. Finn, Jr.** *What Do Our 17-Year-Olds Know? A Report on the First National Assessment of History and Literature.* **Harper and Row, 1987. ISBN: 0-06-015849.** In 1986, eight thousand seventeen-year-olds were tested on their knowledge of history and literature. The test was funded by the National Endowment of the Humanities. The data gathered about the students—study habits, home life, hours watching TV, etc.—were correlated with the test results, providing remarkable information about performance.

**Rudin, Claire.** *The School Librarian's Sourcebook.* **R. R. Bowker, 1990. ISBN: 0-8352-2711-1.** From library management to serving and educating the student, this remarkable sourcebook guides the librarian to the best in professional reading.

*School Library Journal.* **Serial. Bowker Magazine Group. ISSN: 0362-8930.** For selection of materials and professional news.

**Sierra, Judy and Robert Kaminski.** *Twice Upon a Time: Stories to Tell, Retell, Act Out, and Write About.* **H. W. Wilson, 1989. ISBN: 0-8242-0775-0.** Ages 8–12. Introduces storytellers to creative techniques. This resource is useful for classroom teachers, drama teachers, and librarians.

**Slote, Stanley.** *Weeding Library Collections: Library Weeding Methods.* **Third edition. Libraries Unlimited, 1989. ISBN: 0-87287-633-0.** Covers every aspect of weeding as a library procedure. The author works with mathematical models and thoroughly analyzes the literature related to weeding, explains the criteria and processes to employ, and presents four methods, including a computer-assisted method. Emphasizes the importance of sound—preferably automated—weeding policies. A glossary and a bibliography enhance this comprehensive study.

**Smith, Jane Bandy.** *Library Media Center Programs for Middle Schools: A Curriculum-Based Approach.* **ALA, 1988. ISBN: 0-8389-0500-5.** The wealth of practical information and advice in this manual is applicable to most school settings.

**Streiff, Jane E.** *Secondary School Librarian's Almanac: Month-by-Month Activities, Displays, and Procedures For the Entire School Year.* **The Center for Applied Research in Education, 1989. ISBN: 0-87628-783-6.** A useful resource for the beginning librarian, providing a school calendar approach to professional tasks and planning.

**Vogel, Betty.** *A Librarian Is to Read.* **Milestones Publications, 1988. ISBN: 0-888925-877-5.** Library humor, written by a librarian with ten years' experience.

*The Wired Librarian's Newsletter.* **Edited by Eric Anderson.** There is a light touch to this periodical, and the reviews are worthwhile.

*Young Children.* **Serial. National Association for the Education of Young Children.** Focuses on the education and care of children from birth to age 8. Free lists of books, brochures, videos, and posters are available and useful for the vertical file and for selection.

# List 6–2.  Professional Materials: Reproducible List

*Apple Library Users Group Newsletter.* Apple Computer, Inc.

Aversa, Elizabeth S. and Jacqueline C. Mancall. *Management of Online Search Services in School.* ABC-CLIO, 1989.

*The Book Report.* Serial. Linworth Publishing Company.

*Booklist and Reference Books Bulletin.* Serial. ALA.

Breivik, Patricia and E. Gordon Gee. *Information Literacy: Revolution in the Library.* Macmillan, 1989.

*Choice.* Serial. Association of College and Research Libraries.

*EPIEgram.* Serial. Sterling Harbor Press.

*Horn Book.* Serial. Horn Book, Inc.

*Information Power.* ALA, 1988.

*Information Searcher.* Serial. Datasearch Group, Inc.

*Journal of Youth Services in Libraries.* Serial. ALA.

Klasing, Jane P. *Designing and Renovating School Library Media Centers.* ALA, 1991.

Kurzweil, Raymond. *The Age of Intelligent Machines.* MIT, 1990.

*Library Hotline.* Serial. Library Hotline.

*Library Talk.* Serial. Linworth Publishing Co.

Lurie, Alison. *Don't Tell the Grownups: Subversive Children's Literature.* Little Brown, 1990.

*The New York Times Book Review.* Serial. New York Times.

*Online and CD-ROM Databases in School Libraries.* Compiled by Ann Lathrop. Libraries Unlimited, 1989.

Ravitch, Diane. *What Do Our 17-Year-Olds Know?* Harper and Row, 1987.

Rudin, Claire. *The School Librarian's Sourcebook.* R. R. Bowker, 1990.

*School Library Journal.* Serial. Bowker Magazine Group.

Sierra, Judy and Robert Kaminski. *Twice Upon a Time.* H. W. Wilson, 1989.

Slote, Stanley J. *Weeding Library Collections: Library Weeding Methods.* Libraries Unlimited, 1989.

Smith, Jane Bandy. *Library Media Center Programs for Middle Schools: A Curriculum-Based Approach.* ALA, 1988.

Streiff, Jane E. *Secondary School Librarian's Almanac.* Center for Applied Research in Education, 1989.

Vogel, Betty. *A Librarian Is to Read.* Milestones Publications, 1988.

*The Wired Librarian's Newsletter.* Serial. Edited by Eric Anderson.

*Young Children.* Serial. National Association for the Education of Young Children.

# THE SCHOOL LIBRARIAN'S DICTIONARY

Over two hundred years ago William Cowper complained that "the sounding jargon of the schools/Seems what it is—a cap and bells for fools." Nevertheless, for the practicing school librarian it pays to know the jargon. Here are some of the acronyms, phrases, and words we use and read each day but may feel at a loss to define. From "AACR" to "YA," you may now speak with confidence, just as the pro you are.

## List 7–1.   The School Librarian's Dictionary

| | |
|---|---|
| **AACR** | *Anglo-American Cataloging Rules,* publication of the ALA, used as a tool for bibliographic description of materials |
| **AASL** | American Association of School Librarians |
| **ABA** | American Booksellers Association |
| **abridged** | shortened, abbreviated |
| **abstract** | summary of a document |
| **access** | to retrieve information from storage |
| **access point** | the term under which a record is stored |
| **accession number** | a discrete number assigned to an item in a collection for control and record-keeping; generally selected in chronological progression as materials are received |
| **added entries** | additional points of access to a bibliographic record |
| **AECT** | Association for Educational Communications and Technology |
| **ALA** | American Library Association |
| **alphanumeric** | in computer programming: consisting of characters representing both numerals or letters |
| **analytics** | entries in the bibliographic record which provide access via parts of works |
| **authority file** | a list of headings in use in your collection |

| | |
|---|---|
| **automated circulation system** | circulation record stored in a computer database |
| **AV** | audiovisual |
| **baud** | unit of measuring speed of transmission in the telecommunications process |
| **bibliographic record** | the cataloging record of an item; traditionally shown on a catalog card |
| **bibliographic utilities** | computer databases of bibliographic records; largest is OCLC |
| **bit** | the smallest unit of computerized data |
| **bug** | a defect in a computer program |
| **CAD** | computer aided design |
| **CAI** | computer assisted instruction |
| **call number** | number assigned to an item to identify its location |
| **card catalog** | the index to a library's collection |
| **CAT** | computer assisted training |
| **CCD** | cooperative collection development; a process by which library professionals build their collections cooperatively, with sharing of resources |
| **CD** | compact disc |
| **CD-ROM** | compact disc-read only memory |
| **CIP** | Cataloging in Publication; now generally available on the back of the title page in most books. CIP offices are located at the Library of Congress. |
| **circulation** | use |
| **circulation system** | system for locating materials and making them accessible to patrons; may be manual or automated |
| **classed catalog** | catalog in which materials are grouped by subject |
| **closed shelves** | the housing of library materials which prohibits access by persons other than staff |
| **COM** | computer output microform, generally applied to a catalog of materials in microfiche or microfilm format, produced from an electronic database |
| **cross-reference** | entry in a catalog which refers the user to another entry |
| **CRT** | cathode ray tube (your computer screen) |
| **cumulative index** | index prepared from successive editions of indexes |
| **Cutter, Charles** | inventor of a cataloging code while a librarian at the Boston Athenaeum Library (1875); author of *Rules for a Printed Dictionary Catalogue* |

| | |
|---|---|
| **Cutter author table** | alphabetical arrangement of materials within a classification, generally the first three letters of the author's last name or of the main entry word |
| **databank** | information organized for quick use, usually on a computer; contains files of data |
| **DDC** | Dewey Decimal Classification: a code for classifying materials into ten major classes; named for Melvil Dewey |
| **Dewey, Melvil** | the librarian who developed the most widely used library classification system; allows for relative location of materials in a collection |
| **dictionary catalog** | catalog where all entries are interfiled, in alphabetical order |
| **directory database** | printed directories that have been transferred to electronic format |
| **divided catalog** | a manual catalog which is divided, usually into two parts: author/titles and subjects |
| **DOS** | disk operating system |
| **dumb terminal** | a computer terminal which can receive or transmit signals but has no internal processing capability; important to consider when automating library procedures |
| **easy books** | generally, picture books for young children |
| **electronic catalog** | the catalog of a collection entered into a computerized databank |
| **ERIC** | Educational Resources Information Center; a specialized database |
| **etymology** | the history of a word |
| **floppy disk** | magnetic medium for programming computers and storing machine-readable data |
| **flowchart** | diagram of a process or procedure which shows the relationships among and progression of tasks |
| **format** | the physical appearance of material (book, tape, computer software); the way the material is arranged |
| **glossary** | alphabetical list of a collection of specialized words with definitions |
| **GMD** | general materials designation; refers to the physical class of materials to which an item belongs, e.g., globe, filmstrip |
| **headings** | the words placed at the head of an entry to provide the access point to that entry |
| **hypermedia** | interactive software systems that allow the user to create programs |
| **hypertext** | electronic links of texts allowing the user to arrange and rearrange information |

| | |
|---|---|
| **icon** | the graphic representation of a computer command |
| **ILL** | interlibrary loan |
| **input** | transference of data to computer memory |
| **interactive video** | user and computer software respond to one another |
| **interface** | the linkage between systems or components of a computerized system |
| **interlibrary loan** | circulation among different libraries |
| **inventory** | an accounting procedure by which records of holdings are checked against a shelf list |
| **ISBD** | *International Standard Bibliographic Description,* publication which reformed descriptive cataloging in 1974; an international format for description of materials |
| **ISBN** | International Standard Book Number |
| **ISSN** | International Standard Serials Number |
| **keyboard** | the input device for typing characters which will generate a computerized record |
| **LC** | Library of Congress |
| **LCSH** | Library of Congress Subject Headings |
| **LCLSH** | *Library of Congress List of Subject Headings,* a standard list of subject headings |
| **Library Bill of Rights** | policy statement on functions of libraries, developed by ALA |
| **Library of Congress Classification** | system for classifying materials; uses twenty-one letters |
| **main entry** | the heading on the first line of the principal bibliographic record |
| **MARC** | machine-readable cataloging |
| **MARC Distribution Service** | cataloging data on magnetic tape, supplied by LC to subscribers |
| **medium** | a means of communication |
| **microcomputer** | a computer designed for a single user |
| **microfiche** | a flat sheet of microfilm, usually 4 inches by 6 inches |
| **microfilm** | film which contains a reduced photographic copy of material |
| **microform** | any type of film which carries microphotographic images |
| **modem** | (from modulate/demodulate): the modem translates computer data into a signal which can be sent over phone lines |
| **mouse** | a computer peripheral which can be used instead of the keyboard to effect commands |

**multimedia** an item that combines more than one medium (e.g., audio/visual media with the printed word)

**network** group of organizations or individuals linked through communications, hoping to accomplish common goals

**OCLC** Online Computer Library Center, Inc.

**omni catalog** catalog which provides access to an entire collection, print and nonprint, in a single integrated file

**online search** getting information from a databank through the computer

**open entry** an entry in the catalog for which there will be other publications to add (a serial, for instance)

**open shelves** the housing of materials which permits the user to browse and to retrieve from the collection

**original cataloging** assigning a classification to materials

**password** a code by which the user may access a database

**Phoenix Schedules** revisions to the first (1876) DDC tables

**Precis** Preserved Context Index System, a computer-assisted system used to index a variety of bibliographic records and catalogs; developed by the British National Bibliography

**RAM** random access memory; electronic storage of data which provides access to any location in the computer's memory

**ROM** read only memory; storage of electronic data in which the user cannot alter the data or program

**recto** the right-hand pages of a book; the odd-numbered pages

**relative index** an index (as in the DDC) which indicates the relationships among topics

**retrieval** the process by which materials or data are selected and extracted from a collection or database

**RIC** Reader Interest Classification, developed in the Detroit Public Library to meet the needs of patrons who select through browsing a collection

**SEARS** *Sears List of Subject Headings*

**security system** detection system providing a mechanism which will alert you if items are not properly signed out

**selection policy** policy statement outlining criteria for selecting materials for the library collection; essential

**serials** materials published periodically and regularly (magazines, almanacs)

**shelf list** the authority file for your collection; the entries represent the order of titles

| | |
|---|---|
| **SLSH** | *Sears List of Subject Headings;* a standard list of subject headings |
| **smart terminal** | a computer terminal which can transmit and receive signals and can process information without being connected to the power of another computer |
| **software** | programs which require equipment (hardware) to be used; e.g. computer programs |
| **standard "cat"** | those catalogs developed by H. W. Wilson to guide selection in building a basic collection |
| **standard subdivisions** | Table 1 of the DDC; an auxiliary table |
| **storage capacity** | the amount of information your computer is capable of storing |
| **subject heading** | access point by topic |
| **tele-communications** | receiving and transmitting information and data by electromagnetic means such as radio and telephone |
| **title entry** | entry to data by title of the publication |
| **tracings** | subject headings and analytics which indicate added access points to the main entry; listed at the bottom of a catalog card and in the bibliographic record |
| **truncated record** | abbreviated form of the full bibliographic record |
| **UDC** | Universal Decimal Classification, derived from DDC; an international numerical code for classifying ephemeral materials |
| **unabridged** | comprehensive edition of a work; not shortened |
| **union catalog** | a catalog which brings together the contents of several catalogs, usually the collections of several libraries |
| **user program** | computer program written for a particular user |
| **utility program** | software program for the computer which allows the user to perform routine operations |
| **VCR** | videocassette recorder |
| **verso** | the left-hand pages in a book; the even-numbered pages |
| **vertical file** | subject file of pamphlet material |
| **weeding** | eliminating items from your library collection |
| **WORM** | write once, read many times; compact disc upon which one may enter data but thereafter not change |
| **YA** | young adult |

# PROFESSIONAL DICTIONARIES

If the glossary in this book failed to offer the definitions you need or generated further interest, the following list of professional dictionaries may be valuable to you. To quote Albert Jay Nock (*Memoirs of a Superfluous Man*), "As sheer casual reading matter, I still find the English dictionary the most interesting book in our language."

## List 7–2.  Professional Dictionaries

**Chandor, Anthony.** *The Facts On File Dictionary of Microcomputers.* **Facts On File, Inc., 1981. ISBN: 0-87196-597-6.** Defines 2,500 of the most commonly used microcomputing terms. Helps to demystify those terms and acronyms with specialized applications. Italicized terms clearly indicate cross-references within the dictionary.

**Rosenberg, Jerry.** *Dictionary of Computers, Information Processing, and Telecommunications.* **Second Edition. John Wiley & Sons, Inc., 1987. ISBN: 0-471-85558-8.** More than 10,000 entries in this reference define terms used in the information age. Commonly used symbols, acronyms, and abbreviations are given.

**Rosenberg, Kenyon and John J. Elsbree.** *Dictionary of Library and Educational Technology.* **Third Edition. Libraries Unlimited, 1989. ISBN: 0-87287-623-3.** This dictionary, written for the "nonspecialist," defines terms related to all aspects of work with audiovisual materials, hardware, and new storage technologies.

# section 8

# WHERE TO OBTAIN MATERIALS

## List 8–1.  Distributors

BAKER & TAYLOR COMPANY
Box 6920, 652 East Main Street
Bridgewater, New Jersey 08807

BRODART COMPANY
500 Arch Street
Williamsport, Pennsylvania 17705

FOLLETT LIBRARY BOOK COMPANY
4506 Northwest Highway
Crystal Lake, Illinois 60014

HOTHO & COMPANY
Box 9738, 8916 Norwood Street
Fort Worth, Texas 76107

SCHOOL MEDIA ASSOCIATES
2700 N.E. Expressway, C-800
Atlanta, Georgia 30345

SCIENCE NEWS BOOKS, A DIVISION OF
SCIENCE SERVICE
1719 N Street, NW
Washington, D.C. 20036

SMALL PRESS DISTRIBUTION, INC.
1814 San Pablo Avenue
Berkeley, California 94702

## List 8–2.  Periodicals

*BOOKLIST AND REFERENCE BOOKS
BULLETIN.* AASL
50 Huron Street
Chicago, Illinois 60611

*BULLETIN OF THE CENTER FOR
CHILDREN'S BOOKS.*
CENTER FOR CHILDREN'S BOOKS
University of Chicago, Box 37005
Chicago, Illinois 60637

*CHOICE.* ASSOCIATION OF COLLEGE
AND RESEARCH LIBRARIES
100 Riverview Center
Middletown, Connecticut 06457

*EDUCATIONAL RESEARCH QUARTERLY*
University of Southern California,
Phillips Hall, University Park
Los Angeles, California 90089-0031

*ENGLISH JOURNAL.* NATIONAL
COUNCIL OF THE TEACHERS OF
ENGLISH
1111 Kenyon Road
Urbana, Illinois 61801

*HORN BOOK.* HORN BOOK, INC.
Park Square Building,
31 James Avenue
Boston, Massachusetts 02116

INSTRUCTOR MAGAZINE. EDGELL
  COMMUNICATIONS, INC.
7500 Old Oak Blvd.
Cleveland, Ohio 44130

JOURNAL OF YOUTH SERVICES IN
  LIBRARIES. ASSOCIATION FOR
  LIBRARY SERVICES TO CHILDREN
  AND YOUNG ADULT SERVICES
  DIVISION, ALA
50 Huron Street
Chicago, Illinois 60611

LIBRARY JOURNAL
249 Seventeenth Street
New York, New York 10011

MEDIA AND METHODS. AMERICAN
  SOCIETY OF EDUCATORS
1429 Walnut Street
Philadelphia, Pennsylvania 19102

MULTICULTURAL REVIEW.
  GREENWOOD PUBLISHING
  GROUP, INC.
88 Post Road West
Westport, Connecticut 06881-5007

PHI DELTA KAPPAN
Box 789
Bloomington, Indiana 47402

THE READING TEACHER.
  INTERNATIONAL READING
  ASSOCIATION
Box 8137
Newark, Delaware 19714

SCHOOL LIBRARY JOURNAL.
  AMERICAN ASSOCIATION OF
  SCHOOL LIBRARIANS, ALA
50 Huron Street
Chicago, Illinois 60611

SCHOOL LIBRARY MEDIA QUARTERLY.
  AMERICAN ASSOCIATION OF
  SCHOOL LIBRARIANS, ALA
50 Huron Street
Chicago, Illinois 60611

THRUST FOR EDUCATIONAL
  LEADERSHIP. ASSOCIATION OF
  CALIFORNIA SCHOOL
  ADMINISTRATORS
1575 Old Bayshore Highway
Burlingame, California 94010

VOYA: VOICE OF YOUTH ADVOCATES.
  SCARECROW PRESS
52 Liberty Street
Metuchen, New Jersey 08840

WIRED LIBRARIAN'S NEWSLETTER
393 E. Huron
Jackson, Ohio 45640

## List 8–3.   Posters, Promotional Materials

ALA GRAPHICS, ALA
50 East Huron Street
Chicago, Illinois 60611


ARGUS
P. O. Box 6000
Allen, Texas 75002


THE HUMOR PROJECT, INC.
110 Spring Street
Saratoga Springs, New York 12866

INTERNATIONAL READING
  ASSOCIATION
800 Barksdale Road, P. O. Box 8139
Newark, Delaware 19714-8139

JACKDAW PUBLICATIONS, DIVISION OF
  GOLDEN OWL PUBLISHING
P. O. Box A03
Amawalk, New York 10501

KNOWLEDGE UNLIMITED
Box 52
Madison, WI 53701-0052

NATIONAL WOMEN'S HISTORY
 PROJECT
7738 Bell Road
Windsor, California 95492-8518

SCIENCE SERVICE
1719 N Street, NW
Washington, D.C. 20036

UPSTART, DIVISION OF FRELINE, INC.
32 East Avenue
Hagerstown, Maryland 21740

VARITRONIC SYSTEMS, INC.
P. O. Box 234
Minneapolis, Minnesota 55440-8993

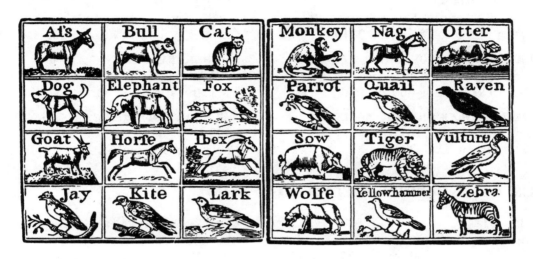

## List 8–4.   Films and Videos

AIMS MEDIA, INC.
6901 Woodley Avenue
Van Nuys, California 91406

AMBROSE VIDEO PUBLISHING, INC.
381 Park Avenue South
New York, New York 10016

BEACON/ALTSCHUL FILMS
930 Pitner Avenue
Evanston, Illinois 60202

BILLY BUDD FILMS
235 E. Fifty-seventh Street
New York, New York 10022

CAROUSEL FILM AND VIDEO
260 Fifth Avenue, Room 705
New York, New York 10001

CHURCHILL FILMS
12210 Nebraska Avenue
Los Angeles, California 90025

CORONET/MTI FILM AND VIDEO
108 Wilmot Road
Deerfield, Illinois 60015

DIRECT CINEMA
P. O. Box 69799
Los Angeles, California 90069

FILMAKERS LIBRARY
124 E. Fortieth Street, Suite 901
New York, New York 10016

FILMS FOR THE HUMANITIES AND
 SCIENCES
Box 2053
Princeton, New Jersey 08543-2053

FILMS, INC.
5547 N. Ravenswood Avenue
Chicago, Illinois 60640-1199

GOLDEN BOOK VIDEO
1220 Mound Avenue
Racine, Wisconsin 53401

HI-TOPS VIDEO
2730 Wilshire Boulevard, Suite 500
Santa Monica, California 90403

LEARNING CORPORATION OF AMERICA
108 Wilmot Road
Deerfield, Illinois 60015-9990

NATIONAL GEOGRAPHIC SOCIETY
Seventeenth and M Streets, NW
Washington, D.C. 20036

PYRAMID FILM AND VIDEO
Box 1048
Santa Monica, California 90406

PBS VIDEO
1320 Braddock Place
Alexandria, Virginia 22314-1698

SOUTH CAROLINA ETV
P. O. Drawer L
Columbia, South Carolina 29250-2712

SUNBURST COMMUNICATIONS
39 Washington Avenue, Box 40
Pleasantville, New York 10570-9971

WILL VINTON PRODUCTIONS, INC.
1400 NW Twenty-second Avenue
Portland, Oregon 97210

## List 8–5.  Publishers/Producers

ABC-CLIO
130 Cremona Drive, Box 1911
Santa Barbara, California 93116-1911

ALFRED A. KNOPF, INC.
225 Park Avenue South
New York, New York 10003

ATHENEUM
866 Third Avenue
New York, New York 10022

AVON (HEARST PUBLICATIONS)
105 Madison Avenue
New York, New York 10016

BANTAM BOOKS
666 Fifth Avenue
New York, New York 10103

BRADBURY PRESS (MACMILLAN)
866 Third Avenue
New York, New York 10022

CAROLHODA BOOKS, INC.
241 First Avenue North
Minneapolis, Minnesota 55401

CENTER FOR APPLIED RESEARCH IN
    EDUCATION
West Nyack, New York 10995

CHARLES SCRIBNER'S SONS
    (MACMILLAN)

CLARION BOOKS/TICKNOR AND FIELDS
215 Park Avenue South
New York, New York 10003

CLEARVUE/EAV
6465 North Avondale Avenue
Chicago, Illinois 60631-6299

CONGRESSIONAL QUARTERLY BOOKS
1414 Twenty-second Street, NW
Washington, D.C. 20037

CRESTWOOD HOUSE (MACMILLAN
    CHILDREN'S GROUP)

CROWN PUBLISHERS (ALFRED A.
    KNOPF)

CURRENT LEADERS PUBLISHING
    COMPANY, INC.
815 Scott Way
Lancaster, Pennsylvania 19446

DAVID R. GODINE
300 Massachusetts Avenue,
    Horticultural Hall
Boston, Massachusetts 02115

DELACORTE PRESS
666 Fifth Avenue
New York, New York 10103

DIAL BOOKS
2 Park Avenue
New York, New York 10016

DIALOG INFORMATION SERVICES
3460 Hillview Avenue
Palo Alto, California 94304

DOUBLEDAY AND COMPANY
    (DELACORTE)

E. P. DUTTON
2 Park Avenue
New York, New York 10016

ENCYCLOPAEDIA BRITANNICA
    EDUCATIONAL CORPORATION
310 South Michigan Avenue
Chicago, Illinois 60604

FACTS ON FILE, INC.
460 Park Avenue South
New York, New York 10016-7382

FARRAR, STRAUS & GIROUX
19 Union Square West
New York, New York 10003

FRANKLIN WATTS, INC.
387 Park Avenue South
New York, New York 10016

G. P. PUTNAM'S SONS
200 Madison Avenue
New York, New York 10016

GALE RESEARCH, INC.
P. O. Box 33477
Detroit, Michigan 48232-5477

GREENWILLOW BOOKS (WILLIAM
    MORROW)
105 Madison Avenue
New York, New York 10016

GROLIER EDUCATIONAL
    CORPORATION
Sherman Turnpike
Danbury, Connecticut 06816

HARCOURT BRACE JOVANOVICH
1250 Sixth Avenue
San Diego, California 92101

HARPER AND ROW
10 East Fifty-third Street
New York, New York 10022-5299

HARPER/COLLINS PUBLISHERS
10 East Fifty-third Street
New York, New York 10022-5299

HARRY N. ABRAMS, INC.
100 Fifth Avenue
New York, New York 10011

HENRY HOLT & COMPANY
115 West Eighteenth Street
New York, New York 10011

HOLIDAY HOUSE, INC.
18 East Fifty-third Street
New York, New York 10022

HOUGHTON MIFFLIN COMPANY
2 Park Street
Boston, Massachusetts 02108

H. W. WILSON COMPANY
950 University Avenue
Bronx, New York 10452

INFORMATION ACCESS COMPANY
362 Exchange Street
Wylie, Texas 75098-9990

INFORMATION PLUS
2812 Exchange Street
Wylie, Texas 75098-9990

LIBRARIES UNLIMITED
P. O. Box 3988
Englewood, Colorado 80155-3988

LINWORTH PUBLISHERS, INC.
Suite One, 5701 North High Street
Worthington, Ohio 43085-9851

LITTLE BROWN & COMPANY
34 Beacon Street
Boston, Massachusetts 02108

LOTHROP, LEE & SHEPARD BOOKS
  (WILLIAM MORROW)

LUCENT BOOKS
P. O. Box 289011
San Diego, California 92198-0011

M. EVANS & COMPANY
216 E. Forty-ninth Street
New York, New York 10016

MACMILLAN PUBLISHING COMPANY
866 Third Avenue
New York, New York 10022

MARGARET K. MCELDERRY BOOKS
  (MACMILLAN)

MCFARLAND AND COMPANY, INC.
Box 611
Jefferson, North Carolina 28640

MONITOR BOOK COMPANY, INC.
P. O. Box 3668
Beverly Hills, California 90212

NEW YORK PUBLIC LIBRARY
455 Fifth Avenue
New York, New York 10016

ORCHARD BOOKS (FRANKLIN WATTS)

ORYX
4041 North Central at Indian School
  Road
Phoenix, Arizona 85012-3397

OXFORD UNIVERSITY PRESS
Walton Street
Oxford OX2 6DP, England

PARTNER PRESS
Box 124
Livonia, Michigan 48152

PENGUIN BOOKS
40 West Twenty-third Street
New York, New York 10010

PFEIFER-HAMILTON
1702 East Jefferson Street
Duluth, Minnesota 55812

PHILOMEL BOOKS
200 Madison Avenue
New York, New York 10016

PIED PIPER MEDIA
1645 Monrovia Avenue
Costa Mesa, California 92627-4404

POCKET BOOKS (SIMON AND
  SCHUSTER)

PRENTICE HALL
Englewood Cliffs, New Jersey 07632

R & S BOOKS (FARRAR, STRAUS &
  GIROUX)

R. R. BOWKER
121 Chanlon Road
New Providence, New Jersey 07974

RANDOM HOUSE
225 Park Avenue South
New York, New York 10003

ST. JAMES PRESS
233 East Ontario
Chicago, Illinois 60611

SAMPLER RECORDS LTD.
P. O. Box 19270
Rochester, New York 14519

SCARECROW PRESS
P. O. Box 4167
Metuchen, New Jersey 08840

STERLING HARBOR PRESS
146 Sterling Avenue, P. O. Box 28
Greenport, New York 11944

SCHOLASTIC INC.
730 Broadway
New York, New York 10003

SHAMBALA PUBLICATIONS, INC.
Horticultural Hall
300 Massachusetts Avenue
Boston, Massachusetts 02115

SIMON AND SCHUSTER
Rockefeller Center
1230 Avenue of the Americas
New York, New York 10020

SOCIAL ISSUES RESOURCES SERIES, INC.
P. O. Box 2348
Boca Raton, Florida 33427-2348

SUPERINTENDENT OF DOCUMENTS
U. S. Government Printing Office
Washington, D.C. 20402-9325

TECHNOMIC PUBLISHING COMPANY
851 Holland Avenue, Box 3535
Lancaster, Pennsylvania 17604

THOMAS Y. CROWELL (HARPER AND ROW)

VIKING (PENGUIN, INC.)

WILLIAM MORROW & COMPANY
105 Madison Avenue
New York, New York 10016

WINGS FOR LEARNING
1600 Green Hills Road
P. O. Box 660002
Scotts Valley, California 95067-0002

WORKMAN PUBLISHING
708 Broadway
New York, New York 10003

# section 9
# TITLE INDEX